# GOOGLE AND THE CULTURE OF SEARCH

D0145357

*What did you do before Google?* The rise of Google as the dominant internet search provider reflects a generationally inflected notion that *everything* that matters is now on the Web, and *should*, in the moral sense of the verb, be accessible through search. In this theoretically nuanced study of search technology's broader implications for knowledge production and social relations, the authors shed light on a culture of search in which our increasing reliance on search engines influences not only the way we navigate, classify, and evaluate Web content, but also how we think about ourselves and the world around us, online and off.

Ken Hillis, Michael Petit, and Kylie Jarrett seek to understand the ascendancy of search and its naturalization by historicizing and contextualizing Google's dominance of the search industry, and suggest that the contemporary culture of search is inextricably bound up with a metaphysical longing to manage, order, and categorize all knowledge. Calling upon this nexus between political economy and metaphysics, *Google and the Culture of Search* explores what is at stake for an increasingly networked culture in which search technology is a site of knowledge and power.

**Ken Hillis** is Professor of Media and Technology Studies in the Department of Communication Studies at the University of North Carolina at Chapel Hill. He is author of *Digital Sensations: Space, Identity, and Embodiment in Virtual Reality* (1999) and *Online a Lot of the Time: Ritual, Fetish, Sign* (2009). He is co-editor of *Everyday eBay: Culture, Collecting, and Desire* (2006).

**Michael Petit** is Director of Media Studies and the Joint Program in New Media at the University of Toronto Scarborough. He is author of *Peacekeepers at War* (1986) and co-editor of *Everyday eBay: Culture, Collecting, and Desire* (2006).

**Kylie Jarrett** is Lecturer in Multimedia at the National University of Ireland Maynooth where she is the program coordinator of the BA in Digital Media.

# GOOGLE AND THE CULTURE OF SEARCH

*Ken Hillis, Michael Petit, and Kylie Jarrett*

Routledge
Taylor & Francis Group

NEW YORK AND LONDON

KH

First published 2013
by Routledge
711 Third Avenue, New York, NY 10017

Simultaneously published in the UK
by Routledge
2 Park Square, Milton Park, Abingdon, Oxon OX14 4RN

*Routledge is an imprint of the Taylor & Francis Group, an informa business*

© 2013 Taylor & Francis

The right of Ken Hillis, Michael Petit, and Kylie Jarrett to be identified as
authors of this work has been asserted by them in accordance with sections
77 and 78 of the Copyright, Designs and Patents Act 1988.

Library of Congress Cataloging-in-Publication Data
Hillis, Ken.
Google and the culture of search / Ken Hillis, Michael Petit, Kylie Jarrett.
pages cm
Includes bibliographical references and index.
1. Google. 2. Web search engines—Social aspects. 3. Internet searching—
Social aspects. 4. Internet users—Psychology. 5. Information technology—
Social aspects. I. Petit, Michael. II. Jarrett, Kylie. III. Title.
ZA4234.G64.H56 2012
025.042'52—dc23                                    2012003462

ISBN: 978-0-415-88300-9 (hbk)
ISBN: 978-0-415-88301-6 (pbk)
ISBN: 978-0-203-84626-1 (ebk)

Typeset in Bembo
by Cenveo Publisher Services

SFI® Certified Sourcing
www.sfiprogram.org
SFI-00453

Printed and bound in the United States of America
by Edwards Brothers, Inc.

6/25/13

Attempt the end, and never stand to doubt;
Nothing's so hard but search will find it out.

(Robert Herrick (1591–1674)<br>"Seek and Find," The Hesperides, 1647)

Search On.

(Google, 2010)

# CONTENTS

# LIST OF FIGURES

# ACKNOWLEDGMENTS

This book is an outcome of our multi-year research adventure into the many intersections among Google, search engines, Web-based identity practices and techniques, political economy, metaphysics and questions of power and agency on the commercial Web. An outline of this project took shape in the form of a 2008 conference panel on Google at the Copenhagen annual meetings of the Association of Internet Researchers (AoIR) and we thank the colleagues and friends we meet each year at AoIR meetings for their sustained interest in and support for our project. These meetings require organization. AoIR's executive is made up of volunteers and we salute them for laboring tirelessly to make these meetings happen in the productive and collegial fashion that they do. Research for this book was supported by the University of North Carolina (UNC) at Chapel Hill, Ken Hillis' home institution. Work was greatly advanced during 2011 by UNC's award of a William N. Reynolds Research Leave and a separate UNC research and development leave from teaching.

Many individuals supported us during this period. Our sincere thanks to the editors at Routledge who helped marshal this book toward publication—particularly Matt Byrnie, Erica Wetter, and Margo Irvin. At UNC, Communication Studies department chair Dennis Mumby was enthusiastic in his material and intellectual support for the project. At UT-Scarborough William Bowen, chair of the Department of Humanities, offered Michael Petit encouragement at key moments. At National University of Ireland, Maynooth (NUIM), Kylie Jarrett's colleagues at the Centre for Media Studies provided invaluable support, both formal and informal, for carving out the time for research and writing. We appreciate the pointed critique and helpful commentaries provided by anonymous readers during the process of review.

No book is written in isolation, and our friends and colleagues provided many different forms of kindness and assistance. Thanks to Ricky Barnes for the many links to articles and cartoons that enlivened our thinking about the culture of search. In particular, we wish to thank Jane Anderson, Feona Attwood, Big Boy, Jennette Boehmer, Paul Couillard, Jillana Enteen, Philip Hartwick, Sal Humphreys, Martin Keck, Ben Light, Astrid Mager, Catherine O'Leary, Stephen O'Neill, Caroline O'Sullivan, Susanna Paasonen, Connie Petit, Denise Rall, Randall Styers, Jenna Titsman, and Michele White.

Portions of this book began as papers given at three consecutive Association of Internet Researchers conferences in Copenhagen, Milwaukee, and Göteberg; the Academy of American Religion; the Joint Programme in Communication and Culture, York University, Toronto; University of Wisconsin-Madison; the University of North Carolina at Chapel Hill; the Third Digital Cultures Workshop, University of Salford; Console-ing Passions Conference, Adelaide, South Australia; University of Salford; Picteilín conference, Dundalk, Ireland, and the Dublin Business School. We extend sincere appreciation to all concerned.

# PREFACE

Justin Esch and Dave Lefkow are friends who have long shared a love of all things bacon. Their quest to find a way to make *everything* taste like bacon reveals much about how a culture of search operates. In 2006, they decided to turn Justin's idea for a bacon-flavored sea salt-based condiment into a marketable product—Bacon Salt. They first searched the U.S. Patent Office database. Bacon Salt was not a registered trade name. Finding nothing like their idea on file, they developed and launched the product with minimal marketing—a website and an email to 200 friends and family. Search engine crawlers soon found and indexed their quirky site, followed shortly thereafter by people searching "bacon." There are a lot of bacon lovers on the Web, and within two weeks the fledgling business had sold out its initial production run of 700 units. Today the salty start-up sells several bacon-flavored products, including baconnaise, bacon pop corn, bacon croutons, bacon gravy mix, and even bacon lip balm. Its product line has moved onto the shelves of U.S. chain grocers such as Kroger, Albertsons, and Walmart.

Justin and Dave's excellent bacon adventure illustrates how search is instrumental to the way the Web works. Search allows us to make sense of the internet and, for many, including Justin and Dave, the everyday world within which we dwell. The two friends were featured on a 2007 episode of *The Story*, a U.S. radio program produced by American Public Media. Their interview with host Dick Gordon reveals a key aspect of the culture of search. Gordon asks the two men how they took their idea and sold it on the Web, what Gordon refers to as "the poor man's marketing plan."

JUSTIN: First of all, business-wise, if anyone wants to start a company, the single, most powerful tool that you'll ever have at your disposal and ever use is Google—I mean that thing got us through everything. Whenever we needed bottles or we needed,

like, lids for our product or label manufacturing or anything ... we'd just jump on
Google ...

DAVE: Well, see, Justin thinks of this as this magic box where we just instantly found
things. So I was doing consulting [in the online recruiting and employment industry]
at the time. So I was actually the one who was digging into this magic box and trying
to figure out, you know, how do we get things manufactured, how do we get it
bottled ... I'll just tell you, Justin, it wasn't as easy as just typing a couple of things
into Google ...

(American Public Media 2007)

Two broadly defined, seemingly contradictory, ways of viewing Google and
search are on offer. Justin sees Google as "the thing" that got them "through
everything" and points to it as indispensable for locating various business products and services. Dave, who views Google as a tool and less as an answer to all
prayers, uses the phrase "magic box" to counter what he sees as Justin's magical
thinking. When online search enters the picture, business practice and the world
of political economy often intersect and overlap with metaphysical ways of thinking about the world of the divine and magic. By probing the intersection of
material and metaphysical forces that drive the culture of search and the information machines upon which it relies, this book examines why this might be so.

# INTRODUCTION

## Google and the Culture of Search

What did you do before Google? Answering the question demands that you not only consider how, or perhaps whether, you retrieved information, but also which particular search tools you may have used before the popularization of Google search. Taking these factors into account should prove revelatory of the astonishing naturalization of the process of search in your everyday life. If you were an early internet adopter, you may recall typing in telnet addresses to access online communities of knowledge from which you gathered information, including the kind that entertains. You may remember going to a public library, using card indexes, reference materials and resources, or asking librarians for guidance in person or by phone. But when you consider *how often* you may have made such trips to the local library, especially if you did not have ready access to research facilities at institutions of higher learning, the question of whether you would actively retrieve information becomes important epistemologically and even ontologically. Epistemologically in that while you may have made the round trip to the public library to research a particular health concern, would you have done so to determine whether it was Jason Bateman or Kirk Cameron who starred in the 1980s sitcom *Growing Pains*, or to satisfy a passing interest in what a high-school sweetheart was doing twenty years after graduation, or any of the other everyday searches we conduct on our ubiquitous Web devices?

Or, as is satirized by the *Chuck & Beans* cartoon (Figure 0.1), would you have resigned yourself to not knowing and the nagging discomfort of an unresolved debate or, worse still, have felt lost, not knowing how to proceed without networked information machines to answer your pleas? At a more ontological level, would the kinds of question that now can seem so pressing even have come

**FIGURE 0.1** "Life before Google." Brian Gordon, artist. © Hallmark Licensing, LLC. By permission, Hallmark Cards

to mind? That today we retrieve information ranging from the life-altering to the trivial as a matter of course is illuminating. But illuminating of what? To search has become so natural and obvious a condition of using the Web, and the Web such a natural and obvious feature of the internet, that the specific contingency of these everyday practices has become obscured. Search is the ultimate commodity fetish. Often it will take a technical breakdown to expose the myriad moments of your everyday life almost instinctively or autonomically given over to some kind of search activity or device.

What did you do before Google? One of the authors of this book was asked this question by a fellow researcher. Despite having researched various aspects of the internet since 2000, being an early adopter of internet technologies, and able to name many prior and persistent search technologies, she was unable to name any she used *on a regular basis*. While aware she had conducted searches and relied on other forms of Web navigation, she could not recall them with any specificity. Her persistent use of Google had pushed aside recollection of any other search engine. And she is not alone. Typing into Google "What did you do before Google?" reveals this is an oft-asked yet just as oft-unanswered question on newsgroups, lists, and blogs. And, indeed, many younger people have no experience of the Web before Google, which they first encountered as their browser's default search engine, and for whom the question makes little sense. This is also to say that Google has become so naturalized it no longer seems to have an origin. It's as if it always was—and therefore always will be—a part of us. To understand the ascendency of search and its naturalization, therefore, requires historicizing and contextualizing Google's rise.

## Google You, Google Me

Google is search's most powerful innovator and driver. From its late 1990s inception, the algorithm PageRank™, which underpins Google's search technologies, transformed the practice and conceptualization of what it was to search the Web. Google established many of the ideological parameters of the culture of search. As an innovator through its famously relaxed corporate culture intended to foster engineering creativity, the firm actively encourages the kind of blue-sky thinking that produces a continual range of new services—including such "game changers" as Gmail, Google Street View and Google Translate, alongside spectacular flops such as Google Wave and Google Buzz. Google hires the brightest engineers and, when unable to secure first-mover advantage, purchases and absorbs the talent of an array of avant-garde technology start-ups, adding to its own pool of intellectual capital. It has been at the forefront of generating online advertising revenue, and it continues to "tweak" its main generator of capital, the PageRank algorithm. In September 2010, for example, it introduced Google Instant, a predictive search technology that provides instant feedback by automatically filling in potential keywords as searchers type. Achieving the autopoietic dynamic of a virtuous circle, digital search has increased in capability and sophistication as search practices and techniques have evolved in tandem, and Google and its suite of ever-changing, ever-growing technologies are at the core of an expanding culture of search.

Search remains the most performed internet activity.[1] In July 2011 alone, Americans conducted 19.2 billion core search queries, and Google processed 12.5 billion of them, commanding 65.1 percent of the U.S. search market (comScore 2011).[2] It processed 91 percent of searches globally during the same month (StatCounter 2011). Google's economic advantage currently rests on twin pillars: it has the best publicly available search engine, and its Android[3] platform ensures that everything available through Google search is accessible through mobile smart phones. The Android platform already provides Web connection for 150 million mobile devices worldwide, with 550,000 new activations daily (Page 2011) and Google processes 97.4 percent of mobile search worldwide (StatCounter 2011). This near monopoly on mobile search perhaps explains why the firm is developing self-driving automobiles in which, happily cocooned and online all of the time, we will efficiently navigate a mobile future dominated by artificial intelligence, robotics, and location-based advertising while we do even more searching, gaming, chatting, and purchasing—in short, becoming ever more linked to the world exobrain.[4]

Google's centrality to the culture of search makes it the automating first among equals, yet we are mindful that Google-the-firm is but one component of the larger cultural dynamic we assess. At times we use "Google" to refer specifically to the firm and at others as a synecdoche for digital search and the culture of search it enables. The *Oxford English Dictionary* authorizes this understanding by listing "to google" as a transitive verb meaning "to search for information about (a person or thing)." At the beginning of the Web's rise, one of its more utopic promoters, Kevin Kelly, observed that the Web's logic relies on a shift from nouns to verbs: "A distributed, decentralized network [such as Google] is more a process than a thing ... It's not what you sell a customer, it's what you do for them. It's not what something is, it's what it is connected to, what it does. Flows become more important than resources. Behavior counts" (1994: 27).[5] Kelly's ruminations allow us to highlight that search is foremost an activity well on its way to becoming a telos in and of itself. It is worth further noting that nouns-turned-verbs also operate to standardize responses to complex issues. Turning Google-the-firm into "googling" and "googled" points to at least three broad issues: 1. the central role of search activities as new forms of knowledge acquisition, production and meaning making; 2. the changing relationship and status of individuals and society to digital forms of information; and 3. the failure of political will to invest in public information infrastructure and the concomitant rise of private search corporations as principal drivers of issues 1. and 2.[6]

Yet search as an activity extends far beyond googling, Google Maps, Google Earth, Street View, and Google Books. It is operationalized across the Web as a way of life, and most of us have become in some way searchers—whether by researching family heritage on ancestry.com, seeking a date on sites like eHarmony and chemistry.com, looking for a job on monster.com or LinkedIn, seeking religious or spiritual guidance and inspiration through sites such as beliefnet.com, or electing to follow breaking news through hashtags on Twitter. Search makes it possible to play Chatroulette, to conduct academic research in electronic databases, to locate old friends on Facebook and classmates.com, to find allies willing to harvest crops in FarmVille or go on a quest in World of Warcraft. Search as a way of life further extends to automated personalized algorithms that suggest items for purchase on sites such as Amazon, eBay, and Netflix. It is the driving logic behind Apple's Genius, Pandora, and similar services that search databases to recommend songs users may like based on first having searched the content of their playlists. Apps such as Listen and SoundHound do the opposite by sampling an unknown song transmitted through a mobile device with sound capture capability and then returning search results on its title and artist, with appropriate links to purchase and download. Search steps out of the screen when old friends meet f2f (face-to-face) after thirty years; when a person is fired after her employer finds an incriminating tagged photograph on Facebook; when the commodity found and purchased on eBay arrives direct via FedEx at the front door.

Search exerts powerful and myriad socio-economic and political influences on contemporary culture. As historian of the book Robert Darnton notes, "Search is the way we now live" (2009: 45), while theologian Philip Clayton calls our lived world a "Google-shaped world" (2010: 9). Search is increasingly understood as a public utility: "When you turn on a tap you expect clean water to come out, and when you do a search you expect good information to come out" (Swift 2009). Indeed, a profound transformation in the structure of feeling of our common world has taken place. The transformation is ongoing, yet there has been insufficient attention to what these changes may mean and how they articulate to a broader confusion between or conflation of information and reality.[7] More precisely, contemporary networked search practices at times exemplify the ways that reality itself seemingly has been subsumed into the informational sphere.

Online and mobile search practices and the algorithms that determine results are accepted by most searchers as utilitarian—though widely understood to be powerful, their very ubiquity has quickly naturalized them into the backgrounds, fabrics, spaces, and places of everyday life. As practices, they are above all efficient and convenient and therefore conceived as politically neutral as if efficiency and convenience were not *the* meta-ideologies of the contemporary technicized, consumerist conjuncture. The conception of search as purely utilitarian and therefore, for many publics, as politically neutral, extends to the purportedly neutral technologies upon which it relies. As if the sociometric search algorithms had somehow designed themselves.

It is humans who design these entities which can seem to take on lives of their own. Search algorithm coding, however, reflects the dispositions, the habitus, the assumptions of its coders. They operate within fields of engineering and technology development and diffusion that are in direct encounter with free market, libertarian, autocratic, democratic, utopian, and globalizing ideologies. One such disposition designed into these machines, exemplified by Google's broad ambition to organize the world's information and thereby achieve something like a hybrid steward–owner relationship to a global universal index or archive, is the West's progressive interest in automating the quest for enlightenment through technology. If we are beginning to incorporate "the searcher" as a component of personal identity, then we are also on the way to confirming search as a moral duty that calls on each searcher to contribute, in the form of her or his search and retrieval history, to the everlasting construction of a universal index or archive of which he or she already is a part. Easy, efficient, rapid, and total access to Truth is the siren song of Google and the culture of search. The price of access: your monetizable information.

## Google Techno-Utopia

Broadly understood, in one way or another we have always been searchers, whether hunter-gatherers or information retrievers, and Google did not invent the technology of internet search. For these reasons neither the culture of search nor Google is totally "revolutionary." Rather, Google operates as a nexus of power and knowledge newly constituted through extremely rapid changes in networked media technologies and equally rapid changes in the social expectations and desires attending to them. The firm's rise reflects and benefits from a generational-inflected growth in the perception that *everything* that matters is now on the Web and that almost everything is already archived in some online database and *should*, in the moral sense of this verb, be accessible through search. We see this increasingly naturalized assumption reflected in many of our undergraduate students, for whom the internet and Google and the #hashtag now constitute their primary access to information.[8] Yet if everything that matters were available through searching the publicly accessible parts of the internet, it would be possible to make the Borgesian argument that the Map had swallowed the Territory. A service such as Street View, however, does seem to depict this impossibility as materially real, and there is a clear and widespread techno-utopian interest in collapsing distinctions between representation and referent, the network and life this side of the screen, by extending the parameters of search ever wider and in every direction, much like the intersecting ripples generated by splashing stones skipping across the surface of a tranquil pond.

Beginning in the 1920s and continuing into the early 1930s, IBM's motto developed by founder Thomas J. Watson, Sr. instructed us to "THINK." In the late 1990s Apple appropriated the instruction by asking potential consumers, through a series of highly successful advertisements featuring famous creative people, to "Think Different." If there is now such a thing as Think Google, it depends on the increasing apotheosis of networked information machines and the techniques and practices they enable. Business journalist Ken Auletta's history of the firm comments repeatedly on the driving force of the technological idealism and missionary zeal of Google founders Sergey Brin and Larry Page (2009: 22, 100–101, 114, 213–214, 289–291). Auletta quotes Brin in the firm's 2004 *Prospectus*: "[Google's aim is] greater than simply growing itself as large as it can be. I believe large successful corporations … have an obligation to apply some of those resources to at least try to solve or ameliorate a number of the world's problems and ultimately make the world a better place" (ibid.: 289). In "Letter from the Founders," submitted as part of Google's 2004 Initial Public Offering (IPO), Brin and Page declare, "Google is not a conventional company." Instead, Google would "focus on users, not investors" and would "be concerned not with 'quarterly market expectations' or paying dividends but rather with protecting Google's 'core values'" (ibid.). These core values center more on a belief in humanity's betterment through technology than on matters of business.

Eric Schmidt, Google's CEO from 2001 to 2011, until superseded by Page, echoes this sentiment: "Our goal is to change the world," he states (ibid.: xii), and Auletta reports he "sometimes lapses into speaking of Google as a 'moral force,' as if its purpose were to save the world, not make money" (ibid.: 22).

Many critics dismiss such utopic comments as arrogance, hubris, or misplaced messianism because the founders' comments seem to violate capitalism's implicitly sacred trust that a corporation's first goal must always be to increase value for its shareholders. But in so doing such critics buy into a kind of economic essentialism predicated on the assumption that there exists some kind of "natural," even universal, distinction between non-economic social relations and practices and those identified as economic. For example, in a *New Yorker* article on Google's "moon shot" to build a digital universal library, Jeffrey Toobin writes that "Such messianism cannot obscure the central truth about Google Book Search: it is a business" (2007). Here Toobin's binary thinking has it exactly backwards. Capitalism is not a unitary or singular formation; that Google is a business success should not obscure a central truth about the firm: its corporate messianism—a combination of technological idealism and missionary zeal suffused with corporate pride and capitalized overtones to be sure, but messianism nonetheless. About his fellow employees, Alan Eustace, Google's director of engineering, insists, "I look at people here as missionaries—not mercenaries" (Levy 2011: 146). Google's techno-utopian vision of organizing and providing timely access to the world's information in the form of a universal index available to anyone with an internet connection, already partially actualized through current search technology and mobile devices, is precisely one of the reasons Google has achieved what we argue is its socially *consecrated* status.

A central premise underlying our inquiry is that there is something beyond the purely economic or political that animates Google's success. Google has achieved consecrated status in part because of the distinct traces of Idealist forms of thinking that attach to it and which are, in constellatory ways, both cause and effect of the firm's dominance within the field of search (we discuss search as a field in chapter 1). We deploy "consecration" in two senses: 1. sanction by law, custom or usage; and 2. the setting of something apart by rendering it hallowed, sacred or divine. "Consecration is a name given to the apotheosis of the Roman emperors," states the 1837 *Penny Cyclopaedia of the Society for the Diffusion of Useful Knowledge*—itself a cosmic product of the early Victorian era's attempt to provide an archive of universal knowledge. The entry notes that both earthly and sacred senses of consecration are encapsulated by the apotheosis and deification of Rome's dead rulers through legal decree by the *Senatus Populusque Romanus*—the "Senate and People of Rome." The *OED* further notes that "coins and medals commemorating these events have the inscription *Consecratio*."

Materially, it should be noted, the thing consecrated remains the same. The *Penny Cyclopaedia* states that "Consecration is generally understood to change not the nature of the thing consecrated, but merely the *use* of it" (1837: 465).

The consecrated candles and holy water at the altar of a Catholic church, for example, remain materials composed of wax, string, and water. The ritualized social act of consecration, and not any intrinsic material quality in the items themselves, *produces* them as sacred. The transubstantiating dynamic is similar to the magical thinking inherent in granting the power of animation to the fetish itself (Hillis 2009), and also in the Catholic belief that "with respect to the consecration of the Eucharistic bread and wine … a complete change is effected in the thing consecrated" (*Penny Cyclopaedia* 1837: 465). Consecration, then, in philosopher John Searle's terminology (1995), is a social and not a natural or brute fact in its own right, even though, as a social fact, it often leads to significant material change. Consecration is richly symbolic, and the exchange value of consecrated items comes to far exceed their use value. Consecration can therefore be understood as a method or process by which we come to accord high, even sacred, value to people, places, and things.

Google has achieved consecrated status in the two senses offered above. It is a business corporation, part of the overall economy, and as such is not set apart from Wall Street, financial markets, and the bottom line. And, the way we use it and have come to rely on it—the multitude of searchers, the population of individuals making up "Wall Street," the corporation, the state, and you, dear reader—has collectively transformed it from being merely useful to a sacred portal for information, the communion wafer of contemporary Do-it-Yourself life. Even the most critical academic scholars of Google are intimate with its functionalities. They have been invaluable to the writing of this book, and we are hard pressed to imagine, for example, how the U.S. Justice Department could research its current anti-trust investigations into Google without the use of search. Simply put, while many of us may wish for search engines more responsive to cultural and linguistic nuances, or less surveillant and "instantly" responsive to commerce's hidden hand, Google works so well at so seemingly small a fee that it has become consecrated through custom and usage, if not by law. A private firm now enjoys institutional status. We, the *Populus Scrutatus*—the "People of Search"—have recognized and legitimized the consecrating nostrum of our very own culture of search.

## Google Metaphysical

Google's scheme to organize the world's information in one universally accessible database conforms to the meaning of a metaphysical first principle. Metaphysics can be conceptualized as "theoretical philosophy as the ultimate science of being and knowing" (*OED*). As part of the "effort to comprehend the universe … somehow as a whole" (Copleston 1960: 199), metaphysics incorporates the study of phenomena beyond the scope of scientific inquiry so as to arrive at an understanding of its "hidden order" (ibid.). As a branch of philosophy, metaphysics deals with first principles, also referred to as ultimate truths. First principle questions are originary or ontological ones pertaining to issues of being, space and time, identity, form, cause, and change (*OED*). Our use of the related term "metaphysical thinking" refers to forms of thought that trade in, *knowingly or otherwise*, a priori, innate, Idealist, immaterial, imaginary, transcendental, and supernatural ideas and forms of association. We focus on proposals, schemes, and ideas that explicitly or implicitly advance the idea of a Universal One across time and space such as Google's ultimate vision to organize all information in one place at one time, which, if ever realized, would be equivalent to archiving the universe.

Ralph Waldo Emerson might have been articulating the metaphysical ideas that underlie Google's vision when he wrote in his journal on May 18, 1843, "Machinery and Transcendentalism agree well" (1911: 397). Transcendentalism draws on aspects of Neoplatonism and "founds itself upon what Aristotle and Kant and Hamilton have called intuition, self-evident truths, axioms, first principles" (Cook 1878: 4). It subordinates reason as a way of knowing to a belief in an innate human spirituality that nevertheless does not reject Enlightenment ideals of scientific experimentation and social progress (Myerson et al. 2010: xxiv). For Emerson transcendence is becoming a "transparent eye-ball" that allows "the currents of the Universal Being [to] circulate through me; I am part and parcel of God" (1904: 374). To transcend, then, is to simultaneously lose one's sense of individual identity and yet see and know all and become one with the Universal. Kevin Kelly, strongly influenced by American Transcendentalism and other variations of Neoplatonic thought, defines himself as a "techno-transcendentalist" who views technology as "transcending in the sense of connecting to a state of awareness, of living, of being, that transcends our day-to-day life. It's not a withdrawal, it's an emergence" (Lawler 2010: 36).

That both Emerson and Kelly believe machinery and a metaphysical belief in transcendence "agree well" is telling. As David Noble has argued, "technology and religion have evolved together and … as a result, the technological enterprise has been and remains suffused with religious belief" (1999: 5). Noble traces this evolution to the era of Charlemagne's court of the ninth century, when a gradual embrace of machinery and mechanism began to emerge as a way to re-attain the prelapsarian state of perfection enjoyed by Adam. What we now call "technological advance" came to be seen as advancing God's will. The "enchantment with things technological," Noble observes, is "an enduring otherworldly quest for transcendence and salvation" (ibid.: 3). Google's vision to build a universal index is but the latest, and possibly greatest, example.

Technologies are ideas in built form, and they contain within them the archeology of their history, including not only traces of their utilitarian purposes, but also of the philosophical ideas and cultural desires that propel their invention, manufacture, and social and geographic diffusion. The desire for a universal index or library capable of assisting the search for knowledge spans millennia. It has been a marker of both aspirations for world peace and fears that to achieve perfect knowledge is to assume something of the godhead and thereby face catastrophic destruction.[9] Google's vision bears traces of the influence of Plato's Ancient concept of the demiurge from which the Egyptian Roman philosopher Plotinus (205–270 CE) subsequently developed his Neoplatonic concept of World Soul. This history helps explain why Google has achieved the implicitly consecrated status of a global Divine Mind.

In the *Timaeus* (c. 360 BCE), Plato advanced his understanding of the demiurge through reference to the lived world: "this world is indeed a living being endowed with a soul and intelligence ... a single visible living entity containing all other living entities, which by their nature are all related" (29/30). The demiurge is a (conceptual) entity so perfect that it transcends all human ideas, concepts, and categories. In *The Enneads*, Plotinus (2004) subsequently identifies the *nous*, the Divine Mind or Spirit. The *nous* is an "emanation" from the universal and infinite One containing neither division nor distinction. It is, therefore, "the image of the One ... the light by which the One sees itself" (Russell 1945: 289).

Unlike the orthodox Christian belief expressed in the concept of *ex nihilo*, that a deliberative and thoughtful God created the universe out of nothing, Plotinus understood the cosmos as emanating *ex deo* (out of God), and, therefore, that the unfolding of the cosmos is a consequence of the existence of the One and a confirmation of its absolute transcendence; the One is the origin of everything and that which everything strives to join, including the *nous* (Divine Mind), *psyche* (Spirit or soul), and *physis* (natural world).

Plotinus' concept of World Soul, understood to flow from the *nous* or Divine Mind, synthesizes these strands of thought. In the 1930s, paralleling the rise of cybernetics, the idea of networked information machines was couched in informational and metaphysically inflected concepts. Permanent World Encyclopedia, World Brain, Global Brain, and World Mind are legacies of this period. More recently, concepts such as the planetary noosphere, Collective Intelligence, Distributed Intelligence, HiveMind, and the Singularity variously adapt and realign the *nous*, World Soul and Divine Mind in order to posit the "ecstatic" possibilities for humans supposedly on offer through the emanations of humanly created and decidedly earth-bound electronic and digital networks. As an emanationist, however, Plotinus was clear that the transcendent One cannot be "any existing thing" and therefore (not unlike the Derridean trace) is "prior to all existents." However, the modern hybrid or fusion of Neoplatonically- and Enlightenment-inflected desire for a Divine Mind taking the form of an electronic archive that would store all the world's knowledge and intentions sidesteps any conceptual or philosophical difficulty in Plotinus' thought. It does so through its implicit positioning of electronic networks as a first principle—as somehow existing prior to and therefore ontologically and cosmologically constitutive of the formation of being, space, time, form, cause, change, and, increasingly, life itself. The current insistence on the part of Google and other Web-based information content providers that they develop and offer *platforms* on which programs and content operate and circulate not only unwittingly replicates the old Marxist binary of base/superstructure, but is itself a contemporary instance of this metaphysical form of thinking.

The conflation of electronic networks with originary and ontological first principles—a conflation with a history (chapters 3–5)—is crystallized through the thinking of metaphysicians who, in various ways, anticipate, theorize, and promote One universal library, archive, and database. Such metaphysicians include philosophers such as Gustav Fechner and Pierre Teilhard de Chardin, who are well known for the mystical, even religious, aspects of their thought. They also include a second group of thinkers less identified with metaphysics but whose thought is deeply influenced by metaphysical ideas. Members include H.G. Wells, Manfred Kochen, Kevin Kelly, Derek de Kerckhove, Pierre Lévy, Ray Kurzweil, and the folks at Google who interpolate each searcher within their universal, searchable copy of reality rendered as patterns of information. Viewed within this longer historical arch, the entirety of the world's information in *one* searchable database becomes a vision of a unified electronic sublime to which we each and all will turn click-by-tracked-click in ritual genuflection, perhaps in hopes of becoming information—part of the immortal *nous* that somehow remains free and monetized, mundane and Ideal, incarnate and immaterial at the same time.

## Google Progress

Google's techno-utopian vision and earthly appetite for power rest on the foundational Enlightenment belief in progress, "that history only runs in one direction, and the future world must inevitably be better than the past" (Douglas 2010: 206). "Progress," wrote intellectual historian Christopher Dawson in 1929, is "the working faith of our civilization, and so completely has it become a part of the modern mind that any attempt to criticize it has seemed almost an act of impiety" (2001: 15). Yet faith in progress, as both a way that humankind might move "forward" toward greater enlightened understanding, and also as the index or marker of this move, has withered on the vine across many sections of social and political life. "No one claims any more that progress is inevitable or that it will culminate in some state of final perfection" (Lasch 1991: 43). As Antoine Compagnon argues, "progress—an empty value in itself—has no other meaning than to make progress possible" (1994: 51). It is the discourse of progress, itself metaphysical, that serves to actualize the possible, to drive the desire to achieve an earthly utopia through the reasoned application of sympathy, science, and rational critical thinking.

Yet in 1929, with the detritus of modernity's hopes for limitless human social advance still littering the killing fields of World War I, Dawson also felt compelled to note,

If at the present day it is at last possible to trace the history of the idea of Progress and to understand the part that it has played in the development of modern civilization, it is to a great extent because that idea has begun to lose its hold on the mind of society and because the phase of civilization of which it was a characteristic is already beginning to pass away … [I]t would seem that the rate of progress is so slow that any ultimate goal of perfection must lie in the infinitely distant future.

(2001: 15–16)

Though an explicit faith in progress "may have been shorn away by the atavistic shocks of the twentieth century, … still we retain our unconscious belief, if for no other reason than the most powerful: as the historian Sidney Pollard observes, because the alternative would be total despair" (Douglas 2010: 207). Today technology serves as a buffer against such despair. The meanings of technology and progress have become progressively intertwined, and progress itself is now constituted and discursively organized principally through technology and its continuing "advance." Increasingly, moreover, what we largely mean by technology, apart from medical applications and pharmaceutical advance, is networked digital information technology. Shiny new information machines and the ever-expanding and relentlessly digital techniques, practices and forms of agency they enable have become the meta-tag of progress.

Twenty years ago Neil Postman argued that the West, broadly speaking, had become a "culture [that] seeks its authorization in technology, finds its satisfactions in technology, and takes its orders from technology" (1992: 71). Three years later, at the dawn of the Web, Langdon Winner observed that "for a great many [Americans and individuals], technology has become the very center of their understanding. In fact, there is now a strong anticipation—even a yearning—that human beings and technical devices will eventually merge into a single entity" (1995: 67). In 1999, near the peak of the dot.com bubble during which media–corporate hype touted the "friction free" "new economy" that the Web purportedly had wrought, David Jay Bolter and Richard Grusin noted:

That digital media can reform and even save society reminds us of the promise that has been made for technologies throughout much of the twentieth century: it is a particularly, if not exclusively, American promise. American culture seems to believe in technology in a way that European culture, for example, may not … salvation in Europe has been defined in political terms: finding the appropriate … political formula … In America … collective (and perhaps even personal) salvation has been thought to come through technology rather than through political or even religious action.

(1999: 60–61)

Postman, Winner, and Bolter and Grusin all speak to a perceived or actual decline of the importance, value, and relevance of the political sphere, particularly within U.S. contexts, to resolve meaningful issues, both large and small. Since their observations, the yoking of human beings to information machines has accelerated, and the yearned-for merger of technology and humankind is manifested today by technotopian priests such as Vernor Vinge and Ray Kurzweil. Their preaching of the Gospel of the Singularity coming in the "near future" when artificial intelligence will render moot human biology and confer on us eternal life has a decidedly American tilt. Yet American values, for better and for worse, have a way of making their influence felt worldwide, and who could deny that the rest of the English-speaking world as well as Japan, China, the EU, the Middle East—indeed most parts of an increasingly networked planet—are not now also in the thrall of information machines.

Since the 2007 global financial meltdown and the political response (or lack thereof) to it, those who feel that the messy and contingent world of representational politics is corrupt and out of touch have only grown in number. From the world of realpolitik, former Australian Prime Minister Malcolm Fraser wrote in 2011, "With rare exceptions, politics has become a discredited profession throughout the West. Tomorrow is always treated as more important than next week, and next week prevails over next year, with no one seeking to secure the long-term future." At the same time, the ascendant technological boosterism within global market capitalism has worked to render commonsensical the ideological belief that the political in the form of the state should embrace and give way to a technicized neoliberal efficiency also discursively positioned as a force for stability. Enter Google and its search results that—unlike decades of broken political promises—are delivered in a timely, reliable, and cost-efficient fashion through a stable technological platform. Yet in all of this it often seems ignored that the very forces of instability introduced by rapid technological change have "spilled over into the political" precisely because such changes are so pervasive. Their inherently political dimension can no longer be denied.

"All that is solid melts into air." The capitalized modern project and its doppelgänger, the drive to capitalize the LifeWorld™, transform all in their path. Perhaps Marx insufficiently anticipated capital's peculiar forms of resiliency and complex abilities to renew itself at critical moments through concessionary and legislated investments in human capital that lead to the kind of innovation Google represents. Many of us use Google even as we understand that it is one of the key drivers in the next phase of "progress," making what was solid—the bricks-and-mortar library, the state archive, the printed book, the shopping mall, the places of the earth and geography itself—melt into the air of the 24/7, privately administered, universal library-cum-archive.

## Google Magic Box

Industry analyst and *Wired* magazine founder John Battelle has noted that, collectively, our searches and the links we follow as a result generate an almost perfect history of consumer preferences and searched desires. He refers to this aggregate data as a form of material culture he terms the "Database of Intentions"—"possibly the most lasting, ponderous, and significant cultural artifact in the history of humankind." It is the "results of every search ever entered, every result list ever tendered, and every path taken as a result … Taken together, this information represents a real-time history of post-Web culture—a massive clickstream database of desires, needs, wants, and preferences that can be discovered, subpoenaed, archived, tracked, and exploited for all sorts of ends" (2005: 6). In noting this ability and Google's "extraordinary cultural aura," he concludes, "Search has about it a whiff of the mysterious and the holy" (ibid.: 7).

The auratic sense of mystery Battelle detects will strengthen as Google continues to mine its database of searchers' interests and desires in order to improve predictive search algorithms—and already the search strings offered by Google Instant can seem uncannily pertinent. As Google search engineer Johanna Wright puts it, "Search is going to get more and more magical. We're going to get so much better at it that we'll do things that people can't even imagine … Google's just going to really understand you better and solve many, many, many more of your needs" (Levy 2011: 68). Wright's comment points directly to a form of consecration based on more than popularity. This is consecration predicated on search as free and easy access to the divine rendered in technological form. "The perfect search engine," Page states on the firm's "Our Philosophy" webpage, "Ten Things Google Knows to Be True," "would understand exactly what you mean and give back exactly what you want" (Google 2006). This is the voice of the consecrated Google God (Figure 0.2).

For most searchers, the glowing white box into which we type our requests for enlightenment is also a black box, a kind of altar on which the ritual of search is enacted. The winking cursor continually beckons us to join it on a "journey" to—as Google put it in its 2010 U.S. Super Bowl T.V. commercial— "Search On." To search on requires no knowledge of search's inner workings. That a search on, say, "black box" returns, according to Google, about 155,000,000 results in 0.13 seconds only adds to the opaque magic while at the same time offering legitimization through a matter-of-fact calculation—itself more black box magic—that in turn draws on Enlightenment ideals of empiricism and its connection to ideals of progress. For searchers, this is magical empiricism at work, a hybrid that, like Emerson's Machinery and Transcendentalism, points to a consistent (though persistently denied) equating in the American imaginary of technology and access to the divine. That such an event is now part of the global everyday speaks to its viral naturalization. As Jacques Derrida and Gianni Vattimo

**FIGURE 0.2** "The Google God." *Tina's Groove.* Rina Piccolo, artist. © 2008 Rina Piccolo. By permission, King Features Syndicate

have noted, "because one increasingly *uses* artifacts and prostheses of which one is totally ignorant, in a growing disproportion between knowledge and know-how, the space of such technical experience tends to become more animistic, magical, mystical" (1998: 56). We see their observation reflected in Figure 0.2. Tina and her friends' "knowledge of" search without "knowledge about" how it actually works leaves them reliant on the voice of Google-as-oracle at a moment when many forms of traditional authority, apart from the technological, are subject to question, contestation, and even refusal. Google's seemingly Delphic power to deliver an unexpected, even "ridiculous," result seems to confirm its godhood, and in such a way do ridiculous things no longer seem so ridiculous as they transubstantiate into truths.

When we consecrate Google as equivalent to a god, it is we who confer the blessing, yet Google remains the same—a corporation based in Mountain View, California, the electronic tentacles of which now circle the planet as envisioned by H.G. Wells and his demiurgic proposal for a global World Brain (1938). Such consecrating practices might seem to point to false consciousness, but false consciousness is a limited materialist understanding that insufficiently considers the need for human beings to make sense of their place in the world—a making sense that often engages the world of spirit and belief. False consciousness as a concept fails to consider that part of us may *want*, even *need*, to believe in the apotheosis of technology because, given that progress, including moral progress, is now largely subsumed under the banner of technological progress, the alternative would be despair. Advertising understands this well, as does religion. James Carey (1975) notes the nineteenth-century link made by early Victorian American religious leaders between electrical technologies of transmission and the divine. He exemplifies his argument with the telegraph and documents the enthusiasm of religious leaders for understanding it as a manifestation of the divine, an "electrical sublime" fully worthy as a vehicle for spreading Christianity's "good news."

The entangled desire for transcendence through immanence has long been operative in practices of technology ideation and development, though it has often been obscured by competing discourses focused on the bottom line. Toobin, for example, would sever Google's messianic "moon shots"—projects rooted in techno-utopianism and reliant on Idealist principles—from its business model, which happens to bring in many billions in revenue but which the firm also uses to fund its "messianic" research.[10] As Gideon Haigh (2006) observes, "Brin and Page tackle business with such evangelical fervor that one industry observer recently called Google 'a religion posing as a company'." Money talks, and across much of the commentariat, as the remark by Haigh's "industry observer" exemplifies, issues of the political are held separate from metaphysics as if bringing them together would result in a category mistake (chapter 7). In the case of Google and the culture of search, however, metaphysically inflected belief helps fuel the information economy and vice versa; as political philosopher Michael Marder has argued in a different context, "Metaphysics and capitalist economy are in unmistakable collusion" (2011: 470). The desire to separate them has also constructed the insistent modern divide between empiricism and magic, technology and religion, the secular and the sacred, and the "exterior" world of hard facts and the "inner" worlds of desiring subjects. The culture of search, however, brings these worlds together so that they speak to and across each other. Google is the culture of search's ontological platform, a fulcrum through which the world of facts and the world of desire comingle, hence the basis of its consecrated status and considerable power.

## Google Power

Google's database provides an extremely rich record of the contemporary cultural zeitgeist and, potentially, an index of each individual searcher's interests and activities recorded in real time.[11] The capacity of search engine advertising based on such databases to reach consumers at the precise moment their desires are transmitted and tracked through search entries is a key component of the engine's economic advantage. As Siva Vaidhyanathan notes, "The more Google knows about us, the more effective its advertising services can be" (2011: 18). A virtuous circle of cybernetic feedback loops ensues. Search algorithms "learn" about our preferences and desires as they endlessly concatenate information about the personal quests of individual searchers. As algorithms come to "know" more about our search activities, search and targeted advertisements become more effective, which leads to a better understanding of searchers' supposedly "inner" selves, and so on in a recursive circle of adaptation and modulation driven by the algorithms as much as searchers and their desires. Crucially, it is also through these interconnected and looping mechanisms that Google's consecrated power becomes overtly political as its data gathering and data mining practices raise fundamental and as yet unresolved—perhaps irresolvable—questions of privacy and personal security (see Halavais 2009: 139–159).

As search technology has developed along with Google's size and corporate reach through its various acquisitions, the firm's ability to capture data from individual users and track their movements across much, if not all, of the commercial Web, has increased accordingly. The 2007 purchase of online advertising agency DoubleClick for US$3.1 billion allowed Google to move beyond search and contextual text ads by utilizing DoubleClick's advertising industry connections to sell targeted multimedia banner and graphical display advertisements across the Web. The acquisition also gave Google access to DoubleClick's user metrics and allowed it to track users on any site on which Google advertising appears (Fuchs 2011; Kang and McAllister 2011). The firm has been heavily criticized for amassing this collection of private data, which at one time it kept indefinitely. Google now anonymizes IP addresses after nine months and removes cookies in search engine logs after eighteen, claiming this is "a reasonable balance between the competing pressures we face, such as the privacy of our users, the security of our systems and the need for innovation" (Google 2010a). And, we might add, the need to mine this real-time data in a timely fashion to make money.

Google's vast database is not merely a source of economic power; it is a powerful agent in its own right that rests in the hands of a non-representative private corporation. This raises the issue of intrusion into private realms in order to commodify them and the user activities that take place there (Kang and McAllister 2011) along with the question of just how much influence any one firm should have over everyday life. Alex Halavais notes that Google's "treasure trove of private information" (2009: 150–151) renders it a key target for identity thieves and unscrupulous marketers. Kurt Opsahl of the Electronic Frontier Foundation, a U.S. libertarian civil liberties group, similarly argues that search engines have created a "honey pot" of information about searchers. "It's a window into their personalities—what they want, what they dream about. This information gets stored, and that becomes very tempting" (Godoy 2006). Opsahl's comments pertain to a 2006 U.S. Justice Department investigation into online porn use and the Department's request for data from Google on user search habits. The potential of the state and other actors and agents to use Google's database to monitor, understand, target, and make determinations about the activities of particular individuals who have searched through Google makes it a potentially dangerous mechanism of surveillance and social control.

Google's ubiquity, hegemony, and consecration mean that its power *to shape* access to information is unprecedented, and accordingly PageRank has received considerable academic attention. We discuss in chapter 1 the context of PageRank's development and provide an intellectual history of its long-term genesis in chapter 5. The algorithm was first outlined in an academic paper by Brin and Page, "The Anatomy of a Large-Scale Hypertextual Web Search

Engine" (1998), and works by attributing importance, and subsequently a higher ranking in the list of search results, to webpages that have a large number of citations or inlinks (incoming links) associated with them. These inlinks are weighted according to the relative importance algorithmically attributed to sites providing the links, which in turn is determined by the relative value of those sites' own inlinks. A page can rank highly in search results if, "there are many pages that point to it, or if there are some pages that point to it and have a high PageRank" (ibid.: 110). Although PageRank has proven vulnerable to manipulation, its introduction not only effected a paradigm shift in the conception of online search but also in the advertising industry by providing clearer metrics for rank valuation of the vast array of information on the Web. As *Wired* editor Chris Anderson (2008) has observed, "Google conquered the advertising world with nothing more than applied mathematics. It didn't pretend to know anything about the culture and conventions of advertising— it just assumed that better data, with better analytical tools, would win the day. And Google was right." Enter PageRank-the-algorithm as a form of social relation in itself.

The suite of algorithms that constitute PageRank remains the core of Google's technological advantage within the field of search. Google acknowledges,

> PageRank is still in use today, but it is now a part of a much larger system. Other parts include language models (the ability to handle phrases, synonyms, diacritics, spelling mistakes, and so on), query models (it's not just the language, it's how people use it today), time models (some queries are best answered with a 30-minutes-old page, and some are better answered with a page that stood the test of time), and personalized models (not all people want the same thing).
>
> (Google 2008)

The way that PageRank functions, however, along with its relationship to the ever-increasing array of other algorithms and measures Google uses to generate individual search results, remains unclear, as these algorithms are the firm's proprietary trade secrets and its prime assets. It is virtually impossible, moreover, to reverse engineer search algorithms because both they and the Web are constantly changing entities. Google made more than 400 changes to PageRank in 2010 alone, and the entire apparatus has achieved such non-deterministic and stochastic complexity that it is no longer possible to know exactly how any given change affects the algorithmic matrix as a whole (Martinez 2011). Such opacity concerning such an important mediator of the symbolic environment of the Web parallels the generally limited understandings of search engine processes among the general population (Hargittai 2008; Vaidhyanathan 2011). Studies of searcher practices tend to confirm Derrida and Vattimo's observation that the gap between knowhow and knowledge creates possibilities for mystical forms of belief; searchers gravitate towards the most highly ranked returns located at the top of search results and in so doing, like the characters in *Tina's Groove* (Figure 0.2), indicate their high level of trust in Google (Joachims et al. 2005; Pan et al. 2007; Keane et al. 2008). Academics are not immune to this practice. A 2008 study of British scholars' use of networked digital resources to research four topics—terrorism, HIV/AIDS, climate change, and internet research—indicated a bias toward Google. When faced with irrelevant results, respondents preferred to change keywords and search parameters rather than seek another search engine more appropriate to their task (Fry et al. 2008).

Such faith in Google's search results generates a virtuous circle: the preferential placing of a site high in the rankings increases its views, "in turn increasing the likelihood of it being placed first, being clicked on, and so on" (Keane et al. 2008: 52). Halavais, extending an argument developed by Haigh (2006), argues that such "trust is a legacy of teachers and journalists who took their jobs as gatekeepers seriously, and we assume that Google is fulfilling a similar role" (Halavais 2009: 105). Halavais implicitly points to the importance of consecration as a method by which gatekeepers are anointed in the first place. He also notes, however, that "while Google dismisses the search engine's biases as natural outcomes of the ranking algorithm … we would never accept such an explanation from a human charged with providing accurate information" (ibid.). Nevertheless, Google has acquired a significant degree of autonomous, indeed unilateral, power to shape the information received by consumer-citizens.

Critical analysis of the underpinnings of this power is important for, on the Web, findability is everything: "if you are not on Google, you don't exist" is the marketers' refrain. Jim Gerber, Google's former director of content partnerships, has stated that "In the future, the only thing that will get read is something that will be online. If it isn't online, it doesn't exist" (*Economist* 2005). That something or someone might not exist unless confirmed so through search exemplifies the flow of ontological power. Simply put, powers rooted in metaphysical forms of thinking beget material powers and vice versa. Figure 0.3 depicts mock horror coupled with fascination at the deviant isolation of the "ungooglable man," an updating of the freewheeling *flâneur* of yesteryear's urban boulevards, whose downcast expression suggests the loss one faces if unwilling or unable to form a part of the searchable universal index.

Lucas Introna and Helen Nissenbaum point out that "what people (the seekers) are able to find on the Web determines what the Web consists of for them" (2000: 171). This capacity to shape a seeker's informational environment, particularly for a virtual monopoly like Google, accrues to the firm extraordinary influence and power. Search engines have a remarkable ability to both systematically exclude and include ideas gathered from the parts of the Web to which they have access. If particular information, such as that required to expand or to support the socio-political discourses of democratic societies, for example, does not rank highly in Google's search results because it is not

**FIGURE 0.3** "The Ungooglable Man." Roz Chast, artist. *The New Yorker*, March 22, 2010. © Roz Chast/The New Yorker Collection. By permission, Condé Nast.

widely popular, or Google's automated processes determine that it is not a good fit with a searcher's personal database of intentions, it becomes relatively inaccessible and most likely does not show up in the first pages of search results. Such information—Haigh (2006) estimates it may be as high as 70 percent of all information on the Web—is effectively censored as its obscurity is determined not by its relevance or potential importance to society but solely by calculating its lack of sufficient overall popularity.

Search algorithms are general statements about reality that influence that very reality. Yet, despite their clear importance, critical discussion that focuses solely on the intentional logic and inherent biases of algorithms is insufficient on its own to understand the culture of search and Google's place within it. Focusing primarily on the power of PageRank, for example, cannot take into account the multiple and variable ways that we interact with Google. Neither can it help explain the ways that a constellation of political, social, economic, and cultural factors (of which the algorithm is but one) shapes search and cultural responses to it. Attributing causal agency to algorithms that are designed by engineers, moreover, works to sever these necessarily ideological decisions from the broader institutional and socio-economic settings in which such decisions are naturalized and which in the first place have led to the production of algorithms that function in particular ways. Code has important ideological effects but it is equally important to recognize that code itself is an ideological effect. It is not just the decisions taken by particular engineers; it is also the ordering of values within the broader settings in which the search industry and searching practices occur that provides the legitimacy and impetus for those decisions and particular algorithms. Consequently, in order to understand search it is crucial to trace the wider institutional and social logics that extend legitimacy to these algorithms and to the very nature of search itself. Studies of algorithms rely in part on a model of power as "power over" the possible meanings made in our symbolic universe. The history of media and cultural studies, however, tells us that this is a very weak sort of power—the power to control through limits and censorship and negation. As Michel Foucault (1978) argues, this model of power (which he terms the repressive hypothesis) does not explain why we just don't say no. There is clearly more at play to ensure our acquiescence to Google's power within the symbolic realm than only its coding prowess.

## Google Affect

Google implicitly invites each of us to reimagine ourselves as searchers, as contemporary explorers and voyagers, latter-day Vasco da Gamas, Captain Cooks, and Neil Armstrongs navigating the proprietary intersection of the digital realm and bodies-as-information. Much as within the incipiently hypertextual world set forth in Jorge Luis Borges' "The Garden of Forking Paths" (1962a), each interactive online search can be seen to produce a unique path, different from the others not pursued, along which the searcher branches and forks through Google's seemingly ordered universe of data. Selecting which search return, which path to pursue or not, positions searchers as the authors of their knowledge quests and forms part of a broader culture that "fetishises the *recipient* of the text to the degree that they become a partial or whole author of it" (Kirby 2006; emphasis in original). Lev Manovich speaks to this observation when he comments that "computer software 'naturalizes' the model of authorship as selection from libraries of predefined objects" (2002: 129). Finding desired information through interactive search can support the sensation and belief that the searcher him or herself, having "discovered" and "called up" the text in question, is its co-creator. Such a belief conforms to Foucault's observation that, as subjects, we constitute ourselves "through well-ordered practices" (2000: 513). Kelly has gone so far as to argue that "in the library of all possible books, finding a particular book is equivalent to writing it" (1994: 280). The suggestion that a successful search positions the searcher as a text's co-creator offers us a way to understand

Google and search more broadly as a technology of the self that promises a limited form of virtual sovereignty. We return to these issues in chapter 7.

A search query result, like any media product, is not a singular text and always encounters the politics of difference at the moment of its consumption. This is especially true for Google because of its use of personalized predictive algorithms such as Google Instant. Because Google records each searcher's IP address, it remembers previous searches and customizes future searches based on past individual patterns and the aggregation of prior user choices and personal preferences. Past becomes future. Personalization produces what Richard Rogers terms an "inculpable engine": it "takes the search engine off the hook, because the 'blame' or responsibility for the results is partly one's own" (2009: 183). Multiple searches by multiple searchers multiply this effect, and as search results are generated, received, and acted upon in so many varied contexts, it is difficult to define how—or even whether—Google's power is operant in each instance. The desires of a searcher seeking, for example, information about a rare disorder such as aquagenic urticaria (google it) differ from those of another using search to play the online game *Six Degrees of Kevin Bacon*.[12] One shows how search has become a potential lifeline. The other exemplifies how the activity of search itself has become a form of media entertainment and content. Each set of results will be subject to different levels of critical appraisal and garner different affective reactions. That these searchers could, in fact, be the same person engaged in different articulations of search activity adds further layers of complexity to understanding the extent and efficacy of Google's power to control symbols and meanings.

Vaidhyanathan observes that "We trust Google with our personal information and preferences and with our access to knowledge because we trust technology that satisfies our prejudices" (2011: 59). His insight speaks directly to Google's ability to give back to us what it knows we want. Indeed, it seems to know us. It knows the disparate geographic locations of the three authors of this book so that entering the same search term on our individual home computers produces results specific to our search histories and respective national locations. Google Instant predicts that for one of us typing "first m ..." indicates a desire for the online academic journal *First Monday* and offers the link accordingly; for one of us searching through Google.ca, it offers First Markam Place, a large pan-Asia shopping mall in the Greater Toronto Area; for another of us it offers First Merit, a bank serving eight states in the American Midwest. Yet, for all of us, "f" is for Facebook. This push–pull between the generic and the personal (sometimes uncomfortably so, as when Gmail places eerily accurate ads next to one's inbox) works to suggest Google is an active agent, a friend and a constant companion we call upon from our mobile devices to answer questions ranging from the trivial—"Who was the guy in that movie?"—to the practical—"How do I get to this location?"—to the vital—"First aid information at the scene of an accident."

Those of us who *do* remember searching the Web before Google's emergence in 1998 will also recall the frustration and tedium of scrolling multiple screens of spam in order to find a webpage relevant to our interests or, perhaps more fondly, recall the serendipity required to find information by surfing link threads or following directory lists. One might also recall the clutter of portal sites such as yahoo.com, the main goal of which at that time was to corral users within their "sticky" confines or shepherd them to partner sites where they were bombarded with information for unrequested services ranging from stock quotes to horoscopes, from weather to movie reviews (Rosenberg 1998). Google's emergence in such circumstances proved revelatory. That using the Web, and accessing information, could be this convenient and for search results to be seemingly this accurate was almost shockingly affective. And for the start-up that produced this revelation also to be a quirky, seemingly non-corporate entity was also highly satisfying for the "plugged-in" digerati who were its early adopters before the site's official launch in 1998. In beta mode, the site was already attracting three-and-a-half million searches per day and had a loyal fan base, drawn by the simplicity and elegance of its search function and ability to cut through the clutter of the then-dominant commercial portal search (Rosenberg 1998; Brown 1999).

In the intervening fourteen years, Google has become a consecrated hegemon. Figure 0.4 depicts the dis-ease this engenders for the many who can't give up Google even though they recognize the leviathan it has become and understand at some level the parastatal status and qualities of governmentality it has achieved along with the almost cosmic authority that comes with this.

If there is any consolation in this, Google's influence and power are bound inextricably to its capacity to please its searcher multitude. Its consecration is affectively produced and can be "de-produced." Even the greatest of emperors cannot forget the constraints of *noblesse oblige*—that the ruler or rulers must give back to the people, at least the minimum required to prevent revolution. Those who forget that such constraints are *precisely* what make their opportunities possible will at some point be dethroned or worse. Today Google feels like a good deal to most of its users. It is free, easy to use, and doesn't require a searcher to reveal his or her ignorance about a subject in front of another human being such as a librarian. But the firm only rules at the behest of these self-same consumer-citizens and, as its self-policing mantra "Don't be evil" implies, can fall from grace at any time. Collective attitudes can evolve or even suddenly shift so that we may come to see a corporation, technology, or social practice differently than we do now. If Google were to fail to maintain alignment with the shifting trust demands of searchers; betray them by too often failing to keep private data safe (the 2010 Gmail hack[13]); too frequently release such data to state agencies ("Google Gives User Data to Government in Most Cases"[14]); fail to maintain the libertarian "information wants to be free" values that support its consecration, then its legitimacy could be lost. Pierre Bourdieu

# GOOGLE

An overpowered hero with a near infinite amount of abilities. Everyone relies on him more than they should while secretly hoping he'll never flip out and use his powers for evil.

## POWERS
Way too many to ever use.

## NEMESIS
Yahoo

**FIGURE 0.4** "The Internet Justice League." Caldwell Tanner, artist. By permission, College Humor

observes that consecrated legitimacy is bestowed by the "dominant factions of the dominant class" as expressed through public and state institutions, and by the choice of "ordinary consumers," whom he also terms the "mass audience" (1993: 51). With the passing of Fordism as an economic construct and social compact, and the rise of our neoliberal Web 2.something era, the value of the idea of mass consumer and its subsequent actualization has given way to the hybrid identity of the "prosumer." Prosumers, the geeks who play with the gadgets designed by the nerds, are savvy shoppers, and Google's current domination of search remains open to challenge from other players within the field of search who articulate the informational ethos more effectively—who design the machines that best reflect and serve the Just In Time diktat of an economy predicated on efficiency, convenience, and obsolescence.

Google nevertheless continues to maintain its consecrated status and thereby its brand value. To do so it must be satisfying and even perpetuate specific forms of searcher desire. We ask, therefore, what desires and which beliefs now shape this drive by Google to generate increasingly individualized and relevant search results? How are these desires and beliefs further shaped by the broader social, economic, and metaphysically inflected milieus in which Google operates? What does it mean when large sections of society come to believe that *all* needed information is available through online search? Is there now an implicit ideal of search that underpins the beliefs of searchers and that enables them to place such trust in a single information provider and its particular process of information gathering? What is the average individual looking for, and *finding*, in the practice of search? These questions animate our interrogation of the political, material, economic assemblage constituted by Google and the culture of search.

## Google Methods

> The more we claim that present capabilities are unprecedented, the more we oblige ourselves to study the past, otherwise how do we know what is or is not unprecedented?
>
> (Duguid 2009: 23)

The chapters that follow offer an intellectual history and a form of media archeology attentive to the ideas, techniques, and practices that inform the culture of search and its undergirding networked technologies. "Media archeology," Geert Lovink proposes, is "a hermeneutic reading of the 'new' against the grain of the past, rather than a telling of the histories of technologies from past to present" (2003: 11). Our approach to media archeology understands that the "old"—older media and technology forms, older ideas and philosophies, older embodied and theoretic practices and techniques—belongs to all of us and more about it should be known so that we understand more about right now. Researching our common heritage in technology allows us to better understand how the forms of thinking, invention, and desire attached to older technologies get remediated into the "new."

The question of distinguishing between the empirically verifiable, recent past of an idea (or technology), and more longstanding philosophical and discursive influences or historical matrices within which ideas and technologies have gestated is an important issue with which contemporary scholarship on new media and information machines continues to wrestle. Most histories of technology support empirical and teleological interpretations. Materialist accounts of the cinema, for example, may detail a progression of earlier devices such as the magic lantern, the panorama, and the praxinoscope that can be seen to contain within themselves, together with the expectations attached to them, aspects of the later technology we now call cinema or film or perhaps video. Fewer accounts concern themselves with theorizing the relationship between an emergent technology and the practices and techniques to which it gives rise, and the broader influence on this technological assemblage of longstanding ways of thinking creatively about the world and our meaningful place in it. Again with respect to cinema, we identify the relative lack of interest in, for example, the various ways that Ancient and medieval theories of light as a divine source that transmits truth and an idea of the good, or as a first principle of the universe (see Blumenberg 1993), might have inflected the cultural sensibilities of those who imagined, then engineered and consumed cinema and its predecessors.

These are two distinct ways or methods often deployed to explain and assess the emergence of new forms and ideas. The first positions a particular form or an idea as having an empirically traceable ancestral lineage that conforms to the logic of universal history, a logic marked by the idea of a coherent whole governed by immutable principles (such as, for example, God or dialectical materialism). The second way or method posits the recent past of an idea or form as influenced by the technical and cultural contributions made by long-standing ideas, desires, and philosophies. Such longstandingness may seem, to those with an empirical bent, to have scant relevance for understanding the rise of the contemporary idea or form in question; however, this is an encrusted logic we challenge. Instead, we proceed from our understanding that *both* recent events, ideas, and inventions *and* germane longstanding philosophies and theories are crucial to understanding the emergence, rise, and social reception of any technology, search included.

The Platonic notion of a "hidden order of history" (Bell 1973: 173) is not one to which we subscribe. Teleological and metahistorical narratives too often serve authoritarian purposes. Instead, we understand that all historical accounts are also forms of criticism as all histories, if they are to be written, are necessarily edited representations of reality. Their truths are always politicized truths, including any unearthed in the historicized accounts we offer in the following chapters. Yet we also acknowledge that certain human interests hold fast or "true" across time and radically opposing ideologies, geographies, and discursive formations. One such interest is held in the phrase "we have always been searchers" even though, like a constellation, what is sought, how it is sought, how it is recognized when found (if it is found), and how its finding is communicated to others varies enormously in both form and content across time and space. We therefore avoid an information-driven account that would confirm the ill-starred but persistent idea that the history of search runs "from closed to open, from bounded to free information, from ... a benighted past to an enlightened future" that would inadvertently "enroll the past in an endorsement of present interests" (Duguid 2009: 15).

Examining earlier practices and techniques, both modern and Ancient, allows us to better understand and therefore explain as well as theorize Google and search as a contemporary constellation and field of forces that both makes a break with the past and recuperates it in sometimes novel ways. In so doing, and inspired by Walter Benjamin's philosophy of history (1969), we intend our account of search as a way to allow readers inundated with implicit and explicit messages that the past is "a dead letter" to bring it and the present (and therefore ideas about the future) into better practical and theoretical alignment. "It's not that what is past casts its light on what is present, or what is present casts its light on what is past; rather … what has been comes together … with the now to form a constellation … For while the relation of the present to the past is a purely temporal, continuous one, the relation of what-has-been to the now is dialectical" (Benjamin 1999: 462).

Search is not an isolated phenomenon and we intend the ways we organize historical ideas, along with our discussion of historical figures and their own relationships with other constellations that may not impinge directly on what it means to search, to generate insights about search that also apply across a range of settings that, like search, gather together the economic and the metaphysical, the practical and the Ideal, and the local and the global. In offering this discussion, we wish to make clear that we do not suggest Google's ideal index has been realized or that it ever fully could be. Similarly, our identification of this drive toward a universal index in no way indicates support for the Idealist, Neoplatonist-inflected philosophies and politics undergirding such desires. To the contrary: our examination of the metaphysically inflected desires fuelling contemporary search practices demonstrates the ongoing (though largely under acknowledged) importance of metaphysical or Idealist thinking to capitalist forms of accumulation such as Google's database of intentions. Google's drive to develop a searchable universal index-cum-library-cum-archive, along with that of other agencies variously interested in "total information recall," relies on metaphysically inflected forms of thought in order to advance the economic and cultural agendas of these players. As N. Katherine Hayles argues, "when bodies are constituted as information, they can be not only sold but fundamentally reconstituted in response to market pressures" (1999: 42). In the case of search, therefore, we identify how contemporary amalgams of cultural, social, and economic forces are in the process of transforming information itself into an ontological first principle.

Reg Whitaker notes that the concept of information is a placeholder made to stand in for the more specific entities to which it variously refers. Though this insight is easily obscured, information is always "about something, it is not that thing itself" (1999: 65), an observation consonant with Jane Bennett's finding that the "violent hubris of Western philosophy … has consistently failed to mind the gap between concept and reality, object and thing" (2010: 13). Even so, the contemporary perception of information—its many meanings ranging from entropy, to the patterned results obtained from various forms of data processing, to intelligence and news, to knowledge communicated about an event, subject, or fact—renders it the virtual lifeblood that courses rhizomatically through networked humankind and its lively online avatars. Idealist projects, however, almost always fail, even though they may visit chaos on humankind before or as they do, and self-reorganization necessarily remains a continual process without completion or end. While there have been projects to "build the new man" and so forth in the past, no ultimate telos exists to which humankind propels itself as an end in itself. No discourse can ever fully interpolate everyone, the discourse of search included. Resistance remains possible, including resistance to the conflation of information with reality itself.

## Chapter Organization

*Google and the Culture of Search* is organized into this introduction and seven chapters. The first, "Welcome to the Googleplex," provides a history of Google to contextualize our discussion of how the firm has come to achieve consecrated status within the field of search. More than sheer economic power is at stake, and we draw from Pierre Bourdieu's field theory and the work of other theorists to discuss the ways in which Google operates as a power–knowledge nexus capable of shaping and reshaping the stories that constitute the realm of information, knowledge, and meaning. Google, we argue, helps produce the kinds of cultural relevancies and symbolic capital that it needs to accrue to itself.

In chapter 2, "Google Rules," we turn to "relevance," a key concept underlying the logic of all contemporary search algorithms, including PageRank. Google's enactment of particular forms of relevance has made it ever more relevant in many everyday lives; given a widespread and growing belief that *everything* that matters is now on the Web, how "relevance" is determined has important epistemological implications for how we come to know and what we mean by knowledge in a culture of search.

Chapter 3, "Universal Libraries and Thinking Machines," traces the influences of individuals and belief systems that subscribe to variations of what we now call universal history: biblical accounts of humankind and its history as governed by the will of God manifested in each and every allegorical event; the mythic status of the Royal Library at Alexandria; Neoplatonist assumptions of humanity as a unitary, coherent unit; and information theory and other modern understandings of mechanization, digitization, computerization, and networks as somehow providing a mechanism for achieving the promised land inherent in Plotinus' Ancient ideal of World Soul.

Chapter 4, "Imagining World Brain," focuses on twentieth-century scientific and metaphysical ideas that, in retrospect, can be seen as furthering the thinking about how to envision and develop a global and searchable universal library. We organize discussion through highlighting and contrasting H.G. Wells' utopian proposal for a World Brain and Jorge Luis Borges' dystopian account of the Library of Babel.

Chapter 5, "The Field of Informational Metaphysics and the Bottom Line," traces the contributions of mid-twentieth-century information scientists such as Vannevar Bush, Eugene Garfield, and J.C.R. Licklider to the eventual formulation of online search. These "pioneers," often in competition with one another for material and status advance, implicitly rely on transcendental forms of affective appeal to promote the saliency of their ideas. And, as we have noted, in the West ideas eventually get built as technologies.

Chapter 6, "The Library of Google," focuses on Google Books as both the latest manifestation of the metaphysical quest for one universal library and as exemplifying how metaphysically inflected desires for universal solutions to complex problems and capitalist economic practices can profitably "intersect". It further argues that the meanings of a library and an archive, once held distinct, intermingle and blur in online networked settings.

Chapter 7, "Savvy Searchers, Faithful Acolytes, 'Don't be Evil'," examines Google's unofficial motto. We discuss Google as a techno-theological assemblage and the online Church of Google as a cultural response to the powers of revelation searchers have come to believe it offers. If "the truth will set you free," knowledge and relevance, however manipulated in advance their provision may be, coupled to salvation *efficiently* delivered, constitute a collective first principle of the culture of search. At a moment of widespread cynical disavowal of many forms of traditional authority, this coupling works to position the firm as an oracle of stability searchers believe they can trust and is why so many Search On.

An epilogue assesses how faith in Google allows the purportedly separate psychic fields of trust, seduction, and faith to conjoin.

# 1

# WELCOME TO THE GOOGLEPLEX

What kind of an entity is Google? It is a technology firm, a media corporation, an automated ad agency, a platform, a financier of automated vehicles and alternative energy projects. The list is not exhaustive and in its hybridity Google is all of these and more than the sum of its parts. The firm's power and influence operate across many intersecting fields and Pierre Bourdieu's theorization of society as organized into overlapping arenas or *fields* of practices (1993, 1996) offers us a helpful way to theorize the human dynamics at play in, across, and among different fields. Field theory occupies a middle theoretical ground that straddles textual analysis, cultural studies, and structuralist criticism (Calhoun 1995) and can be applied productively across the social, cultural, and economic fields that Google also spans.

At base, field theory argues that reality is a social construct and that to exist is to exist socially in relationships with others. What is real, Bourdieu observes, is always relational and everyone understands themselves and their position in the world through becoming aware of the relational differences and similarities between and among the practices and objects they perceive. Such proposals are reasonably straightforward and, indeed, form the implicit, though mostly unstated, bases of many people's everyday understanding of the world around them and how power and influence circulate in it.

A precise definition of a field is elusive. In many ways Bourdieuian fields are arbitrary and defined tautologically by the recognition of their existence by actors and stakeholders within the field (Warde 2004). In this way fields are like phenomenological theories of geographic place that rely for their efficacy on the relational positions among human and non-human actors in any one place, as they are made up of individuals who are related through distinct networks of practices that organize the field. A field is semi-autonomous, its boundaries porous, and Bourdieu's examples include politics, economics, education, technology, science, art, literature, and religion. To this list we add search. Any field's constitution is shaped by its own internal rules, hierarchical ordering of values, forms of agency and prestige that Bourdieu terms cultural capital (Bourdieu and Wacquant 1992), and by power dynamics external to the field. As Nick Couldry (2003) has noted, such external forces most often incorporate the dominant economic and political fields, and when field theory is applied to media organizations (such as Google) include fields occupied by media audiences and consumers. The intersection of competing power relations originating within a field (endogenous) and those originating from outside it (exogenous) together produce an ordering of values (the field's implicit rules) within the field in question. Differences in what is valued (such as what constitutes prestige, status, access, success, failure, and so forth) and how value is determined may be unique to each field, but all facets of society are marked by similar interpenetrating and systematic organizations of economic and cultural forms of capital. The attendant relationships to social power that follow from such organization are inseparable from and embedded within the form of organization itself.

Each field has its own affective beliefs and logics that roughly concord with those of its actors or stakeholders. For example, stakeholders in the field of technology include firms such as Google and Microsoft, researchers and scientists working for them and other employers, business people interested in technology and its financing and development, government regulators, those who use technology, those who oppose its use, and so forth. While their relational positions within the field clearly differ, all stakeholders, including those who oppose technology, agree in differing though interpenetrating ways that it is important to them. Struggle within any field, then, is a given. Within the framework of field theory as it applies to cultural producers such as Google, "the real locus of struggle over meaning lies not in the relation between any particular set of cultural producers and their audiences, but among fields of cultural production (both producers and homologous audiences) that vie among themselves over the power to produce legitimate knowledge about the social world" (Benson 1998: 487).

In many ways, a field is a zone of power, as nebulous as "the cloud" and equally powerful. The following sections draw from this brief and selective outline of field theory as part of historicizing Google's rise and contextualizing its current dominance within the field of search. Our account considers the overall cultural matrix from which the early Web arose—a matrix that can variously be termed its "structure of feeling," "zeitgeist," or, following Bourdieu (1993), "habitus." Developed respectively within English, German and French academic traditions, each expresses a similar idea. A structure of feeling refers to "the felt sense of the quality of life at a particular place and time: a sense of the ways in which particular activities combine into a way of thinking and living"

(Williams 1960: 64-65); zeitgeist is "the spirit or genius which marks the thought or feeling of a period or age" (*OED*); and a habitus, as a product of history and a code of culture, is generated by the interplay among myriad ways of acting, skill sets and taken-for-granted everyday cultural temperaments, dispositions, embodied tastes, styles, skills, and values. The stakeholders who constitute any one field, then, share a similar habitus or perceived sense of "the rules of the game." The rise of the search industry and Google within the context of mid-1990s engineering culture and the early commercialization of the Web is a case in point. We examine the tensions between "nerds" and "suits" that were produced by yoking the specific kind of libertarian Californian ideology of computer engineers believing that technology would resolve all social ills to the business plan and marketing logic of venture capitalists and MBAs focused on transubstantiating ideals into hard cash. Google's ability to successfully navigate these tensions is a key factor in explaining the firm's currently consecrated status.

## Commercializing the Web

The search industry emerged as a semi-autonomous field in tandem with the first steps to commercialize the internet. In 1991, the U.S. National Science Foundation (NSF) loosened restrictions on commercial use of the internet. In August of that year, Tim Berners-Lee built the first website at the Geneva-based CERN. The Web achieved mass popularity beginning in 1993–1994 following the release of Marc Andreesen's Mosaic Web browser. Its rapid diffusion not only introduced many people to the internet (and Web) but also pointed directly toward the internet's untapped economic potential (Kenney 2003: 38). The NSF's 1993 decision to discontinue subsidizing the internet's architecture after 1995 further encouraged the Web's commercialization.

This commercializing process ran counter to the social qualities of the early internet which was marked by a Do-it-Yourself (DIY) culture associated with home enthusiasts and the nurturing of the network within key U.S. academic institutions such as UCLA, UC Santa Barbara, Stanford University, and the University of Utah. The specific kinds of libertarian notions held by early DIY adopters—the "Californian ideology"—drew on radical ideas of direct democracy that emerged from countercultural movements and "a profound faith in the emancipatory potential of the new information technologies" (Barbrook and Cameron 1996). Adherents to this Californian way of thinking saw in the internet the potential for restoration of a public sphere constituted in democratic deliberation, as well as opportunities for generating individual empowerment through the increased agency provided by a relatively uncontrolled media system.

These principles, espoused by important technicians and policy advocates such as John Perry Barlow and the Electronic Frontier Foundation, informed the development of technical infrastructure marked by plurality, access, and a rejection of hierarchical controls. "By insisting on decentralization, multiplicity, plurality, and identity fragmentation, these movements rejected traditional forms of institutional authority (parental, educational, state) that were considered to be constraints on individual emancipation" (Ouellet 2010: 182). While this anti-statism, coupled to a belief in the inherently progressive social value of applied technologies as solutions to the problems of the present, ultimately may have reconciled itself with the thinking of the reactionary right (ibid.), the trace of anti-statism nevertheless generated a tension and resistance that inflected the early phase of the internet's and Web's commercialization. The internet's origins in public funding, academic inquiry, and community involvement fundamentally contradicted the tenets of economic markets (Barbrook and Cameron 1996). The rejection of authority and centralized control during this period, moreover, led to what Alex Halavais describes as "an unofficial ban on commercial activity on the internet, enforced by cultural pressures" (2009: 71)—a ban not lifted until 1993–1994, when the Web experienced its great takeoff.

Elizabeth van Couvering's 2008 history of the search field is useful in illuminating the context of the struggle between the libertarianism espoused by Californian ideology and Web commercialization. She identifies three overlapping periods of search development. The first, 1994–1997, is one of technical entrepreneurship in which digital search (as in the engineering of information retrieval) typically developed within academic and other non-commercial settings. Many start-ups associated with early search sought funding primarily from venture capitalists yet often found it difficult to identify a successful business model. For engines such as AltaVista, Excite, and LookSmart licensing was the preferred model for revenue generation, yet advertising tied to searches dominated the market. The goal of early stakeholders in the field was to attract large audiences measured by impressions or the number of times a website is visited.

Web commercialization at this time was exemplified not only by ubiquitous pop-up and banner advertising but also by the rapid increase in speculative capitalism that led to the late 1990s high-tech boom. The emerging discourse of "knowledge economies" within state policy, industrial settings, and the work of management theorists began to shift focus to supply-side technical innovation so that, by the mid-1990s, computing and networked media were deemed central to economic growth in post-industrial "information economies" (Lister et al. 2003: 187). The so-called "new economy" based on digital media technologies was embraced by existing corporations as a new way to market products and services to the Web's early adopters. The rise of these same media technologies, moreover, offered the crucial promise of high profits from technical innovations. By early 1994, entrepreneurs and venture capitalists had started to seed start-ups, the numbers of which grew rapidly in tandem with the ever expanding multitude of Web users. Early market successes, often based on projected earnings from untested technologies and business plans, fuelled further speculation and resulted in the relentlessly feverish dot.com boom of the late 1990s. As the bubble of high-tech stocks grew ever more distended, academic institutions once allied to the non-commercialization principles of the Californian ideology started developing and investing in e-commerce start-ups. As Martin Kenney puts it, "the ensuing 'dot.com' fever made entrepreneurship an important career goal for students and faculties" (2003: 39).

The bubble burst in 2000. The NASDAQ technology index lost 40 per cent of its value within six months and to date has never regained its lofty heights. Our current experience of the internet, and particularly the Web, remains irrevocably shaped by this pre-millennium dot.com boom (Lister et al. 2003), and despite its libertarian and non-commercial roots the Web and search today are decidedly commercial media and cultural forms.

The second period of search development that van Couvering identifies, 1997–2001, straddles the dot.com boom and bust. It is characterized by the consolidation of high-traffic sites through the development of portals. Portals such as AOL and Excite@Home provided a search function, but their focus was on content and creating audiences that could be sold to advertisers. Their search functions, therefore, were often seen as "good enough" in that these portals did not wish search engines to operate so effectively as to direct audiences away from their sites. While this was a logic that Google was to blow out of the water with its superior technology, during the late 1990s e-commerce literature had argued extensively for building mechanisms into site design to keep customers engaged exclusively with a site and its corporate partners. The goal was twofold: to generate disincentives to leave a site and thereby maintain a stable consumer base; and to activate a virtuous circle wherein as more users remained "stuck" to a site, its value for all users (and the site's owners) increased. In such contexts, "community" became the "killer app." Creating stickiness was conceived as the preferred mechanism to generate and sustain audience engagement with the portal (Armstrong and Hagel 1996; Hagel and Armstrong 1997; Kelly 1998; Tapscott 1998; Shapiro and Varian 1999; Yap 2002). Portals also sought to generate audiences by becoming ISPs, yet the ways such sites organized data needed to be very closely aligned with portal content and that of strategic partners: "a proprietary 'walled garden,' or secondary Internet, could be created which might be owned by a single company" (van Couvering 2008: 186). Commercial portals used licensed search technology within their walled gardens while stand-alone advertising-supported search engines such as HotBot developed as a unique market. Advertising sponsorship, partnerships, takeovers, and mergers continued even though many portal sites could not develop viable business models (Halavais 2009). The 2000 dot.com crash, however, limited the range of possible sponsorship partners within the high-tech industry and induced a major rethink of the Web economy.

The third and current period of search industry development, from 2002 onwards, involves further consolidation and virtual integration. It is characterized by the rise of Google's dominance in the field and a withdrawal of established and "legacy" media and telecommunication companies from search development, a return to licensing of technology as a source of revenue and the rise of the pay-per-click advertising model (Laffey 2007; van Couvering 2008) discussed below. The current period features a reinvigorated online advertising industry that has shown consistent growth since 2002, save for the peak of the global economic crisis in 2009 (IAB 2010). According to the Internet Advertising Bureau, in the second quarter of 2010 the U.S. online advertising industry revenue totalled US$6.2 billion. Of this total, search-related advertising revenue accounted for 47 percent and has remained the principal form of online revenue generation since 2005. Display advertising is in second place, with 36 percent of total revenue generated online (IAB 2010). Since 2002, it is not only large corporations whose faith in the commercial Web has been restored. The viability of what Chris Anderson (2004) refers to as "the long tail" of online commerce—selling large amounts of commodities, each of which is sold in relatively small quantities to niche audiences, as exemplified in different ways by Amazon.com and eBay—was evidence of, and served to consolidate, the Web-based presence of small retailers and advertisers. Retailers' and advertisers' overall success worked to support the rise of the search industry as a separate advertising platform. The development of successful, ad-based business models allowed actors within the field of search to consolidate their businesses, as seen by Yahoo!'s 2003 purchase of search company Overture Services for US$1.6 billion. The acquisition allowed Yahoo! to "control both key elements to search success: good content to pull users in and good ads to help pay for the service" (Sullivan 2003). The parallel syndication of advertising networks has allowed for virtual integration of these networks, and a single search engine can be deployed seamlessly across various sites (van Couvering 2008: 199).

One can easily trace Google's rise across the periods van Couvering outlines. In 1997 Brin and Page developed Google's search engine as Ph.D. students at Stanford University in Palo Alto. Like other start-up principals, they turned to venture capitalists. Yet, despite the growing pressures of commercialization within the field of search, Google has negotiated a path that allows it to maintain some of the idealistic qualities associated with the early search industry and which continue to inform the broader social and cultural forces shaping the Web's commercialization. Google's model of search has been operationalized as industry best practice, and its current legitimacy in part flows from a combination of having aligned itself with these dominant norms and from also having "led the charge," as an early adopter, to normalize them as best practices. The next section examines Google's negotiation of the at times contradictory, at times mutually constitutive, forces of libertarianism and commercialization at play within Web settings. A key hybrid value formation that emerges from this contestation is technical autonomy, a disposition that inflects Google and search as a field.

## Technical Autonomy

Brin and Page's stated objective in their paper outlining PageRank was to replace the "black art" of search and its commercially corrupted results and "push more development and understanding into the academic realm" (1998: 109). Their goal was to make search as useful as possible, and they forcefully expressed an aversion to paid search. More useful search results, the founders argued, would benefit not only Google's users but would encourage them to search more often. This, in turn, would generate ever greater volumes of data necessary for further academic inquiry into search activities. "Usage was important to us," they wrote, "because we think some of the most interesting research will involve leveraging the vast amount of usage data that is available from modern Web systems" (ibid.).

Given the very active role Brin and Page take in shaping product development, Google's suite of products is stamped with their temperaments, dispositions, and values. Their experience of collegiality as graduate students within the habitus of 1990s Stanford engineering culture inflects their approach to engineering and the culture of their firm. Google has succeeded not only because of its well-conceived search engine, but also because "it forged teams of engineers who were not territorial, who formed a network, communicating and sharing ideas, constantly trying them out in beta tests among users, relying on 'the wisdom of the crowds' to improve them" (Auletta 2009: 113). Ken Auletta's (2009) exploration of Google, made possible by his impressive access to Brin and Page, repeatedly confirms that engineering principles shape the firm (see also Edwards 2011; Levy 2011). Page's appointment in 2011 as CEO, replacing Eric Schmidt, reinforces the core of engineering values at the heart of the firm. Google actively cultivates engineering abilities, and between 33 and 38 percent of its workforce is employed in engineering capacities. Google allows its engineers (or at least a privileged subset of them) to devote up to 20 percent of their work time to "blue-sky" research and side projects. While this practice has been associated with the problems of work/life balance to which critics of Google's "cool" corporate culture have pointed (Stabile 2008), the firm's shaping by its atomistic, libertarian, neo-Llullian (chapter 3) engineering culture leads to a corporate habitus marked by objective rationality, utility, efficiency, and supreme faith in technological fixes.

From the outset, the search engine was designed to avoid the subjectivity, maintenance expense, slow speed of indexing and limited scalability common to human-maintained directory sites (Brin and Page 1998: 107). Google continues to assert the independence and objectivity of its search results. For example, in response to the controversy engendered by an anti-Semitic website featured prominently within Google's U.S. search results for the term "Jew," the firm claimed impartiality: "The beliefs and preferences of those who work at Google, as well as the opinions of the general public, do not determine or impact our search results" (Google 2011). The firm, however, did respond to complaints by inserting a disclaimer, framed like a paid ad, at the top of U.S.-based search results for the term. It reads,

> A site's ranking in Google's search results relies heavily on computer algorithms using thousands of factors to calculate a page's relevance to a given query. Sometimes subtleties of language cause anomalies to appear that cannot be predicted. A search for "Jew" brings up one such unexpected result … We apologize for the upsetting nature of the experience you had using Google and appreciate your taking the time to inform us about it.
>
> (Google 2011f)

As Adrian Mackenzie notes, "an algorithm selects and reinforces one ordering at the expense of others" (2006: 44); therefore, while the neutrality that Google claims for its results may not actually exist, this discursive frame does underscore the disposition toward objectivity at the core of Google's search engine design.

Regardless of search engine algorithms' ability to select and reinforce certain orderings of information, this "objectivity" is now a core value within the culture of search. We can trace the emergence of the field of search as we recognize it today to the victory of (ostensibly) automated search engines such as Google's over humanly indexed directory services. Yahoo!'s abandonment of its directory service in 2004 was a pivotal development in the restructuring of the field. Driven in part by the increasing difficulty of human indexers to keep up with the Web's exponential growth, Yahoo!'s decision also responded to increased consumer competence and expectation. Searchers now placed a premium on search models that could provide near-instant results combined with deeper searching of individual pages across an increasingly complex Web. The shift from thematic aggregating of websites, with each site considered a single corpus, to the indexing of individual pages and individual keywords enabled the deep linking that could provide more comprehensive results. The field's values had evolved from an emphasis on managed support for consumer "discovery" to managed "data recovery" (Battelle 2005: 61). In this context, Google's idealistically informed, automated search engine was available as an efficient and transparent means of ensuring seemingly precise results from search queries and was thus perfectly positioned to gain advantage from this shift in the values of the field.

We noted that Google's engineering culture is shaped by the Californian ideology's anti-statist, pro-technology, quasi anti-economic agenda. Lawrence Lessig describes the early Google as "part of an engineering tribe that defined itself as the anti-Microsoft ... Microsoft's approach was: 'You're going to live by my rules.' The opposite is: 'No, I'm going to build it and you're free to use it however you want. I'm just going to empower you to do what you want.' It's the Unix philosophy: Give me a little pile of code and you can plug it into anything you want. That was Stanford in the nineties" (Auletta 2009: 41). Fred Turner also documents how the libertarian, freewheeling, neo-hippy DIY ethos of the Burning Man festival has proven integral to the "ethos of benevolent peer production" (2009: 78) actively fostered within Google's famously positive corporate culture. Turner suggests that this reframing of engineering as a form of "artistic creativity" has allowed the firm's workers to "reimagine themselves collectively as autonomous creators and restore to their labor, if only for a while, the sense of social value that is so often falsely claimed for it by corporate marketers" (ibid.: 88). He also suggests that the 20 percent time allows engineers to "stop thinking of working for Google as just a job and reimagine it as a way to pursue individual growth" (ibid.: 79). While this may be only an ideal that contrasts markedly with the firm's sharper business practices, it also speaks to a general disposition to value the kind of autonomous production long associated with writers, artists, and high art. We pursue this association in the following section.

While Google has managed to remain true to certain ideals associated with the Californian ideology, it is also a publicly traded corporation in the business of making money for itself and its shareholders. Engaged by the rules and values of the dominant field of economics, it cannot operate entirely sequestered within the subfield of autonomous artistic production that would allow it to focus exclusively on developing search algorithms and other products *solely* for higher ideals. In a 2002 interview with John Battelle, then-CEO Eric Schmidt described Google as being in the "technology business." One year later he greeted Battelle with the words "Isn't the media business great?" (Battelle 2005: 3–4). While its core asset is search, and though what it actually sells is keywords (Lee 2011a), Google's revenue stream relies on an established economic model shared by broadcast mass media—the audience is the commodity sold to advertisers (Smythe 1981). In recent years between 96 and 97 percent of the firm's revenue has been attributable to advertising from both Google-owned sites and networked partners (Google 2010, 2011a). Google is profoundly shaped, therefore, not only by its technology-loving and altruistic engineering culture that values autonomous production, but also by the field of advertising and its contradictory emphasis on large-scale production and short-term financial gain.

Following the dot.com crash, the pressure for digital media firms to engage in large-scale production of audiences was intense, particularly as venture capitalists increasingly required start-ups to identify feasible revenue models before the inevitable IPO. Google was not immune to these pressures. During its early days, "Page and Brin had spent nearly all of their time improving the service.

Increasingly, however, the founders were pulled into debates about business models, sponsorship deals, partnerships, and even the prospect of going public— a preordained event for companies that took money from high-profile VCs during the late-1990s Internet boom" (Battelle 2005: 91). This exogenous economic pressure led to Page stepping aside as CEO and the hiring of Eric Schmidt as his replacement in 2001, seen as necessary "adult supervision" because of Page's limited business experience (Levy 2011: 81–82). In selecting their "supervisor" Brin and Page rejected dozens of "suits" in favor of Schmidt who was at least an engineer and spoke their language. The founders also inserted terms into the IPO's S1 public offering document that indicated their adherence to values associated with autonomous production. "At filing, Google declared it would sell $2,718,281,828 worth of its shares—a seemingly random number, which was, in fact, the mathematical equivalent of e, a concept not unlike pi that has unique characteristics and is well known to serious math geeks. By manipulating the actual offering to provide this knowing wink to nerd humor, Google was in effect declaring: *the geeks are in control*" (Battelle 2005: 216–217; emphasis in original).

HotWire started selling banner advertising in 1994, which some mark as the beginning of the online advertising industry (Evans 2008). Banners became the predominant online ad form and a cost-per-thousand (CPM) metric that measured the number of times users viewed an ad determined their value. Business literature noted the possibility inherent in interactive media of using click-through rates to accurately measure advertising effectiveness. "While other forms of advertising could be measured through response (e.g., the number of calls to a dedicated telephone number), the Web enabled immediacy. Users could click on a banner to be taken directly to an advertiser's website" (Laffey 2007). The transparency this technological change made possible revealed that people mostly ignored banner ads (just as they did and do with much offline advertising). Those who did click through did not reliably generate sales (McStay 2010: 45). Faced with an audience increasingly rejecting attempts to be marshalled by media (the empowered e-commerce prosumers), marketers lost faith in standard approaches to advertising (ibid.: 43–46). Between 2000 and 2003 the percentage of online advertising revenue attributed to banner ads plunged from 48 to 21 percent. The very survival of the online advertising industry was at stake. It required a more effective means of ensuring positive customer engagement with online ads, and of assuaging clients' concerns that their marketing dollars be well spent. This was especially important for search companies as "users would not stay [on their sites] long enough to justify high advertising rates" (Laffey 2007: 213).

This difficulty in establishing a viable way to make money through online advertising was surmounted through adoption of the native internet pay- ment model whereby advertisers are charged based on the transparency of

click-through-rates (CTR) using the "cost-per-click" (CPC) model rather than
the CPM model. In the CPC model, advertisers are charged the cost of the ad
*only* when clicked on by users, leaving impressions to be free of charge (van
Couvering 2008). The adoption of CTR and CPC, in turn, fed into the development of search-specific advertising; in 1998, Goto.com (later renamed Overture
Services) introduced paid performance (van Couvering 2004) also referred to as
paid search (Laffey 2007). Paid search brought engineering efficiency to how
advertisers were charged. The more often consumers clicked through ads associated with a particular keyword, the higher the cost to advertisers but also
the higher ranking of this advertisement in results on searches for this keyword.
This new model offered two key advantages. First, the added transparency of
CTR and the cost equity of CPC reduced advertisers' risk. They would no
longer pay for unwanted or unacknowledged advertising. Second, paid search
provided direct access to consumers at the very moment when they sought specific goods and services, again reducing advertisers' risk. "The key virtue of search
advertising for advertisers is that it targets consumers when they are interested and
searching for information about products and services. For consumers, the upside
is that they do not receive irrelevant information about products and services
they are not interested in. This is a system that is intended to work for consumers
and advertisers alike" (McStay 2010: 51). The CTR/CPC model's introduction
coincided with an increase in e-commerce and in information searching as the
internet's user base continued to broaden, broadband infrastructure strengthened,
and an increasing array of producers correspondingly developed Web presences
(Fallows 2005).

Google's hybrid CTR/CPC model was distinct in its incorporation of
certain mechanisms intended to maintain the firm's relationship to autonomous
production. In 2000 the firm supplemented the sponsored links of large advertisers with AdWords, its scalable DIY automated keyword service that fixed
prices for ads relative to their ranking in an overall list of advertisements generated through a search but with priority given to those ads with high CTRs.
Doing so discouraged advertisers from buying keywords that did not relate
to their own products. Facing mounting pressure to generate greater revenues
from its advertising (Levy 2011), in 2002 Google adopted, arguably cloned,[1]
Overture Services' use of keyword auctions for its improved AdWords Select.
This system was still based on the relative transparency of CTR/CPC metrics
but involved advertisers bidding competitively for the ranking of the keyword
rather than purchasing its use for a set cost. Google further introduced two
key in-house innovations. The first was to model a "Vickery's second bid
auction" in which an AdWord's successful bidder is charged only a penny more
than the second highest bidder—a technique that offers advertisers greater transparency and value. The second was to include a quality formula in determining
an auction's winner and the rankings of ads. Using CTR as the sole measure
of advertising costs had introduced incentives for scamming, as advertisers

themselves could improve their rankings by clicking through to their own sites. The introduction of a quality metric based on relevance was designed to prevent scamming of Google's automated system and the biased results such scamming produced for searchers and advertisers alike. While this formula's black box quality reduced transparency for advertisers, it also encouraged them to better attend to the *quality* of their pages and the relevance of their keyword choices in attracting customers. Google viewed the revamped ad system as "a virtuous triangle with three happy parties: Google, the advertiser and especially the user" (Levy 2011: 86).

Beyond these innovations intended to ensure transparency and continuing customer satisfaction, the crucial difference in Google's model of advertising was a result of the firm's insistence on differentiating paid search results from "organic" search results. So that searchers would not be confused or manipulated by advertising replacing the independent, arguably less biased, information generated by the site's search algorithms, Google initially segregated paid listings from other search results by organizing them into a separate list to the right of the main results display. Since early 2010, however, while continuing its policy of placing paid ads in this way, the firm also includes relevant ads at the top of the main results. Google differentiates these ads from unpaid results by placing them within a shaded background box intended to mark them as different from the organic returns listed below.

From the beginning, Google deliberately limited the format of paid ads to lines of plain text in counter-distinction to the annoying, garish pop-up banner advertising common on the early Web (Levy 2011). The ads' stripped-back content not only reduced download times for users but also improved the quality of their search experience because the ads were generated on the basis of keywords searched for by users. Most importantly, segregating advertising maintained the integrity of organic search results. While GoTo.com had allowed advertisers to pay to be included in search returns, this was precisely the "black art" practice the founders decried in their 1998 paper. Google insisted, and continues to insist, on not allowing advertisers to pay for inclusion in its index, asserting that the automated democracy of its index produces best value for searcher-consumers. The clear metrics of the advertising model eventually adopted by Google as well as the model's ability to target consumers with appropriate content at appropriate times makes it not only a cost-effective and transparent medium for advertisers (McStay 2010), but also retains the firm's effective status as a neutral arbiter for consumers. Within the field of search, these decisions about how to refine its ad model are part of Google's work to generate a position of trust with consumers. This issue gained prominence in 2001 when Consumer Alert, a U.S. anti-commercialism group, filed a case with the U.S. Federal Trade Commission asking it to test whether search engines were breaching prohibitions against deception (Commercial Alert 2001). While the FTC's conclusion was ambivalent as to whether paid inclusion violated the FTC Act, it did suggest that businesses needed to clearly disclose this practice and issued consumer alerts (Federal Trade Commission 2002).

Google's pre-emptive decision to reject paid inclusion is noteworthy, as it constitutes an attempt to establish a transparent and trustworthy relationship with a particular type of user. According to 2005 and 2011 Pew Internet & American Life studies, more frequent searchers are more skeptical of search engines' fairness and more aware of their biases; frequent searchers are also likely to be younger and have higher levels of education and income (Fallows 2005: 15). Such individuals, however, are a minority, as 62 percent of searchers are unable to differentiate paid search from organic results. The studies confirm that a user's class and educational status correlate with ability to grasp the inner workings of internet technologies, including search engines (Hargittai 2008). In being so rigorous with the purity of its search results, therefore, Google was responding not only to market demand but also to a set of elite users' demands as a way to accrue legitimacy. By domesticating advertising's influence in such a way, Google established a viable economic model that did not impede its ongoing accrual of the symbolic profits generated from its elite audiences' appreciation. Along with the influence of the Californian ideology, these decisions indicate that the firm continues to see value through its association with the sphere of restricted, autonomous production.

## Autonomous Production and Symbolic Capital

We have noted Google's high engineering culture and its disposition to value the kind of autonomous production associated with writers, artists, and high art. In *The Field of Cultural Production* (1993) Bourdieu draws on the fields of art and literature to contrast autonomous artistic production against large-scale production intended for the marketplace. While he did not theorize how a for-profit corporation's practices might adhere to the logic of the fields of art and literature, in this section we extend some of his observations to connect the two models of production offered in the proceeding section's account and thereby further account for Google's consecrated status. Any theory is part of its own habitus and is distinguished by its historical context and objects of analysis, and Bourdieu's approach does not adequately address the contemporary field of mass media production (Hesmondhalgh 2006). Nevertheless, his ideas have been adapted by other media theorists who also find the core ideas of field theory a useful analytical tool.

Bourdieu writes that, "At one pole, there is the anti-economic economy of pure art" (1996: 142). In this realm of highly restricted production, economy centers on accumulating symbolic capital ("art for art's sake"). Symbolic capital is best defined as prestige or recognition. Accumulating it is the means by which an actor secures and maintains a dominant position within the fields of art and literature; in recursive fashion, acquiring prestige and recognition induces legitimacy from peers and elite audiences. Significantly, Bourdieu refers to this form of cultural legitimation as *consecration*. Like a feedback loop or virtuous circle, this resulting consecration in turn enables an actor to define what constitutes a field's best practice and in so doing also to influence the field's internal dynamics.

In addition to accumulating symbolic capital by maintaining its nerd status and roots in Californian ideology, Google does so through its unofficial corporate slogan and cornerstone of its brand identity, "Don't be evil" (chapter 7). Accumulating symbolic capital is part of the firm's "higher calling" and is evident in the extensive range of philanthropic, environmental, and social justice issues that Google supports financially and practically, and which also animate significant components of its research and development agenda. It is committed, for example, to the development of alternative energy sources and to improving the environmental footprint of its many data centers and their voracious appetites for electricity. It maintains a philanthropic arm, Google.org, which oversees such diverse technical projects as developing energy meters for individual domestic use and mapping influenza and dengue fever search trends to aid in pandemic controls.[2] The firm maintains Google Grants, a program that offers free AdWords to charitable organizations, as well as dedicated YouTube channels for non-profit organizations. It promotes volunteering by its staff and provides grants, scholarships, and donations for various educational, cultural, and social initiatives.

Google also provides an array of services intended to support people's involvement in everyday events simply because they are "cool." For instance, it provided a live stream of the June 2011 lunar eclipse for those unable to directly view the event simply to "brighten someone's day" (Google 2011h). While it is easy to be cynical about such corporate philanthropy—and it is vital to recognize the value of these activities as branding exercises—Google is nevertheless deeply engaged in developing products that offer it no immediate, short-term financial gain. Instead they provide value by helping the firm maintain its dominant position within the field.

At the other end of the spectrum from autonomous production is production of the commercial kind, a production shaped less by the endogenous forces of symbolic capital internal to the field than by exogenous forces of the fiscal economy. The logic of commercial production emphasizes short-term economic profit and confers "priority on distribution, on immediate and temporary success" (Bourdieu 1996: 142). Bourdieu maps the fundamental properties of this organization in the form of the following grid (Figure 1.1).

Bourdieu places mass-produced cultural goods such as vaudeville and journalism within the field of cultural production that is most organized around economic capital. This subfield of artistic production is also the most heteronymous, as it is the most subject to laws and rules imposed by the external fields of economics and politics. The powerful agents within the subfield of large-scale

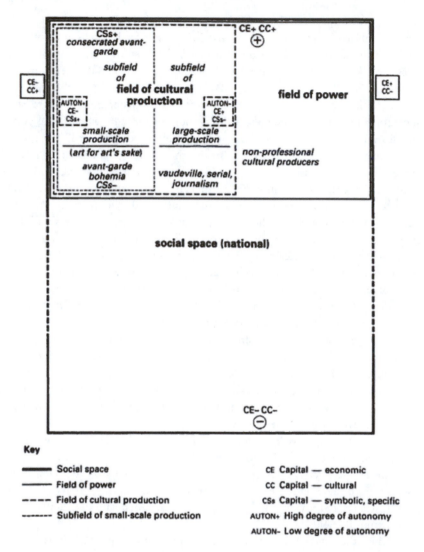

**FIGURE 1.1** Bourdieu's Field of Cultural Production in the Field of Power and in Social Space. *The Rules of Art*, 1996, p. 124

production are those who primarily accrue economic capital that is then parlayed into social power. We can think here of media barons such as Rupert Murdoch, whose economic capital from News Corporation's many holdings has enabled his many significant interventions into the field of politics across the globe. The other subfield of restricted or small-scale production, which includes bohemia and the avant-garde, is oriented toward the accumulation of symbolic rather than economic capital and is therefore a more autonomous field of production less influenced by, and often transgressive of, the established order of power relations. Here are located the avant-garde artists whose products often extend or challenge accepted norms and in so doing demonstrate disinterest in or disdain for the commercial marketplace. Within this subfield of restricted production is also found a set of elite artists whose work is accorded the status of "high art" but who garner institutional recognition through awards, grants, and citations. These artists are those *consecrated* artists whose products have the auratic presence of disinterested art but whose values and creative output align sufficiently with prevailing elite tastes and institutional formations to be accorded by them the status of high art. These artists have high symbolic and cultural capital, and because they are culturally consecrated they have the power within the field to determine and validate the artistic merit of other artists in the field. Their power in social space further increases as they achieve effective control over the terms of entry into the field for all new actors.

The increased influence of economics and its specific forms of determinism on media industries has shaped the ways in which the media field operates (Couldry 2003: 658). Accounts of contemporary journalism, for example, have used field theory to exemplify how journalism synthesizes, often uneasily, restricted, or disinterested "high" forms of cultural production with the subfield of large-scale production and marketing. As Manuel Castells argues, the more that commercial imperatives shape a media organization, the more its journalists will be required to make editorial decisions or define best practice in ways that support commercial interests. In advertising-supported industries, this means that attracting a large audience becomes not only an institutional goal but also a "a source of professional influence" (2009: 200). "The more the actual course of events permeates into the media, the more media influence expands, as people recognize themselves in what they read or watch" and "what is attractive to the public boosts audience, revenue, influence, and professional achievement for the journalists and show anchors" (2009: 200–201). Such a virtuous (or vicious) circle leads to a situation where, for example, political reporting is considered institutionally successful if it "maximizes the entertainment effects that correspond to the branded consumerist culture permeating our societies" (ibid.). Such are the pressures that organize the sensationalist infotainment of contemporary news media, and it is also alignment with these regrettable features that enables access to the field of communication by actors such as politicians or corporations. In effect, it is economic pressures within the field of media production, rather than any conscious ideological agenda, that establish a set of ideal communication forms, the possession of which serves as "media capital," which Couldry (2003) defines as the capacity to influence and shape media form and content.

Media capital, in turn, can be converted into economic, political, or social capital by actors within the field as well as those operating with fields that intersect with it. In this framework, important sites of resistance to these effects of such forms of capital are part of "an inside game, produced within the field of small-scale production among avant-garde [producers], and among the corresponding fragments of the dominant classes, who in their own struggles for distinction, take up these new products" (Benson 1998: 485). It is, moreover, the relative lack of intersection with the fields of power by small-scale producers such as the alternative press that ensures they retain the autonomy to provide news without attention to commercial imperatives and to construct professional values that support alternative forms of journalism. Yet this very autonomy and lack of mainstream consecration ensures that such forms of journalism—precisely because they eschew sensationalist, personalizing infotainment—are less able to affect the terms of media capital that benefit politicians and therefore less able to instigate change to the mediated political landscape.

The media or journalistic field is a pivot within the wider field of cultural production precisely because it disseminates to publics the information and opinions that deeply influence how publics come to understand the field of cultural production itself (Couldry 2003: 657). Search, we suggest, occupies a similar pivotal position. While Google's search engineers might not seem to labor within the same settings as the garret-bound artists and avant-garde writers studied by Bourdieu, they nonetheless produce cultural artifacts in the form of refined algorithms and other software offerings that have challenged and extended accepted norms as to what search might yield. And they do so within a firm that, by asserting the ongoing purity of its search results, evinces a quasi-disdain for market concerns. Like mainstream journalism, however, Google search is also commercial search and part of large-scale production; it is available to general audiences rather than just specific cultural elites (Benson 1998: 465–466). This means that slightly different logics than those identified by Bourdieu are at play.

If mapped directly onto Bourdieu's grid in Figure 1.1, Google as a set of technologies and as a firm does not situate entirely within either the subfields of autonomous or large-scale production that Bourdieu suggests are structural features of all fields of cultural production. Google instead occupies a hybrid position that effectively straddles both subfields: it generates mass audiences and huge profits *and* maintains its association with non-economic imperatives. Associating with non-economic imperatives, such as refusing to mix paid and unpaid advertising, helps Google build the consumer trust and legitimacy that allows it to accumulate economic *and* cultural capital. It is the elite audience of savvy searchers that confers the cultural capital involved. It also does not hurt that Google is the largest player in the field. This helps it crowd out competitors and easily access spaces of power[3] while maintaining a form of legitimacy akin to that of an idealistic and disinterested artist. The very breadth of this hybrid form of cultural and economic capital further consecrates Google's industry dominance.

For some readers such hybridity of large- and small-scale production may seem contradictory. For Bourdieu, any legitimacy accrued within fields of cultural production is anchored in different forms of consecration by socially hierarchized audiences. The first form is the legitimacy granted by other high-art producers of that field and the field-specific value system within which they operate. In this context, any accumulated profits are purely symbolic—they take the form of prestige and respect by peers. The second form is that provided by bourgeois taste and the institutions of that class fraction. Here Bourdieu references awards and citations from academies and salons that "sanction the inseparably ethical and aesthetic (and therefore political) taste of the dominant" (1993: 51). The final form of consecration flows from consumers' widespread acclaim of the cultural product in question. In the fields of cultural production studied by Bourdieu—primarily literary production—the third form of legitimacy reduces the first (high art) form's claims and the symbolic profits it confers. The second (bourgeois) form of legitimacy has a more complex relationship to prestige, with the particular type of institutional acknowledgment—whether the institution itself has high cultural capital in the field—shaping its effects. In fields of restricted production such as high art, some forms of institutional acknowledgment and, most importantly, popular appeal move the producer from a position of autonomous production to one of dependency on his or her audience. Such a move overtly declares the relationship of symbolic power to economic and social capital, thereby highlighting its illegitimacy. This leads to a "relationship of mutual exclusion between material gratification and the sole legitimate profit (i.e. recognition by one's peers)" (ibid.: 50). Consequently, symbolic dominance in the fields of art and literature requires ongoing negotiation of a position where, somewhat hypocritically, one expresses (cultural) disinterest in and disdain for the very (economic) interests that mark one's successful domination.

As our analysis of Google reveals, however, cultural and economic forms of capital accumulation need not negate each other in the field of search, and therefore the logic of commercial search does not fully dovetail with the logic of the fields of art and literature within which economic and political forms of capital may be distinct from, and mutually exclusive of, symbolic capital. As David Hesmondhalgh (2006; see also Lopes 2000) notes, contemporary cultural industries such as the recorded music industry are distinguished by the proliferation of complementary subfields of restricted production *within* the dynamics of large-scale production. Commercial search, like other culture industries, is necessarily located within the field of large-scale production as it requires mass appreciation to be economically viable and not merely the attention of critical, cultural elites (Benson 1998: 465–466). Nevertheless, field theory's identification of the leaky boundaries between semi-autonomous and intersecting fields, its identification of the ways that actors act out their dispositions within their field, and its concept of the habitus as always historically situated remain valuable insights precisely because they account for the complexity of everyday human interactions at the level of the corporation *and* of everyday life that search as a business and as a social practice necessarily entails.

## The Necessity of Hybridity

We have argued how it is possible for Google to possess both symbolic and economic forms of capital. It is, however, not only possible—it is *essential* that it do so. The combination of the Californian ideology's influence on the development of Web technologies, Google's overt articulation of ethical parameters over definitions of good search, and wide-ranging cultural expectations about the public utility of information generates a requirement that any firm attempting to make money in the search industry also must remain aware of search's crucial social role as a cultural and social mediator. The importance of accruing economic *and* cultural gains—consecration by institutions, mass markets, elite consumers, and industry alike—is indicated by tensions within Google itself. Yet these different kinds of gain need not contradict, an understanding that was flagged from the outset of Google's commercialization. As noted in the introduction, in their "Letter from the Founders" that formed part of the firm's IPO registration, Brin and Page indicated that Google would continue to be driven by higher principles.

> Google is not a conventional company. We do not intend to become one. Throughout Google's evolution as a privately held company, we have managed Google differently. We have also emphasized an atmosphere of creativity and challenge, which has helped us provide unbiased, accurate and free access to information for those who rely on us around the world.
> (Google 2004)

The letter further declares Google's long-term focus and disavowal of short-term gain.

> As a private company, we have concentrated on the long term, and this has served us well. As a public company, we will do the same. In our opinion, outside pressures too often tempt companies to sacrifice long term opportunities to meet quarterly market expectations. Sometimes this pressure has caused companies to manipulate financial results in order to "make their quarter."
> (ibid.)

This second point is then reiterated in terms of innovation: "We will not shy away from high-risk, high-reward projects because of short term earnings pressure." Brin and Page top it all off with their commitment to not be evil.

Don't be evil. We believe strongly that in the long term, we will be better served—as shareholders and in all other ways—by a company that does good things for the world even if we forgo some short term gains. This is an important aspect of our culture and is broadly shared within the company.

(ibid.)

That this document, which stands as the essence of the firm's corporatization and proof of the influence exerted on it by the exogenous economic order, should carry such commitment to autonomy, future value generation, and principles of philanthropy and social good reflects the firm's development of a hybrid value system that speaks congruently to political, economic, and metaphysical concerns.

A specific instance of this congruity is found in Google's attitude toward collecting user data. Earlier in the chapter, we referenced Brin and Page's claim that usage would be important to the firm because aggregating the vast quantity of user data available on the Web would allow it to produce "some of the most interesting research" (1998: 109). The founders noted that "there are many tens of millions of searches performed every day. However, it is very difficult to get this data, mainly because it is considered commercially valuable" (ibid.). As a consequence, Google developed its search engine architecture to compress and store user activity data specifically to support "novel research activities on large-scale Web data" (ibid.). While such non-commercial intentions doubtless informed the search engine's development, this same ability allows Google to gather extensive data about its multitude of searchers today. This data allows for the generation of personalization functions (chapter 2) that arguably benefit both consumers and advertisers. It is, therefore, precisely *because* of Google's long-term, anti-economic focus that it was (and remains) able to collect data or generate products before it fully understood how to generate revenue from these mechanisms. In such a way we can see how the automated collection of data so valuable to Google for its future research projects, and which emerges from the rational dictates of search efficiency, can profitably and productively co-exist with the short-term economic benefits of personalized marketing.

Managing this hybridity, however, has not always proved an easy task. To successfully negotiate between the Scylla and Charybdis of disinterested autonomous production and profit-focused large-scale production, Google must respond effectively to its own corporate growth. Its increasing heft within the field of search makes its heteronymous, somewhat Janus-faced qualities more visible and shifts its model of consecration away from the symbolic capital of the fully autonomous producer. Like the broader field of search in which it is the first among equals, Google's recent history has been marked by increasing consolidation and growth that have been based on virtual integration and strategic purchases. The success of Google's advertising syndication model, for example, has allowed it to expand its advertising network through partnerships (van Couvering 2008). Recently, however, Google has extended its own service provision through technological innovation. From search-based services such as Google Books, Google Instant, and Google Goggles, to its development of cloud computing platform services and into the mobile internet and locative media markets with its Android operating system, Google has expanded the sites upon which it generates ad revenue and augmented its ability to amass a history of individual search activities that is crucial both to its marketing agenda and its ability to use this data to improve "search for search's sake."

Since inception, Google has acquired over 150 businesses. Three key purchases are those of YouTube (bought in 2005 for US$1.65 billion), Double Click (bought in 2007 for US$3.1 billion), and Motorola Mobility (bought in 2011 for US$12.5 billion). Acquiring YouTube was crucial, as its first mover advantage in the field of video sharing gave YouTube an unassailable position of market dominance, despite Google's earlier attempt to counter YouTube with its own video-sharing site. Such high-profile expansion through buyouts, however, exposes the firm to criticism ranging from anti-trust suits—the 2007 purchase of DoubleClick and, at the time of writing, ongoing investigations of its search monopoly by the U.S. Federal Trade Commission; the U.S. Senate Subcommittee on Antitrust, Competition Policy and Consumer Rights;[4] and the European Union—to settlements for copyright breaches (*Viacom v. YouTube*), to accusations of abuses of privacy and consumer trust (see Halavais 2009: 139–159), to the now rejected Google Books Amended Settlement Agreement (chapter 6). The list continues to grow.

Given Google's dominant position in the field, such clear tendencies towards market imperatives (and consolidation) require careful management and provide examples of revealing discursive shifts. For instance, Chris Hoofnagle (2009) ana-lyzes the rhetoric of Google's media statements in relation to privacy concerns about increased behavioral marketing. His research reveals the use of trade-off arguments whereby the firm claims that privacy concerns are mitigated by the obvious (at least to Google) social benefits derived from technical innovation. Through such trade-off arguments the firm appeals to those also holding to the apparently disinterested belief in technological progress inherent within the Californian ideology, but the need to maintain consumer trust through this kind of spin also speaks to the necessity for Google to continually maintain the tricky balance between corporate interest and its cherished autonomous production.

This same defensive posture is on view in the firm's controversial decision to enter the lucrative Chinese market. By compromising its search results to satisfy the censorship demands of the Chinese government (despite many such compromises made by other actors across the search industry), the firm revealed too strong an orientation toward economic profit. Expressions of outrage from human rights organizations and criticism from many commentators that Google had breached its promise to "do no evil" (Johnson 2010; Pal 2010) sparked a concerted PR campaign by the firm to reframe its decision as a question of user rights. Google claimed that it continued to contribute to the greater good by providing at least some access to search for Chinese users, again relying on the implicit assumption of the Californian ideology that information access produces democratic social change (McLaughlin 2006). Its subsequent decision later in 2010 to shutter the Mandarin-language Google.cn site and redirect users to its still-censored Hong Kong-based site was similarly spun as an ethical stand for human rights. This decision was applauded by the U.S. government and the same human rights organizations that had criticized Google's initial entry into the Chinese national market. That Google's decisions in 2010 did not result in its disengagement with the Chinese government was poorly understood. Google continues to maintain a corporate presence and business partnerships in China, and its decisions seemed shaped by issues of data security rather than concern for human rights (Grim et al. 2011; Vaidhyanathan 2011: 117–121). While from a PR perspective neither of these decisions was wholly successful as damage control operations, what is important is that they reveal that the tension between economic and symbolic cultural capital remains constant.

## Consecrating Google

Google's legitimacy depends upon constant maintenance of the (perceived) equilibrium between economic and symbolic profits, and this balance in turn sustains a particular model of search—the one that Google most clearly articulates. In a self-reinforcing dynamic, Google's symbolic power and legitimacy normalize its particular model of search as the very definition of search itself. As Bourdieu notes, to be consecrated within a field is to be doubly articulated. On one hand, the qualities of a consecrated agent flow from the ordering of values within that field, with an actor achieving consecration by his or her unique ability to articulate a position that encapsulates those values. On the other hand, to be consecrated is also to be a generator (and maintainer) of that same order. To possess symbolic capital is more than having the ability to influence or shape social activities through the production of symbols. It is the power to *construct* social reality through the misrecognition of the arbitrariness of the particular symbolic system operationalized by an actor who has accrued significant amounts of capital and power (Bourdieu 1993: 75). Symbolic capital enables and sustains power by normalizing practices or modes of thinking—in Bourdieu's terms, doxa—that make it seem "only natural" to support the goals of already powerful agents. Symbolic power such as Google now holds to generate systems that classify knowledge gives it the epistemological power to shape worldviews so that such systems achieve wide acceptance and pervasive use, and as an outcome of its consecrated position, Google's symbolic capital offers it the power to reproduce the conditions that favor its continuing domination.

The legitimacy to define the contours of orthodox thinking and best practice is the prime goal within any field of cultural production. With reference to the field of literature, Bourdieu argues, "In short, the fundamental stake in literary struggles is the monopoly of literary legitimacy, i.e. inter alia, the monopoly of the power to say with authority who are authorized to call themselves writers; or, to put it another way, it is the monopoly of the power to consecrate producers or products" (1993: 42). To be consecrated, therefore, is also to have the power to consecrate others, to reinforce particular modes of practice and to exclude others. Google's nimble maintenance of its consecrated position is ultimately concerned with sustaining this legitimacy to define and dictate the terms of good search and effectively declare who else can call themselves good search providers. It is not merely Google's economic capital that contributes to its monopoly of the search field. It is also its symbolic capital—arguably a misrecognition of its economic and cultural capital, but not reducible to only this—that enables the firm to successfully define "good search" and to embed its model as the favored means of accessing Web-based information.

If one seeks to understand the culture of search, it is important to first understand the particular qualities of Google's model of best practice and the ways that this model influences search activities. Understanding the model not only fosters insight into the field and the mechanisms through which Google maintains its industrial and cultural dominance, but also sheds light on the first principles encoded into Google's search algorithm. An important argument advanced throughout this volume is that Google *actively* shapes how we encounter information and therefore how we come to know. The way in which we encounter information provides us models for action. To recall the question posed in the introduction—What did you do before Google?—such models make it difficult for us to imagine or even remember how we acquired information "before Google." *How* we come to know through Google's mechanisms is just as important as *what* we come to know, for how we come to know directly influences what it is that we know. The next chapter unpacks the contingent qualities of Google's model of good search and its focus on the notion of relevance, and it further explores the epistemological and at times ontological first principle framework that underpins our interaction with information in the "Age of Google."

# 2

# GOOGLE RULES

> When all information is available all the time, everywhere, it is the process
> of selection and analysis that gives it value through relevance.
>
> (de Kerckhove 1997)

People who use the Web have developed a set of expectations about information
retrieval inculcated and shaped by their ongoing engagement with search engines.
The spare white rectangular box at the top of so many webpages seems intuitive,
simple, even natural. We know how to use it and we know what it's for: "Not
only do people expect to see a search box, they expect it to behave in standard
ways: anything outside of the expected will frustrate the average web user"
(Halavais 2009: 9). For most searchers, such expectations have been set and then
satisfied by Google. Its models of a good search engine, a good search result, and
good algorithmic logic have become normalized as *the* industry standards. Because
of its consecrated status, Google rules, and, as such, the rules set by the ruler
define the parameters of the culture of search.

The prime factor organizing these rules, as well as the content of this chapter,
is the concept of relevance and in particular how it has been operationalized
by Google. The search industry appropriated the concept of relevance from
the discipline of information science "where it forms the bedrock of several
traditional measures of information retrieval quality, including, for example,
recall and precision" (van Couvering 2007). This observation is confirmed by the
most cursory search of industry literature and commentary, which reveals the
search industry's close embrace of the concept. A freighted term, relevance is
now encoded in every algorithm and application that extends search capability.
In the current technological conjuncture, algorithms constitute statements
about reality that have the ability to influence reality itself; because networked

search constitutes a process of knowing, any conception of relevance encoded algorithmically by engineers affects how we come to know. Moreover, given the widespread and growing metaphysical belief that *everything* that matters is now on the Web, what the search engine reveals through its list of returns increasingly becomes equivalent to what we *can* know. As we argue in the sections below, in the algorithmic culture of search, relevance equals epistemology.

## The Relevance of Relevance

Relevance is a persistent topic on The Official Google Blog, which provides "insights from Googlers into our products, technology, and the Google culture."[1] A February 2011 post states, "Our goal is simple: to give people the most relevant answers to their queries as quickly as possible. This requires constant tuning of our algorithms, as new content—both good and bad—comes online all the time" (Google 2011f). The post subsequently announces that Google has made "a pretty big algorithm improvement" that will affect 11.8 percent of all U.S. search queries. Without offering details other than this precise percentage, the post explains,

> This update is designed to reduce rankings for low-quality sites—sites which are low-value add for users, copy content from other websites or sites that are just not very useful. At the same time, it will provide better rankings for high-quality sites—sites with original content and information such as research, in-depth reports, thoughtful analysis and so on.

The post positions relevance as the opposite of "not very useful" and associates it with rational-purposive action and functional utility, and it exemplifies how Google conceives the search experience as an academic interrogation driven by purposive agendas (Halavais 2009). Sites that do not satisfy Google's assumptions of relevance, regardless of any potential value they may otherwise contain, receive lower rankings. Google's relevance privileges *utilitarian* value as a way of understanding, and it yokes utility to quality of search experience. The yoking is made clear in many posts on the blog. "This week in search 4/29/11" touts "more relevant predictions in Recipe View": "In the past," before the introduction of Google Instant, in September 2010, "you'd see the same search predictions that you'd see on the main web results page, which wasn't always helpful. Now ... you'll see more relevant search predictions. For example, typing [c] will give you predictions for [chicken] or [cake] versus [craigslist] or [cnn], and typing [co] will predict [cookies] or [coconut]—and maybe inspire you to make coconut cookies." The post associates relevance with predictive utility and a quality search experience that involves less typing (Google Instant claims to be "faster than the speed of type" (Google 2010a)) and which also may lead to algorithmically inspired creativity and personal fulfillment. Implicit is the suggestion that achieving perfect relevance would be akin to the technology seeming to read one's mind. Such perfection would actualize the desire expressed in Page's declaration that "The perfect search engine would understand exactly what you mean and give back exactly what you want" (Google 2006).

Page's interest in "perfect search" and his firm's steady revisions to its algorithm exemplify David Rothenberg's "circle of technological practice," an interpenetrating dialectic or feedback loop circling among human intentions and desires, the development of new technologies to express those intentions and desires, and the new intentions and desires these technologies help authorize: "Those who use the tool begin with their own intentions, and the more they accept the technology, the more their desires are changed" (1993: 18). Brin and Page did not root their graduate research in the idea of reading minds—at least not in their 1998 paper, which offers scant mention of relevance save that its authors "want our notion of 'relevant' to only include the very best documents since there may be tens of thousands of slightly relevant documents" (1998: 109). Relevance had not yet been articulated in the founders' thinking to ideals of utility or the experiential quality of search itself. However, once digital search had been seen to work well—and one must remember that Google has achieved consecration in part because its PageRank algorithm works so well—it begat new imaginaries that pushed the concept of relevance toward some seemingly logical outcome or telos. In this one can see how the rush to new invention and tweaks to existing technologies never supersede the imaginary. The process of new desires unleashed by new uses of new technologies, that in the marketplace seem to only ever temporarily satisfy the desires they stimulate, is part of a cycle or spiral of development that can seem like a self-perpetuating engine of newer technologies and accompanying desires and so forth. Google's technologies of relevance and searcher engagements with them fit the bill.

Page, in a 2004 conversation with Brin, reportedly expressed his belief that search eventually would go beyond reading one's mind to *being* one's mind:

> "[Search] will be included in people's brains," said Page. "When you think about something and don't really know much about it, you will automatically get information."
>
> "That's true," said Brin. "Ultimately I view Google as a way to augment your brain with the knowledge of the world. Right now you go into your computer and type a phrase, but you can imagine that it could be easier in the future, that you can have just devices you talk into, or you can have computers that pay attention to what's going on around them and suggest useful information."
>
> (Levy 2011: 67)

In Brin's vision, mobile voice recognition devices will push "useful" information at us, including Google ads, and *tell us things we didn't know we wanted to know.*

Search becomes a "thinking machine" that knows us better than we know our-selves. The desire to make it so informs Google Instant, a project that Google engineers nicknamed "Miss Cleo" in reference to the American TV spokes-woman famous for her commercials pitching her pay-per-call psychic help line. Page reiterates later in the conversation, "Eventually you'll have the implant, where if you think about a fact, it will just tell you the answer" (ibid.). The aug-mented searcher-cyborg. Brin and Page's comments reveal a desire to enchant relevance by giving it such an automatic quality of liveliness that it would be indistinguishable from a godhead speaking through you. More prosaically, Brin and Page also indicate that the more predictive the technology, the more relevant the searcher's experience. Along the way the money and Google's corporate relevance continue to flow.

In his memoir of Google's early years, Employee No. 59, Douglas Edwards, quotes Arthur C. Clarke's famous aphorism "Any sufficiently advanced technology is indistinguishable from magic" and adds that his job as a member of the UI (user interface) team was to make search "supernaturally simple" (2011: 58). In 2000, Edwards played a role in constructing an April Fool's joke on Google's home page that was part of an effort to boost Google's brand. After securing Brin's approval for the project, Edwards had the thought, "What if Google were so good it delivered results before you even searched?" He composed a FAQ and created a modified home page for a mock technology called "Ante-Temporal search," later rebranded as "MentalPlex™" (ibid.: 97). The imagined technology used "proprietary predictive search algorithms devel-oped through 13 years of research by an international consortium of PhDs in the fields of artificial and pseudo-intelligence, parapsychology and improbability" to return results without requiring searchers to enter a query. "Typing in queries is so 1999" (Google 2000). Although the joke created confusion for some search-ers, it was largely viewed as successful in branding Google as hip enough to make fun of itself. The page remains online (Figure 2.1), and the April Fool's home page has become a Google tradition that continues its branding exercise.

The 2000 April Fool's home page example illustrates two salient points. First, its humor relies on the outrageous proposition of mind-reading search. The FAQ makes clear the page is a joke and the technology the province of magic, yet as his 2004 conversation subsequently would reveal, Page hardly views the merger of mind and search as a joke; while the mythical technology is not even at the beta stage, Page seems quite insistent on its inevitability. The importance of "beta" to the culture of engineering should not be underestimated. Philip Clayton writes about what it can teach the contemporary Christian church, and his inter-pretation directly applies to understanding how Page can easily imagine an idea becoming reality.

> One of the greatest insights of the Google-world is the freedom of Beta. A Beta is more than a product not-yet-ready-for-consumption, but a way

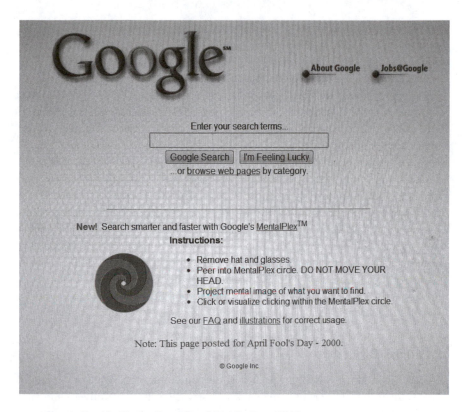

**FIGURE 2.1** Google Home Page, April Fool's Day, 2000

of thinking, creating, and living. It owns being unfinished … For a long time all of culture … believed in the myth of perfection, a closed process of creation, an established finality before completion. Before Beta, a mistake, glitch, virus, or crash was an embarrassment, a failure of the developers. Now these 'bugs' are opportunities for learning and we thank people for pointing them out as they join in to improve.

(2010: 13)

Beta culturally interpolates. It becomes its own first principle. A cycle of self-consecration achieved through seemingly transparent product refinements ensues. Clayton's observations about beta concord with Rothenberg's positing of a circle of technological practice in understanding how technologies at the beta stage of development, and even such imaginary technologies as MentalPlex™, over time can become goals worth pursuing. As the character in Figure 0.2's cartoon strip says, "Ridiculous things aren't so ridiculous when the Google God speaks."

Second, the joke works to incorporate searchers more fully into a nascent culture of search. George Myerson's comments on the mobilization of the telephone are apposite: "[It] isn't really a technological process—it's cultural. The problem isn't to *invent* a machine, but to get us all to adopt it, to feel we need it" (2001: 7). Making searchers part of a knowing in-crowd through branding efforts such as the April Fool's home page is one way to accomplish this. Another is to position search algorithms as magical agents at the service of rationality, the increasing agency of which enriches our lives, never mind any potential downside. Such discursive strategies circulate within capital formations that build demand for new technologies that people don't (yet) know they need. As one Twitterer put it upon the release of Google Instant, "So glad Google finally fixed search. I for one was sick of staring at a blank screen waiting 0.24 seconds for my results" (Smith and Bosker 2010). As the by now apocryphal question "What did you do before Google?" confirms, such technologies quickly become social appendages that "we" can't imagine ever having done without. As such they exemplify Martin Heidegger's broad conclusion (1977) that technology really accomplishes metaphysics by virtue of its capacity to reveal or "bring forth" that which was not perceived or evident beforehand.

## Positivist Objectivity

Google's predictive search technology is one outcome of its focus on a specific kind of relevance. In her study of search industry rhetoric, van Couvering identifies the consistent use of a science-technology schema to frame search quality and technological change more generally as outcomes of a "positivist, experimental science that has objectivity as an essential norm" (2007). Google's corporate philosophy emphasizes the relevance of positivist objectivity to its values: "It is a core value for Google that there be no compromising of the integrity of our results. We never manipulate rankings to put our partners higher in our search results. No one can buy better PageRank. Our users trust Google's objectivity and no short-term gain could ever justify breaching that trust" (Google 2006). We see here, within the frame of objectivity, how Google equates quality and relevance. "From a technical standpoint, then, the definition of a quality search engine is simple: If the search engine gives you results that answer your question, then the search engine has delivered a relevant response and the results are quality results" (van Couvering 2007).

The logical outcome of positivist objectivity is to collect and store as much data as possible, including data about users who, in effect, become informational objects at the service of the firm. While a searcher might interpret the results of her search as quality results if they provide a relevant response to her question, it is also the case that the more Google knows about her in advance, the better the quality and relevance of its answer to her query. In Google's specific pursuit of relevance, then, quality and quantity bleed into each other;

relevant or quality search outcomes increasingly depend on the firm knowing ever more about the searcher to the point where it comes to possess effectively omniscient data. That Google understands this conflation and is taking steps to actualize the possibility of omniscient data is indicated by remarks made by Eric Schmidt: "The power of individual targeting—the technology will be so good it will be very hard for people to watch or consume something that has not in some sense been tailored for them," and "I actually think most people don't want Google to answer their questions ... They want Google to tell them what they should be doing next" (Jenkins 2010). Stated otherwise, Schmidt believes, perhaps even fetishizes, that people want a thinking machine to determine the order and sequence, the general reality of their lives.

The drive for perfect quantification as a precursor to perfectly relevant, satisfying search also powers Page's comment, noted at the top of this chapter, that search "will be included in people's minds." It is a decidedly undelicious, metaphysically inflected irony that the positivist focus on objectivity which fuels the acquisition and storage of ever more data as part of providing individually valued search results ends up with the seeming transcendence or obviation of the imaginative human agency that leads us to seek answers through search in the first place.

We are not alone in noting the ironies that issue from Google's need to achieve Total Information Awareness in order to provide us with relevant search returns. (The irony disappears when we become the commodities Google sells to its advertisers.) The 2010 animated video "Don't be evil," produced by Jamie Court for the organization Consumer Watchdog, captures the surreal outcomes of this quest for totality rooted in positivist objectivity. The video mounts an over-the-top critique of Google's interest in acquiring as much information about as many people as possible. It depicts Schmidt as a lecherous vendor leering down from an ice-cream truck emblazoned with the Google logo. As he offers neighborhood kids free cones, Schmidt informs the virtual camera that nothing is "free" and tells the driver to "give me a dozen full body scans" of the kids gathered at the truck's dispensing window. In a voiceover Schmidt intones,

> Now hold still while we collect some of your secrets. And if there's anything you don't want anyone to know, well you shouldn't be doing it in the first place. Remember kids, you can't believe everything your parents say about privacy. Timmy, does mommy know that daddy spends his whole day surveying sports websites? How about you, Susie? I bet your daddy doesn't know mommy's been googling old boyfriends.

Schmidt's voicetrack runs parallel to a graphics display for an (as of yet) imaginary technology, "Google Body Analytics Scan," which lists Timmy's and Susie's vital statistics, favorite activities, occupations, and other personal details (Figure 2.2). Donning creepy shades, Schmidt continues, "Now kids, I want to share our

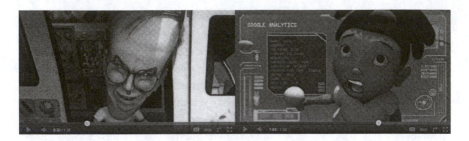

**FIGURE 2.2** Still Images from "Google: Don't be evil," (Consumer Watchdog 2010). Privacy Project, Consumer Watchdog. By permission

newest invention. With these Google Wi-Spy glasses, I can see everything." As angry moms and dads appear and start to chase the now moving truck, we hear Schmidt's final refrain, "Remember kids, we put the ogle into Google."

## Relevance and the Limits of Utility

Google's model of relevance merits criticism for its utilitarian bias and overemphasis on a particular mode of searching—academic investigation. The model is privileged at the expense of more socially focused modes of engagement with search that would also lead to "customer satisfaction." For instance, Halavais (2009) notes the loss of serendipity that occurs when search engines mobilizing utilitarian ideals of relevance come to determine information retrieval:

> Serendipity was inherent to the initial metaphor for traversing the web: surfing. The metaphor suggested that while you may be moving through the information, there was room to turn around, to take detours, and that the topography of the information encouraged these actions … There is a particular knowledge that is obtained only through exploration that is, even when goal-oriented, open to peripatetic function.
>
> (2009: 53)

The randomness and non-directional qualities of browsing that produce serendipitous encounters with information are essential to innovation. This effect of the Web, Halavais adds, is diminished by search engines that focus on the direct delivery of information reduced to its abstract utility. Given Google's consecrated position within the field and its consequent ability to reproduce its utilitarian model of search as best practice, such limitations on the types of information made available are of consequence not only to the ways that we, as searchers, understand the world around us today, but also to our ability to imagine the future as plural, multiple, and open. Yet even here Google assumes utilitarian approaches are best, as heard in Schmidt's straight-faced claim, "We have figured out a way to generate serendipity" (Sark 2011).

A number of studies from social, technical, and policy perspectives explore the limiting effects of search engines, including Google's PageRank algorithm (Hindman et al. 2003; Upstill et al. 2003; Finkelstein 2008; Goldman 2008; Hess 2008; Halavais 2009). Such studies often focus on the bias effects of the codes and processes through which search engines collect and organize data. Van Couvering (2007) notes that relevance, when construed as a technical measure, crowds out other measures of quality such as fairness and diversity of information that shape, for example, the field of journalism. Paul Reilly's (2008) study, using a variety of search engines to find the names of Northern Ireland "terrorist" organizations, found difficulty in accessing what he refers to as "controversy-revealing sites." Instead, he identifies the greater likelihood that search engines will direct users to the website of established institutions such as the BBC and universities. Reilly argues that this systematic privileging of established authority marginalizes access to the tools necessary for developing and maintaining diversity of opinion and conflicting viewpoints. Instead, typical search engines provide what he refers to as "more of the same" information, effectively suppressing controversy to the detriment of a rich understanding of issues (see also Gerhart 2004).

Given the culture of search that is upon us, such forms of bias and exclusion constitute one of the more significant, if under-recognized, issues that society faces. As Alejandro Diaz points out, the ideal of democratic deliberation is quite distinct from the pragmatics of actual democratic governance: "Sure, a political democracy generally requires that the aggregated preferences of the majority be put into practice. But this does not imply that only the majority's views should be heard during deliberation, nor does it suggest that popular opinions should be preferred *ipso facto*" (2008: 16). The privileging of institutionalized representations by PageRank, therefore, not only indicates algorithmic partiality to dominant understandings but also an inherently anti-deliberative bias.

It is important to understand that results generated by search engines are not drawn directly from the Web per se, but from cached copies of webpages gathered at a specific moment by a particular search engine's automated data collection bots and crawlers. These pages are stored in an index, and the index is searched, not the Web. Sites not stored in the index are effectively invisible to search engines. In all of this one sees how biases can be generated not only during the implementation of the ordering and sequencing algorithmic logic that generates search results but also in the indexing process itself.

These various biases do not make Google better or worse than any other media firm that filters, organizes, and frames representations in particular ways. What is arguable, however, is that the codes Google uses to construct its searches have a more determining control over content than, for instance, the gatekeeping function of human news editors. As legal and internet society scholar Lawrence Lessig notes, in the case of digital media, code is a totalizing organizer of possibility and action, regulating behavior by absolutely determining the terms of engagement. Code's absolute constraint, like a locked door, prevents any knowledge of what might lie beyond it and therefore inhibits considering why one might want to find the means to pass through the doorway in the first place (2006: 82, 342). In the field of information, the ways by which different codes enable the visibility of different kinds of knowledge have a regulatory effect on the nature of political action associated with that knowledge. Therefore, even if users treat search results with the skepticism with which they now approach traditional news media, the codes of Google's search algorithms retain a significant amount of power to determine the content, if not the actual meanings, generated by user searches. For, when one turns to Google, *one does not initially know what one does not know*. Given that no current search engine can organize information in a way that readily would allow one to determine the gaps in one's knowledge, contemporary search technologies encourage the perpetuation of the most popular and hence most dominant ideas as well as the possibility of their uncritical acceptance. Therefore, as Google works to realize its goal to organize the world's information through its reliance on the positivist objectivity of these automated algorithms, its potential to effect forms of symbolic violence becomes unprecedented.

## Beyond Utility: Extending Google's Model of Relevance

The previous sections assessed Google's particular understandings of relevance and how the firm deploys these understandings through its tripartite emphasis on utility, objectivity, and quality of search. While such principles are inherently utilitarian, Google's model of relevance is also based on other features that influence searchers' modes of engagement with information and, thereby, the broader culture of search and the specific processes of knowing it supports. These features or "rules" are 1. instantaneity, 2. generic individualization, and 3. universal granularity.

### *Rule #1: Instantaneity*

Google's worldwide network of data centers and server farms holds more than a million parallel processors linked via the firm's distributed file system, known within Google as Colossus (Hoff 2010). The largest array of computers in the world together with Colossus' architecture allows for rapid scalable indexing of an ever-expanding Web along with the ability to provide Google Instant's near-instantaneous results. Google prides itself on ensuring speed, boasting that Google Instant reduces the overall time of each search by two to five seconds and, if used globally, would save "more than 3.5 billion seconds a day. That's 11 hours saved every second" (Google 2011c). Google's drive toward instantaneity not only applies to its search technologies but also to its advertising network and browser. Page Speed Online enables webmasters to review their sites' performance and offer suggestions about speeding up the delivery of pages, including to mobile devices (Google 2011e), and Google Code offers webmasters a raft of services to "improve the experience for your users around the world by several seconds" (Google 2011d). A speedy approach is also on view in the Chrome browser speed test videos proudly produced by Google engineers (YouTube 2010; Google n.d.). In inviting developers to share insights into "making the Web faster," Google declared, "From building data centers in different parts of the world to designing highly efficient user interfaces, we at Google always strive to make our services faster. We focus on speed as a key requirement in product and infrastructure development, because our research indicates that people prefer faster, more responsive apps" (Google 2009a).

Urs Hölzle, Google's Senior Vice President of Operations, speaks to this desire, explaining, "Speed can drive usage as much as having bells and whistles on your product. People really underappreciate it. Larry [Page] is very much on that line" (Levy 2011: 185). Hölzle also notes that when people feel search results are too slow to appear on their screens, they become "unconsciously afraid of doing another search, because it's slow. Or they are more likely to try another result than rephrase the query. I'm sure if you ask them, none of them would tell you, but in aggregate you really see that. On the other hand, when you speed things up, they search more" (ibid.: 185–186). Microsoft's experiments with its Bing search engine also "showed that when results are delayed, users respond with their own latency, taking longer to click on links after a search is completed. Presumably, during the half second or more that the results are delayed, the users have begun to think about something else and have to refocus before they get around to clicking on a result" (ibid.: 186).

The concern with speed extends across the search industry, and speed, for Google, is a first principle, an ontological value of the highest order that drives its sense of corporate meaning. This is not only because speed has become a commandment for efficiency-focused engineers, but also because, as Paul Virilio has observed, instantaneity along with ubiquity are attributes of the divine now increasingly applied to human affairs (1997: 70). But in the real world of gaps, technical failures, re-routings, work-arounds, human inattention, and so forth, instantaneous search is an ideal. Belief that it can be realized manifests a form of Platonism that can be seen to imply that instant search—precisely because it lies in the ideal realm of desire—necessarily must remain somewhere else than this earthly plane. We recognize that utopian ideals, including the ideal of instantaneity, can inspire those who seek to improve the real world. But a firm that believes that search could ever actually be "instant" is a firm that privileges "perfect" ideology over the messy contingencies of embodied earthly realities, both machinic and fleshy. It is a firm that has buried its collective head in the virtual cloud and bought into the myth of Plato's Cave in believing that it can, through instant search, lead us out of the Cave and into the "true" and perfect reality of the Platonic Ideal.

In the capitalized real world in which Google operates, users buy into this temporal strategy of speed. Ever more speedy search is a strategy directed toward a metaphysics of instantaneity—a perfect state that, if ever achieved, would leave the first principle dimension of time behind. And here we can see the latent articulations that lie behind the will to instantaneity and Brin and Page's hope that in the future search will go beyond even reading one's mind to *being* one's mind. In the real world, this is an Idealist metaphysics that Google encourages its users to accept. Such a focus places greater value on the utopian desires for machines that provide instantaneity and immediacy than it does on the real world's flesh-based need for accretion or sedimentation of understanding and knowledge over time.

We do not, however, believe that a conscious focus on metaphysical questions of first principle per se operationalizes Google's business decisions. Rather, as we argue throughout this book, metaphysics and the political economy of modern corporate practices are not so far apart as commonly supposed. The corporate ideal of cloud computing is just such an instance of Platonic metaphysics applied to real-world thinking. It seems only natural that Google, with its pivotal role in the development and application of cloud computing practices, encourages its legions of users to store their information in the cloud and then to call on it only when needed. While this information in many ways is a "stand-in" for their embodied selves, unlike actual bodies it need not be retained *in situ*, and neither is this encouraged. Archived results run the risk of diminishing in "relevance" over time. Google's Autocomplete function, which provides suggestions based in part on each user's (or IP address's) previously entered search terms, encourages little user investment in remembering or archiving search terms. Given the ubiquity of Google's search technology across a variety of Web-enabled devices, the necessity to store—to remember—vast quantities of search results or search terms is obviated. With Google so close at hand, it "only makes sense" that its model of good search, indeed its model of relevance, is based on Just In Time delivery that reduces our need to remember.

## Rule #2: Generic Individualization

Generic individualization of search results is a second feature or rule of Google's model of relevance. As users' competencies and the scale of the Web expanded, a key shift occurred away from the "surfing" common to early internet experiences to the more targeted contemporary operation of "searching." This shift can partly be attributed to the increased valuation of speed, yet it also draws attention to the notion that good search focuses on finding what is *already known* about a particular topic rather than on the generation of new knowledges, texts, or objects. Lev Manovich speaks to this point: "By the end of the twentieth century, the problem was no longer how to create a new media object such as an image; the new problem was how to find an object that already exists somewhere" (2002: 35). While the juxtapositions of various retrieved data may indeed create perpetually new objects, at their heart databases—and Google's index is nothing more than a database—are centered on the recovery of *existing* information. Within the field of search and its normalized model of relevance, therefore, increasing importance has been placed on satisfying the expectations of targeted searches and goal-oriented searchers who already have a sense of what they are looking to find. This happens through the provision of anticipated, and thus generic, information.

Genericism is the underlying logic of PageRank, which draws on the so-called wisdom of crowds. Its model of relevance values and hierarchizes information as "relevant" in terms of its *measurable* appreciation by a mass of users, including those institutionalized experts whose valuations receive higher weightings. This occurs in a context where, despite the diversity of the Web, established or already well-known webpages tend to attract the highest number of users. Studies have shown that the Web's structural patterning concords with Zipf's "power law distribution" (Adamic and Huberman 2002; see also Halavais 2009: 60–64). Zipf's law suggests that the frequency of an event is inversely proportionate to its rank, so that the second most frequent event occurs half as often as the first and so forth. Adamic and Huberman argue that this same logic applies to both the popularity of a site (in terms of numbers of hits or impressions) and the number of links associated with that site. The most popular website is twice as popular as the next, with a great number of sites clustering below the median level of popularity. Similarly, while many pages have some links, relatively few contain great numbers of links (Huberman 2001; Halavais 2009: 60–64). As PageRank treats the number of links as evidence of a page's popular approval, more highly linked pages, as noted in the introduction, are more likely to be highly ranked in the search engine's results, and are thus more likely to attract more links, increasing their ranking. This cascading dynamic generates a context of "preferential attachment" (Huberman 2001; Halavais 2009: 67), where greater value is given those who already possess such capital, thereby accounting for the logic behind Zipf's identification of power law distribution. In effect, the underlying structure of the Web and the dynamics of PageRank generate a self-organizing virtuous circle in which attention on the Web is distributed unevenly and in ways that privilege sites with established and authoritative Web presences. Halavais summarizes:

> In order for a website to make it onto the first page of results on Google, it first has to have a large number of links to it. However, without being on the first page of results, few website authors will know that it exists and be

able to link it ... PageRank and related esteem-enhancing search algorithms clearly increase the current imbalance, calcifying existing networks of popularity.

(2009: 68)

This skewed distributional logic and its privileging of "popularity" is a key concern of most critical interpretations of PageRank which in various ways note that the prior choices of webpages by all searchers serve to guide the "active" searcher through his or her own process of information gathering. Measuring relevance through popularity "abandons the goals of actually reflecting a page's 'importance' or 'authoritativeness' on a given subject, and instead aims to mirror the 'common' wishes of users" (Diaz 2008: 17). The way PageRank positions information as relevant typically reflects the most common and commonsense viewpoints of and attitudes towards a particular topic. This means that, within the model used by Google, what gets considered as relevant or valuable information already has a profoundly generic quality. Google Instant incarnates this genericism as it prompts users with typical search strings drawn from the archives of existing searches practices while it simultaneously displays the most common earlier search results for these terms as well. As evident in these technologies, relevance is ultimately about the provision of normatively defined ideas across the field of search. Effectively, there are no relevant surprises in the Googleverse.

Such genericism, though, is tempered by an increasing focus on individuation in search results (Hoofnagle 2009; Rogers 2009). Google collects and aggregates vast amounts of user data. As noted in the previous chapter, this capacity was written into the firm's original algorithms in order to facilitate its own future research into search activities (Brin and Page 1998). Mackenzie notes that "algorithms carry, fold, frame and redistribute actions into different environments" (2006: 43) and each Google search, as a "signal" of consumer activity, is fed back into the algorithm, enabling it to "learn" what consumers define as good results (Levy 2011), which serves as an important agent in generating "relevant" results. PageRank, then, positions the individual searcher as a resource for indicating epistemic difference. This point is also crucial when it comes to advertising revenue. In early 2004 Google began to seriously investigate various means of gathering specific data that would allow it to personalize search results (Zimmer 2008). Once this data could be gathered, it increasingly was used to generate more personalized ways of providing information to searchers and of providing targeted advertising, drawing as it does on information already gathered before the current search (Hoofnagle 2009; Röhle 2009). "Event-based data," generated by logs of user activity including IP addresses, clickthroughs, and browsing data, are combined with other databased representations of activities associated with that user or IP address, as well as with general models of user activity generated from mass data, to craft tailored results for individual users.

Despite this form of personalization, it is important to recognize that the data so generated continue to have a generic quality. While search results may be ranked or selected based on personalization algorithms, they nevertheless reflect only a prediction of the actions a user may take as they are generated solely on the basis of aggregating pre-stated preferences. In effect, Google offers searchers ideas of what to search for based on individual preferences that reference only a generic "vision" of themselves, a point discussed further in chapter 7.

In all of this, the logic of the database underpins Google's index. At the turn of the millennium, Manovich described personalization technologies where users select from a menu of pre-given objects. "Paradoxically, by following an interactive path, one does not construct a unique self but instead adopts already pre-established identities. Similarly, choosing values from a menu or customizing one's desktop or an application automatically makes one participate in the 'changing collage of personal whims and fancies' mapped out and coded into software by the companies" (2002: 129). While Google's targeting technologies are much more sophisticated than the standard pull-down menus Manovich describes, they suffer from an incompleteness of data and a consequent inability to provide truly encompassing definitions of the individual. Such path-dependency ensures genericism of results and renders Google unable to achieve its goal of "understanding what you mean and giving back exactly what you want" (Google 2006). Such understanding may, in fact, only be possible for humans—librarians, for instance—who have a more ready ability to truly personalize search. Google, then, faces a similar difficulty as that faced by advertising-supported broadcast mass media, where uncertainty about how to measure the rich quality of audience engagement has a long history. The perfectly understandable consumer "is the utopian symbolic object that will never be realized, but which audience measurement perpetually strives to approximate" (Ang 1991: 58). While Google's ideal model of relevance may provide perfectly individualized search results, its actual automated model continues to genericize search.

## Rule #3: Universal Granularity

Google anticipates a perpetual project of data gathering. Point 7 of its corporate philosophy claims, "there is always more information out there" (Google 2006), and for Google to achieve universality it is essential that all things, both representational and material, be available for indexing and retrieval. This disposition is evident in the digitization of Main Street on Google Street View, books on Google Books, the human body on Google Body (now Zygote Body), and everything from menus to landmarks to art works to wine labels to commercial logos on Google Goggles. Information on these sites must be searchable, indexable, and measurable at a fine level of detail. Data must be granulated into datum. This leveling of information suggests a kind of universality in which all information is equally 0s and 1s but, because of Google's model of relevance, some information is more highly ranked than others and thus more "visible"—more easily retrieved by searchers and therefore positioned as more worthwhile and worth remembering. For instance, PageRank accords a keyword appearing in a headline a higher ranking than a keyword appearing in text marked up as a caption. Comments on blog posts are systematically discounted in delivery of search results and in page ranking (Rogers 2009), and Google routinely devalues the status of porn sites (Vaidhyanathan 2011: 14). While the need for it to identify and differentiate various kinds of data has become increasingly central, the firm's insistence on, and its development of mechanisms to guarantee, the granularity of information constitutes another way that its model of relevance organizes how we access knowledge and therefore the classification of knowledge itself.

## Contingency and Relevance

It is easy to criticize Google's instant generic results and universal granularity on the basis that they provide decontextualized, and thus readily misconstrued, information to searchers, or that the practice excludes some pages entirely (see Herring 2009; Mayer-Schönberger 2009). It is also possible to lament the lack of surprise or serendipity that results from Google's generic individualism and its circumscribing of our capacity to learn by limiting access to only that which fits with what we already know (Vaidhyanathan 2011: 182). Through their focus on the substantive nature of the search results, these criticisms provide valuable insights. More important to our project, however, is to recognize that the adroit targeting of specific information inherent within Google's model of relevance is just one of several methods possible for engaging with information or knowledge. Such targeting depends on algorithms, the myriad subtle and direct agencies of which we fully acknowledge. We need again to emphasize, however, that algorithms are themselves the outcomes, the products of interweaving and entangled constellations of internal and external forces of fields of practice and structures of feeling. So, too, are Google's particular implementations of genericism and universal granularity contingent manifestations of a culturally inflected set of ideas held by the firm's leaders about the nature of information gathering that has particular consequences for the ways in which we are expected to engage, and actually do engage, with knowledge.

For instance, Rogers suggests that medieval scholars' "search for knowledge began by knowing where they had to go, but not necessarily what was in store for them once they arrived. They knew the sites (the libraries), and from them they eventually would learn the texts (and the key words)" (2004: 35–36). Rather than the granulated instant gratification provided by Google's model of relevance, such pre-modern forms of gathering information were emergent, immersive, and full of potentiality. Indeed we would not even apply the concept of relevance as a valid measure within such information-gathering contexts.

Rogers, however, does propose this "traveller-knowledge scenario" as a model for contemporary collaborative filtering processes such as the social bookmarking site Delicious.com (formerly del.icio.us) that provide an alternative means of storing, sharing, and finding data on the internet. This model is what Halavais calls "sociable search" (2009: 160–180); information gathering follows trails formed through the recommendations of other users. While Google adopts some features of this approach—drawing on collective intelligence forms a key plank of the genericism of its search results—the targeted granularity of its search results denies the serendipity and contextualization inherent within the model described by Rogers.

Rogers proposes a different model of information retrieval when he describes Yahoo! as a web librarian (2009). The distinction Rogers introduces is between, on the one hand, Google's automated "neutrality," universality, and the ways in which granulated information provides satisfying results and, on the other, the clear authority, subjective ordering, and contextualized suggestions librarians provide. The effect of Google's model of relevance on institutional gatekeepers such as librarians has been profound. As librarian Kay Cahill notes, the growth of search engines and information access has changed the way that library patrons conceive of themselves and librarians: "They see themselves as searchers, and they know that the information is out there. And they no longer see librarians as the guardians of information per se. They see librarians as the guardians of the expertise they need to use the tools they know are out there to access that information" (2009: 71).

The shift in the conception of librarians from "guardians" of information to facilitators of access reflects a widespread belief that online search now constitutes a more direct and unbiased mode of engagement with information gathering than possible when one required a librarian and the institutional privilege, and therefore bias, he or she represents to access information. Indeed, one of the great emancipatory promises of the internet and the Web, particularly as articulated through the Californian ideology, is direct individual access to information without the shaping and moderating influence of gatekeepers. As our discussion of the gatekeeping role of hyper-surveillant search engines indicates, however, such a promise is naive at best. In the absence of a more robust and honest discussion on the part of search engine providers of the issues discussed in this chapter, the promise appears increasingly deceptive.

Cahill's discussion of the shift in popular status of librarians points to an important development. Walter Benjamin (1962) discusses the decline of the figure of the storyteller typically associated with oral cultures. For Benjamin, the storyteller's wisdom was rooted in his or her direct, socio-historically embedded, experience of the stories he or she lived to tell. It was storytellers' performative sharing of their oral histories with their audiences that ensured these histories' transmission along with maintaining the storyteller's authority. Beginning with the emergence of the novel, and extending through modernity to contemporary electronic communication, the culturally, temporally, and socially located corpo-reality that provided context and meaning for telling stories has waned. Benjamin notes, for instance, the scalar impossibility of conveying by storytelling the experience of World War I and its inconceivable horrors. As there was no commonly shared historical experience of misery of this magnitude, the story of war was unable to be told as lived experience. It *was* possible, however, to express this horror in the *form* of information which, as Benjamin suggests, requires no validation other than its own verifiability. In the process of information provi-sion, authority is no longer contextualized and instantiated but positive and abstract. For Benjamin, the decline of such located authoring, and authorization, has had a diminishing effect. "In every case the story-teller is a man [sic] who has counsel for his readers. But if today 'having counsel' is beginning to have an old-fashioned ring, this is because the communicability of experience is decreasing. In consequence we have no counsel either for ourselves or for others" (1962: 83). While Benjamin's lament for the decline of authorized speakers and the long yarn of anecdotal experience may grate against contemporary liberal tendencies which refute such claims to authority, our point is that it has not always been illegitimate for information, knowledge, or the stories that shape our world to be directly mediated by actively interested gatekeepers who provide difficult, richly nuanced, and ambiguous narratives drawing upon context, memory, and shared understandings. It is has not always been the case, and nei-ther is it still, that wisdom or understanding are best generated through factual and informational media such as "objective" news services or automated, granular search engines based on the equation popularity = relevance.

The relative merits of these alternative, older models of gathering relevant information, however, are not what is at stake here. Rather it is the shift away from historically or culturally different regimes of encountering information and, by extension, building knowledge that is important to emphasize. As natu-ralized as receiving results within seconds of entering a search term that deeply links you to the particular page hosting that term may now seem, receiving results in this way is not a "natural" or essential quality of Web information retrieval, or of any other information retrieval process. This model is specific to the contemporary field of search in which Google and searchers alike rank instanta-neity, generic individuation, and universal granularity as valuable qualities. Each searcher happy or "satisficed" with the relevance of her personalized search results perpetuates that particular model of relevance as an epistemic framework. Microsoft's Bing search engine, while economically competitive, does not offer an alternative model of relevance and, if it were to usurp Google's status, there would be no resulting major difference in the field's organization of values. Google has accused Bing of directly copying its model of relevance, likening it "to the digital equivalent of Bing leaning over during an exam and copying off of Google's test." Bing does not dispute Google's claim (Sullivan 2011). We need to acknowledge, therefore, that Google's model of relevance is not solely its own. As Bing's copycat activities indicate, Bing rightly "belongs" to the field of search's current organization of values. And it is Google that first, and most successfully, articulated this orthodoxy and on whose symbolic capital its perpetuation since has relied. It will take a seismic shift in the field's values to meaningfully unsettle this model of relevance.

## The Epistemology of Relevance

The effects of Google's doxa—it's "taken-for-grantedness"—works to expand the field of search it already dominates. Search mediates our lives and our mode of engagement with information, and the nature of knowledge and the process of knowing inherent in Google's model of relevance are crucial to understand in terms of one other. All learning happens *in situ* and examining how Google's model of relevance depends upon a particular epistemology that can influence searchers' specific approaches and engagements with information also sheds some light on the broader meaning of search today. In this section we focus on the importance of understanding how specific forms of searcher engagement with Google's model of relevance come to be seen as "natural" ways of learning.

In *Critique of Information* (2002), Scott Lash argues that contemporary media-saturated settings of ubiquitous mediation, such as those generated by digital and mobile technologies, have a particular ontology that he describes as informationalization. Content associated with the newspaper format and, we would add, the 24/7 rolling news of contemporary networked and online television lacks the durational persistence of older media forms. "The news," Lash says, extending McLuhan, is perpetually new. It is composed

> under pressure of a deadline, of no use tomorrow, of value for 24 hours and no longer. Such information loses meaning, loses significance very quickly ... Newsprint, or information, has neither logical nor existential meaning. It is often not subsumed under universals. Its meaning is accidental, ephemeral and very often trivial ... For their part, newspapers and other forms of information ... have no meaning at all outside of real time. Outside of the immediacy of real time, news and information are, literally, garbage. You throw out the newspaper with the disused food and the baby's disposable nappies.
>
> (ibid.: 144–145)

There is much here that is relevant to Google, and indeed probably more so than to the news media Lash discusses. Google's rapid delivery of results has a similar real-time immediacy, which is not necessarily a quality of search results per se. Google's data are not necessarily new—the index and the cache are archives of historically produced data. However, Google's *way of knowing*—the process it provides by which we come to engage with information—is marked by a temporal framework constituted in *immediate* gratification of desire. Online search displays information within moments of being sought and that, by the same logic of immediacy, also can disappear instantly back into the index, or cloud, from whence it came. What Google's model of search proposes is, then, not accretion of knowledge but the immediacy and ephemerality of information retrieval.

The instantaneity of Google's model of relevance can be understood to generate results that are neither universal nor transcendent and, consequently, do not function as ideologies. This does not mean that Google's results are not ideological. Rather, they do not have the same ontological status as metanarratives of ideology. Instead, we encounter them merely as information. "Ideologies were extended in time and space. They claimed universality. They were extended often in the temporal form of 'metanarratives.' … Information [on the other hand] is compressed in time and space. It makes no claim to universality but is contained in the immediacy of the particular. Information shrinks or compresses metanarratives to a mere point, a signal, a mere event in time" (ibid.: 1). Unlike the type of embodied content generated by Benjamin's socio-historically located storyteller discussed in the previous section, Google's results, experienced for specific moments and to satisfy specific purposes, cannot draw upon historical contexts and instantiated meanings. Without the necessary extension across space and time, such results cannot be understood as narrative or even discourse.

Lash defines such non-narrative informational content as "a collage of particulars" (ibid.: 145). This notion is perfectly represented in the disconnected list of ten search results that is Google's default response. The image of a collage further resonates with the personalized search results that flow from generic personalization, as well as the particularity of its model of relevance. As a single corpus, the ever-growing number of search results produced globally or, even those generated for an individual user, lacks narrative cogency. That each set of results is increasingly tailored to an individual searcher's orientations means that no singular, universal narrative for any particular search term is produced. This is illustrated by the way that the geographic location of a searcher's IP address has an important determining role, generating as it does search results particular to that location. Google's index is further broken down into finely grained component parts so that search results are fragmented, often with incoherent relationships between individual results within the list. Each result may individually fulfill the requirement of "relevance" but need not be thematically related to other results. Deep mining of individual keywords extracted from context fundamentally ensures that search results are a "mass of particulars without a universal" (ibid.: 144). For instance, Quick Scroll, an extension to Google's Chrome browser, displays search results on the browser page. The service enables searchers to be taken directly to those individual search terms. Rather than reviewing the entire document and approaching the search terms within the broader narrative of the page in question, searchers adopting this technology instantly link to granulated information. The instant provision of finely grained results marks Google's results as information, not discourse or narrative, or, again, even ideology.

How, then, do Google's search results achieve validity? From their own "facticity." Particularly in the context of soundbite journalism and sites such as Gawker.com, where an audience's capacity to reflect and link back to previous iterations or discussions of a news event is curtailed, or relegated to the fragmentation of hyperlinks, news is not asked to rely on any other authority than its own presence as news for its validity. While this self-serving dynamic may not apply to quality journalism, it has deep applicability for understanding Google's decontextualized yet immediately gratifying results. Their validity does not depend on the historicizing and contextualizing qualities that mark discursive knowledge and discourse. As Benjamin says of information, the "prime requirement is that it appear 'understandable in itself.' Often it is no more exact than the intelligence of earlier centuries. But while the latter was inclined to borrow from the miraculous, it is indispensable for information to sound plausible" (1962: 85). Google's model of relevance directly articulates a way of knowing to believability based on facticity. Its search results gain validity from the performative power of their own "findability" and immediate utility to a specific searcher and not from being based on access to any coordinated sets of knowledge per se.

## Knowing Phenomenologically

Facticity is the important feature of Google's epistemology; information has meaning because of its relationship to the underlying assumptions that organize everyday life (Lash 2002: 90). This is, however, not the everyday of Benjamin's storied storyteller, who takes her tales and authority from personal experience in order to establish connections among generations and places spread across time and space. The temporal immediacy of Just In Time information access differs from the historicized temporality in which the storyteller remembers and tells. Instead, Google's search results and those who utilize them increasingly conform to the logic of the database: "individuals and objects now are no longer stories or even subjectivities but only points or nodes in a network" (ibid.: 134).

Google's model of relevance, as an example of informationalized culture, relies on an epistemological framework whereby individual engagement with information becomes grounded in immediate, experiential relations between subject and object akin to that in the world of play. In play, Lash argues, there is not a "symbolic correspondence" between the player and his or her role; rather, the player *becomes* that role (ibid.: 158). This immersion is the reason why playing a team sport is often more profoundly affective than other activities (such as waged labor) driven by practical need. Utilitarian calculations of value, however, become less central to an informationalized culture marked by dynamics associated with play. In play, the loss of distance between subject and object can place reflexive judgment on shaky ground. "To play is to be *so* interested, *so* involved immediately as to rule out the possibility of judgement. Judgement involves always a separate and neutral instance. It presupposes a culture of representation. Play … does not involve this" (ibid.: 160; emphasis in original). Google's ontology can be similarly described.

This loss of judgment occurs because play presupposes closeness between the subject and object as opposed to the conceptual distance associated with representation and critical interpretation. "The work of art or contemplated nature must be in another space from the viewer in order to be judged. The football match, the agon, is not in separate space but in the space of what Heidegger called 'the there' … It is not to be viewed or painted, but 'played' or followed. The supporters are 'in the world' with their team" (ibid.: 161). It is the immediacy and immersion of such experiences that distinguish them from practices entailing critical judgment. Lash also observes that a judge cannot be called "in the world" with the criminals on whom he or she renders judgment and it is from this distance that the judgment acquires validity and authority. This distance, though, is not available to searchers whose experience of searching, while not necessarily play, is of being engaged in a performative context where meaning is generated through their affective and individualized response to search results. Searchers are necessarily "in the world" *with* their search results, an engagement made more resonant by the personalization technologies that craft those results just for them. In this setting, unlike the positivist scientist or the judge able to step back from the object and world of their study, the searcher cannot generate distance from the search results. She or he cannot generate the objective, reflective, reflexive distanced judgment of the transcendental ego variously set forth by Kant, Hegel, and Husserl. Google's model of relevance does not support an epistemological position from whence one might observe reflexively in order to make aesthetic or critical judgments. Instead, the searcher filters, values, and organizes information through experience. "The experiencer … has knowledge of the object from his/her attitude, from the particular perspective of this intentionality. This knowledge is not through judgement, but takes place in a mode in which judgement is suspended: it is instead knowledge through belief" (Lash 2002: 165). Google's model of relevance occupies a position within the field of search that intersects with ever more mediated ways by which experience and faith supplant reflexive judgment as principal measures of knowledge. Engagement with information becomes more phenomenological than reflexive or rationally evaluative.

It is at this juncture where the broader significance of Google's model of relevance may be found. Google's results provide what the American satirist Stephen Colbert has identified as "truthiness": those performative "truths" that are deemed, in recursive fashion, true or "facts" precisely because one already believes them to be so (Meddaugh 2010). Many searchers trust personalized search results precisely because their contents already are acceptable to and resonate with their expectations. Knowledge generated through such empiricism alone has the potential to change the contours of public debate.

Dominique Mehl (2005), for example, assesses the increased personalization of public discourse as evidenced by confessional talk shows and various forms of mediated audience participation where public deliberation is presented as a comparison or evaluation of preferences or feelings. She argues that such experience-based accounts have either replaced or effectively stifled intellectual debate: "Objections can only be formulated in terms of pseudo-objections, such as: 'I did not react in the same way when I had a similar experience.' A story, which acts as an argument, becomes genuinely impossible to challenge" (ibid.: 25).

While Mehl's argument that truthiness irreparably damages the public sphere is difficult to sustain, her central point resonates with our position. Google's epistemological framework, based on the idea that knowledge is a phenomenological aggregate, follows the logic of Ouroboros and privileges a form of knowing that depends on its own internal validity, and that works to foreclose recognition that the significance of information also depends on the ways that it has been subject to disagreement and debate. The outcome is twofold. First, such a mode of engagement potentially produces subjective, non-rational evaluations of the information searcher's encounter. This may profoundly affect the types of content they deem valid for inclusion in public discourse. Second, as search normalizes truthiness as a mode of judgment it could become the entirely relative touchstone for evaluating public and civic matters, a point we further develop in chapter 7. While Google's own influence may not be sufficient to ensure this secondary effect, it is important to note that the informationalism driving the firm's mode of relevance intersects with 1. current trends toward increased performances of non-rationality, 2. the rise of personal narratives in political and commercial discourse, and 3. the reshaping of civic life given the increasingly leaky boundaries between public and private spheres (Papacharissi 2010). The exclusions and inclusions of algorithms increasingly shape the form of information available in public settings. But, as this chapter's analysis indicates, the underlying epistemology of the model of relevance that shapes *how we know* has an equally profound effect.

It is important to note that the mode of engagement just outlined is allied to principles of neoliberal governance which place a culturally policed premium on the forms of agency implicit in Google's model of relevance and epistemology (Rose 1999; Coté and Pybus 2007; Jarrett 2008). The neoliberal subject is not ideological in the traditional way that ideology has been conceived and understood. Neoliberalism relies, in part, on what Nikolas Rose terms an "ethopolitics" to construct its "active" subjectivities: "By ethopolitics I refer to attempts to shape the conduct of human beings by acting upon their sentiments, beliefs, and values—in short, by acting on ethics" (2007: 27). A combination of cultural, economic, and political forces works to induce individuals to willingly accept complete personal responsibility for their own lives' trajectories. Interactive consumption, and e-commerce in particular, become practices and sites not only for rendering identity markers directly economic but also for encouraging citizen-consumers to understand their lives, "actually or potentially, not in terms of fate or social status, but in terms of one's success or failure in acquiring the skills and making the choices to actualize oneself" (Rose 1999: 87). This is precisely the actively affective searcher encouraged by Google's model of relevance. For Maurizio Lazzarato, this form of subjectivity "ceases to be only an instrument of social control (for the reproduction of mercantile relationship) and becomes directly productive, because the goal of our postindustrial society is to construct the consumer/communicator—and to construct it as 'active'" (1996: 142).

The seductive qualities of this form of active agency germinate through pleasure, play included, and Zygmunt Bauman suggests that the mediated realm of consumption's main attraction is the purported sense of freedom it offers "to people who in other areas of life find only constraints, often experienced as oppression. What makes the freedom offered by the market more alluring still is that it comes without the blemish which tainted most of its other forms: the same market which offers freedom offers also certainty. It offers the individual the right to a 'thoroughly individual' choice; yet it also supplies social approval for such choice" (1988: 60–61). The pleasurable appeal of the "freedom to decide," therefore, constitutes part of the seductive core of Google's model of relevance. The form of search that Google's truthiness-confirming model generates thus works to manage the subjectivity of, and subjection to, dominant forms of power. In the final analysis, perhaps the most important power to which we become subject as we mediate ever more of our life through Google is Google itself as a novel form of parastatal authority and governmentality. While there is diversity in the particular meanings being made from search results as each result is subjected to a personalized measure of individual truthiness, this diversity remains lodged within the overall metaphysical unity of the firm's singular and dominant model of good search.

# 3

# UNIVERSAL LIBRARIES AND THINKING MACHINES

Returning to the notion of an intellectual library, we must concede that … the imagined intellectual material, of which the intellectual library is composed, is interior and could be said to seep through us until it is eventually … exuded in the form of texts, images or other creative acts.

(Jarvis 2008)

How Google and its suite of technologies have achieved cultural relevance, the firm's ability to set industry and societal standards of best practice, its meaningful influence over how knowledge is distributed and understood, and its high economic valuation—these are the foci of chapters 1 and 2. Beginning with this chapter we offer a set of intellectual histories of the longstanding, Idealist desire for a universal library. We begin with the pre-1900 thoughts, desires, theories, and systems of belief that collectively inform contemporary search. The chapter outlines the longevity of the quest for automated knowledge by tracing a history of ideas about storage, code, and classification's intertwining relationships to claims concerning knowledge, value, and truth. We attempt to show how the past—past myths, past technologies, past practices and techniques—still speaks through the present even as we also recognize that the culture of networked search is something new.

In his 1939 essay "La Biblioteca Total" ("The Total Library"), Jorge Luis Borges (1899–1986) provides a brief history of the idea of a total or universal library. Like others, we are indebted to this work and draw on it to help organize this chapter's narrative account. Commenting that "It's a wonder how long it took mankind to think of the idea" (2001: 214), the Argentine writer and librarian identifies the nineteenth-century German panpsychic philosopher and psychologist Gustav Theodor Fechner as the "belated inventor" of the idea and further identifies Fechner's mentee, German mathematician, philosopher, and science fiction writer Kurd Lasswitz as the idea's "first exponent" (ibid.). Borges subsequently mentions the history of correspondences among this idea and Ancient theories of Atomism as well as Renaissance theories of combinatory analysis, and he builds on a suggestion by German author and journalist Theodor Wolff that the total library "is a derivation from, or a parody of" the "thinking machine" designed by the late medieval polymath Ramón Llull as an aid for converting Muslims to Christianity's "true" fold (ibid.).

The contemporary mathematician in Borges limits his account to a discussion of proposals for universal libraries based more on "universal orthographic symbols" and less on "the words of a language" (2001: 215), as if words could not be atomized into 1s and 0s. Our treatment engages a broader range of ideas than does Borges' account. It draws on ideas that do not depend on universal orthographic symbols for their actualization as well as those that do.

## Atomic Value

In "The Total Library," Borges writes that the "'oldest glimpse' of the idea is found in the first book of Aristotle's *Metaphysics*" (2001: 214). In it, Aristotle summarizes the fifth century BCE cosmogony of Leucippus, who, with his student Democritus, formulated the theory of the universe identified as Atomism. For the Atomists, reality consisted in atoms alone, which were "that which cannot be cut finer" (Kitto 1964: 200) and, therefore, "so infinitely small as to be incapable of further division" (*OED*). "When Democritus gave the atom its name, which in Greek means 'indivisible,' he meant that these particles represent the ultimate possible limit to which the breaking up of matter into its component parts could be carried, atoms, in other words, being the smallest and simplest parts of which all materials bodies are composed" (Gamow 1960: 129). The Greek word for atom, *stoicheion*, means "number" *and* "letter." The plural is *stoicheia*, or "elements," and Atomism asserts a "concordance between atoms as the elements of reality and letters as the elements of the world of language" (Scholem 1965: 77).

Atomism's universal explanation of reality relies on the belief that all physical bodies, regardless of individual form, are constituted in *stoicheia*, the differences between these bodies deriving entirely "from position, order, or form" (Borges 2001: 214). Atomist philosophy was, in part, an extension of Pythagorean belief that "visible, tangible bodies are aggregated from a plurality of units equally held to be the points of geometry, the atoms of bodies, and the units of arithmetic" (Hillis 1999: 96). Atoms, possessing elemental materiality, are separated from one another by an immaterial Void that "is always everywhere between the surfaces of [these] different bodies" (Cornford 1936: 225). Ancient Atomism marks the beginning of a connection between metaphysically inflected theory (in the sense of theory constituting a first principle) and the belief that reality not only can be represented adequately by abstraction (whether in the elemental form of numbers or letters of the alphabet) but also that reality *is* universally constituted in abstraction itself.[1] Theories of Atomism, as Hayles has noted, have proved darkly important in that they encourage the fantasy that we can do away with the body because we are, at base, nothing but aggregated bits of information (1999: 12).

By the time of Cicero (106 BCE–43 BCE), the indivisible atomic elements that the earlier Greeks had represented by letters had come to be understood as analogically equivalent to the letters of literature (Mann 1989: 1010). Since the seventeenth century, however, Atomism, with its conceived basis in materialism, has been the accepted scientific interpretation (Reese 1980: 38). The Atomists' distinction between the materiality of atoms and the immateriality of a boundless Void as a natural fact is the basis for endowing abstract space with physical existence, and in Galileo Galilei's (1564–1642) revival of atomistic theory it forms the basis for his then scandalous proposal for an infinitely open space (Hillis 1999: 95–97). The Atomists' distinction between the immaterial void and the materiality of atoms, moreover, parallels and anticipates the binary distinction between 1s and 0s upon which digital computation relies.

Like Hayles, James Gleick discusses the legacy of Atomism and he does so by making the connection between Atomism and the bit (a condensation of the term "**bi**nary digi**t**"), the smallest unit of information. "The bit is a fundamental particle … not just tiny but abstract—a binary digit, a flip-flop, a yes-or-no. It is insubstantial, yet as scientists finally come to understand information, they wonder whether it may be primary: more fundamental than matter itself. They suggest that the bit is the irreducible kernel and that information forms the very core of existence" (2011: 9–10). The Atomists' proposal that reality is constituted in abstraction, then, is foundational. It is an origin myth that anchors the eventual rise of information theory and computer science upon which, in turn, modern forms of search reliant on the building block of Boolean algebra ultimately depend. Atomists' theories, anticipating the bit of information, are the building blocks for coming to imagine how one might reduce the complexity and size of *all* stored information or represented knowledge into *lively* patterns capable of being meaningfully accessed by truth seekers and information searchers. This correspondence is clear in physicist John Archibald Wheeler's assertion that "If and when we learn how to combine bits of fantastically large numbers to obtain what we call existence, we will know better what we mean both by bit and by existence" (1989: 368).

Wheeler, who collaborated with Albert Einstein and Nils Bohr, makes clear his faith, as did the Atomists, that reality, including our embodied existence, wholly depends on the abstraction of number itself. Wheeler's stance concords with Jane Bennett's definition of metaphysics as "a set of aesthetic images depicting the stuff of which all things are made and speculating about how that matter is arranged or is liable to arrangement" (2001: 89) and it also, crucially, aligns with the hybrid mystic–scientific thought of Pierre Teilhard de Chardin (chapter 5) who, in an essay titled "The Atomism of Spirit," argues that "life is the property that is peculiar to *large organized numbers*" (1970: 30; emphasis in original). One might say, then, that Greek Atomism and the Pythagorean first principles upon which it relies are early indications of the longstanding impulse to code that continues to drive twenty-first-century engineering cultures such as Google's; that the binary-like organization of the sticks and stones used by Atomists as placeholders to record the value and position of any one number within a broader array was an early data storage device that anticipated the development of combinatorial logic and bodies-as-code (see this chapter's note 1). Atomism further informs the current conceptualization of knowledge as increasingly divisible but also increasingly recognizable as the patterns generated through that division, a dynamic that, as discussed in chapter 2, lies at the core of Google's particular application of the concept of universal granularity as a means of generating personalized forms of search returns.

## Tower of the Tongue-Tied

A foundational Judeo-Christian myth, the story of the Tower of Babel is often explained by Christian exegesis as a warning against human arrogation of divine power and the hubris inherent in competing with or attempting to exceed the power of the Creator on high. It is also interpreted as directing attention to humankind's fall from grace: "Our earthly Babel is a falling off from the lost speech of Eden: a catastrophe and a punishment" (Gleick 2011: 418). In nonsecular readings it is often understood as an origin story for explaining linguistic diversity and the rise of nations. It is also an inspiration for Borges' 1941 short story "La Biblioteca de Babel" ("The Library of Babel"), in which he offers a fantastical image of the universe-as-library and an allegory for the folly of believing that all knowledge could ever be brought together under one jurisdiction. As Gillian Rose notes (1993: 226–228), the story carried by the myth has been interpreted in many ways and continues to fascinate.[2]

The story is told in the Book of Genesis. Following the Great Flood a tribe migrated from the east to arrive at the land of Shinar (present-day Iraq). Ruled by the tyrant Nimrod (adjudicated the greatest ruler known), the people commenced work on "a city and a tower with its top in the heavens" to make a name for themselves. God, however, after close inspection of the project, proclaimed, "Behold, they are one people, and they have all one language; and this is what they begin to do; and now nothing will be withholden from them, which they purpose to do. Come, let us go down, and there confound their language, that they may not understand one another's speech'" (Genesis 11: 4–8). Sundered into mutually uncomprehending language groups, the city's inhabitants abandoned work on the city/tower and scattered across the Earth. The biblical account of the Tower, then, can also be read as warning against too unified a shared symbol system, such as a universal language, even though shared symbol systems make social and economic advance possible.

One explanation for the name "Babel" is that it derives from the Ancient Hebrew *balal*, meaning "to jumble." The Greek *Bāb-ilim*, however, means "Gate of the God" (Wiseman 1996: 109–110). If one considers both meanings, the myth is Janus-faced. While Babel offers potential access to universal truths of divine knowledge and power, to build it ends up, depending on one's point of view, either sundering the whole or introducing diversity. To sunder may be to punish and to make impossible any access to such truths without translation. To make diverse could be a form of reward. In either case, the builders believed that the Tower would let them make a name for themselves and that through this architectonic form of identity construction they would access the sense-denying but seemingly reasonable "lie of unity" (Nietzsche 1976: 480).

The myth's role as a cautionary against hubris becomes clearest when analysis focuses on its qualities that derive from *Bāb-ilim,* "Gate of the God" meanings. In his cosmologically titled *The Coming of Post-Industrial Society,* Daniel Bell interprets the myth: "Cast out from the Eden of understanding, the human quest has been for a common tongue and a unity of knowledge, for a set of 'first principles' which, in the epistemology of learning, would underlie the modes of experience and the categories of reason and so shape a set of invariant truths" (1973: 265). Yet what are the consequences of such unitary invariance, whether of language or of access to information? The myth instructs that any human power that works to concentrate all power and knowledge into one place or system (such as one language or one universal library) is overreaching and, therefore, subject to corruption, failure and punishment. In his discussion of the Tower, Jarvis notes that "uniformity leads to a pride so great that the society collapses" and "totality suggests an ending in stasis, which is where the lie of unity inevitably takes us" (2008). Commenting on Franz Kafka's use of the Tower as an "allegory of spiritual desolation," Josep Ramoneda interprets the myth as indicating that "The submission of all to a unique and permanent project is the fantasy of all power (in its extreme form we call it totalitarianism), but it runs contrary to the numerous different endeavours that make up a city, which is plurality and not unity" (1999). There is moral, political, social, and genetic value in human diversity but totalizing schemes also can lead to geographical diaspora and chaotic linguistic plurality.

We extend the Tower's interrelated meanings to suggest that there is value in diversifying access to information as a way to diversifying knowledge. While the myth can be interpreted as positing the origin of linguistic diversity, it also can be read as indicating the wisdom of accepting that the reality of different languages and the difficulties of communication and access to information this raises is just the way it is (Ricoeur 2006: 18). Paul Ricoeur notes that linguistic diversity reflects the fractured reality, often including the necessity for translation, within which any basis for understanding and knowledge acquisition of necessity must begin. His observation about the necessity of translation is important, yet if the Tower of Babel is a metaphor of acceptance of linguistic diversity, then it would also constitute a way of stating that any such acceptance is equivalent to borne resignation.

In light of the Tower's many meanings, it is apposite to make note of point 8 of Google's "Ten things we know to be true." Titled "The need for information crosses all borders," point 8 suggests the transcendent, Tower of Google quality inherent in the firm's ambitious project. "Our mission is to facilitate access to information for the entire world, and in every language … We offer Google's search interface in more than 130 languages … Using our translation tools, people can discover content written on the other side of the world in languages they don't speak" (Google 2006). Through using Google's networked architecture we all make names for ourselves, and Google's is the greatest.

We offer the above observations because, within the logic of the myth, linguistic diversity is an outcome of God's anger. Diversity and multiplicity, while doubtless the way things were, are, and will be, are presented in the myth as forms of cultural setback and punishment. This leaves open the question as to whether the story of the Tower has in any way laid to rest the persistent ideal of the unitary One—what will become over time the sense-denying Neoplatonic idealist lie of unity which, nevertheless, continues to inform such universalist projects as Wells' mid-twentieth-century World Brain, Google Translate, and Google Books. Jacques Derrida has argued that Nimrod and his tribe of Jewish nomads were punished for seeking a "unique and universal genealogy" (1991; cited in Bartholomew 1998: 308). Had they succeeded in their quest, "the universal tongue would have been imposed by violence, by force, by violent hegemony over the rest of the world" (1988: 101).

Yet, while the Tower is an encoded message that can be decoded as warning against the hubris attending "one way" approaches, the biblical account does not deny that the desire for universal solutions to human problems is real. The question, then, is where do the politics reside? It is productive to consider Derrida's suggestion that the Tower's completion would have meant the violent imposition of a universal tongue in light of what Jean-Noël Jeanneney has had to say about the intersection of hierarchization and Google Books. Despite Google's global focus, the culturally inflected hierarchization of its search results, coupled with a commercial demand to rank monetizing sites highly in PageRank (chapter 2), "will likely weigh in favour of Anglo-Saxon culture" (2007: 6). Further,

> With respect to works still under copyright … the weight of American publishers may be overwhelming. As for journals and books disseminating

ongoing research, the dominance of work from the United States may become even greater than it is today. What is at stake is language … and we can see how the use of English (in its American form) threatens to become even more prevalent at the expense of other European languages— all of them … I don't … believe there will be any deliberate ostracism or censure, but I do believe there is an overall … tendency that necessarily leads to an imbalance … toward the hyperpower of a dominant civilization.

(ibid.: 7–8, 33)

No deliberate censorship on Google's part, but, instead, a much more unsettling hegemonization of the lived world, which, from Jeanneney's perspective, is the outcome of an intellectual genealogy that positions it as only natural that American exceptionalism, its scholarship and products included, should be first among equals in attaining cultural and economic dominance.

Jarvis, then, in assessing the ways that visual images of the Tower have evolved over time, suggests that "perhaps, we can say that the concept of a universal language has given way, over time, to the concept of a universal library" (2008). It is certainly arguable that the universal library that many believe Google has become contains within itself, as Google Translate exemplifies, the concept, if not the actualization, of an universal language achieved through automation. Early evidence of the giving way to which Jarvis refers is found in the practices adopted at the Royal Library at Alexandria, where scholars charged with developing its collections translated as many foreign language books as possible into Greek, then the known world's lingua franca. The associations with physical infrastructure that the idea of a library (along with the archive) connotes, however, are also relevant. The American essayist Robert Cortes Holiday (1880– 1947) once commented that "Books are simply the material from which the library is fashioned … Now a library is a structure, like a work of architecture, a composition, like a drama or a piece of music; like them it is the intelligible, conscious, and disciplined expression, in a concrete and disciplined expression of an idea" (1919: 196–197). The account in Genesis connects language or voice with the actual building of the Tower of Babel as an architectural work. The book, then, like the Tower, is architecture's rough clay, just as the search queries entered in Google's search box and phrases to be translated entered into Google Translate are building blocks for the firm's database of intentions that has allowed it to make a very great name for itself.

Rose connects the Tower's architecture to Nimrod's tribe's attempt to make a name for itself. Jewish interpretation, she contends, understands the Jews as having been punished for their efforts because, in building the Tower, they were "making and naming a god of their own invention … In this light the confusion of tongues may be understood as the way humankind are taught a lesson about the relation between divine and human power" (1993: 226–227). What might this lesson be? Rose suggests two potential ones: one may be found

in the myth's transmission of the "idea that human powers and their successful execution are dangerous to their perpetrators" (ibid.: 229); the other lesson
lies in the account's implicit communication that language as a signifying system
is distinct from both the law and labor (ibid.: 230). History may "consist of
ineluctable paradox" (ibid.: 232) but, above all, language—the symbolic code
that carries the power to name and hence create—is a law unto itself. Lawrence
Lessig (2006) advances a parallel idea seemingly more applicable for the contemporary conjuncture when he argues that the code that drives digital media also
organizes our actions and possibilities, including the ways we engage with and
through it. This describes a law unto itself whether we realize it or not.

Like the rise of Google, building the Tower of Babel, then, can be understood as an effort to fabricate a form of code that could tower seemingly inde-
pendently over its human makers. The Tower is said to have been clad in
brickwork stamped with cuneiform writing—a storage mechanism for data that,
like modern computation and server farms, fuses architecture and language or
code. This fusion of architecture and code, moreover, reveals an affinity between
the thinking of the Tower's makers and Atomism's insistence that all forms of
reality reduce to the *stoicheia*—elements of number and letter. The Tower, then,
constituted an architecture of language elevated to a first principle that anticipates
the current understanding that electronic networks and the platforms they link
enjoy similar architectural status. Architecture is the metaphysic—the creation
that names. Under the sign of the Tower of Babel, human inventions threaten
their inventors even as they seem to promise salvation.

In considering how the Tower's caveats and lessons might apply to digital
search, two points seem germane. The first is that if any one firm, organization,
or institution controls online access to information in a monopolistic or near-
monopolistic fashion, or if there is only one way or schema of imagining (or
inventing) how information can be archived, accessed, and presented, then
humankind may find itself at the *Bāb-ilim*, the gateway of a God it has created—
whether by Nimrod or Google—in the form of a humanly consecrated information machine that nonetheless threatens humankind with an information
monoculture or, as Jean Baudrillard would put it, "a veritable triumph of uniform
thought ... monothought" (2000: 23–24). This suggests a paradox lodged within
the very idea of a universal library: gathering "all information" can lead to monothought and the creativity and aliveness such a gathering might have been
found initially to support may be inhibited in the rush to code "all" human
memories into *one*, effectively monocultural machine. The second, related, point
is that contemporary search results can be articulated to the complex political
economies attending the aforementioned Law of the Code—the discursive
practices and linguistic framings of search techniques are signifying systems in
their own right. Algorithms powering search have achieved sufficient technical
power so as to be able to "produce" general statements of reality that then come
to influence—some would say even determine—general reality itself. In addition,

search names each searcher—the law of the code is time-stamped onto each searcher's history in the search engine's database every time a searcher searches. This technologically rendered reality-as-signification, however, does not authorize or support any misunderstanding on the part of the searcher that search practices and techniques are somehow apart from the law (in the law's Ancient meaning of "the way") or from the labor that undergirds these practices in the first place. Indeed, as other chapters in this volume make clear, increasingly the discursive practices made possible by search technologies and techniques heavily impinge upon law and labor relations.

To this second point a complementary amendment should be attached. Chapter 2 argued that search results fracture perceived links between information and context—between any information a search engine organizes for display and the contexts within which this information was and is produced. Internet search is, in part, an outcome of a strategy based on hyperlinks; everything online can seem to connect rhizomatically to everything else by hyperlink. Indeed, discursive practices promoting electronic networks as natural phenomena direct users to experience everything as effortlessly linked within an information "ecology." The recursive chain of signification that can result may direct searchers to many different sites. However, within the proprietary algorithmic monothought of contemporary search logic, apart from the original search terms entered by these individuals, a broader explanatory or contextual frame for making sense of any information displayed is not part of the search results. The disconnected search results that a search produces are *comprehensible* as a corpus only because they are organized hierarchically by the search engine's "personalized" yet opaque algorithmic logic. This logic exemplifies Lessig's dictum "Code is Law" (2006). These disconnected results, furthermore, are only rendered *meaningful* through the particular interpretive framework of the particular searcher in question. As chapter 2 argued, this mode of engagement with information lacks the holistic cogency of ideology or metanarrative *except for that provided by the algorithmic logic—by the code*. An important component of sense-making, therefore, including how the mind develops creative associations across seemingly unrelated topic areas (chapter 5), is potentially stymied. We agree with librarian Anne O'Sullivan, who maintains that accessing information in this disconnected manner leads to "an over-emphasis of the particular, with no understanding of the whole" (2010). And we also concur with psychologist Peter Kruse, who expresses his concern with such confounding forms of access by referencing the Tower of Babel myth.

> Imagine a meeting where all the participants speak in English but don't reflect sufficiently on the various cultural contexts from which they come. The words used are then the same, but the basis of understanding is different. The situation is even more difficult than that in the biblical metaphor of the Tower of Babel: people don't understand one another even though

they are speaking the same language. In the Internet the feeling arises much too quickly that you have grasped the message. Genuine understanding requires discourse and context.

(Hütter 2010)

Kruse applies the Tower of Babel's moral instruction about our human dilemma to contemporary networked settings when he suggests that even those who speak the same language become confounded in their search for knowledge when the information they seek arrives decontextualized. To build on chapter 2's discussion of relevance, we note that when, for example, the first several screens of search results for a specific product or well-known individual are heavily larded with links to SEOs (Search Engine Optimizers) and other splogs ("spam" + "blogs"), then ascertaining the value of results is made more difficult. Apart from the investment by Google and others in some creative thinking about how such links might be eliminated or gotten around, SEO-generated links do not stimulate the creative interplay of ideas that has been one of the not-so-implicit promises of digital search. Through this example, however, it is also possible to understand SEOs as a logical response to Google's desire to index all the world's information, which includes advertising that Google asserts can be useful to searchers (Google 2006), because SEOs *do* offer information of a sort—it just happens to be useless or misleading (see Pash 2011). Borges anticipates this possible outcome—a surfeit of information, searchable or otherwise—when he notes that, in the Library of Babel, "for every sensible line of straightforward statement, there are leagues of senseless cacophonies, verbal jumbles and incoherences" that together point to "the formless and chaotic nature of almost all the books" (1962: 53).

What Borges and the Tower of Babel account together suggest is that the attempt (never mind the reality) to organize all information into *one* universal system carries with it not only the risk of producing something like an architectural impasse in the form of information overload but also the danger of babbling despair born of the realization that meaning and information have parted ways. Tom McCarthy has noted that "all code is burial, to dwell within the space of code is to be already dead. But then perhaps the opposite is true as well" (2003: 6). We cannot do without code. While to dwell imaginatively within it, or within atomized, externalized forms of the self, such as medical scans, emails, shopping records, and YouTube videos, is to risk death from extending our sense of self, Narcissus-like, too far from the limits of our material bodies, for some, code and these same externalized and abstracted forms of the self may also herald a sense of being reborn. Google's venture, based on universalizing the precepts of a particular ideology coded into the writing of its proprietary algorithms, may contribute to our embodied human dilemma even as it also may serve to move us "forward" towards a technologically inflected version of the Ancient but impossible Platonic Ideal.

Latter-day metaphysicians such as Kevin Kelly (1994) would argue that algorithmic technologies, in allowing searchers to arrive at meaningful answers to search queries, also allow them to move beyond any despair rooted in a recognition of this dilemma. At times this may be so. Endless loops of spam, however, suggest virtual architectural impasses as instances of the ineluctable paradox of human ingenuity already at work in undermining the first principles of a universal library. Though Philip K. Dick, in his allegorical 1968 Cold War novel *Do Androids Dream of Electric Sheep?*, did not anticipate networked search, the novel's concept of *kipple*—a general entropic decay that, like the ruined Tower, endlessly accumulates around us as the dust of time and in seemingly equal measure to a societal focus on networked screens and a turning away from the environmental realities of the earth—seems apposite to the kinds of digital trash offered to many searchers. Datatrash, a contemporary monocultural distraction, is a logical response to the kinds of search engine ranking strategies that Google and its imitators in the field of search employ. It is an expression of the unavoidable and ever-present limitations and impediments to human understanding lodged within the signifying system of search itself, and it serves to confound reception of the information that a searcher actually may *need* to find in order to "make a name" for him or herself. In every constraint an opportunity awaits; in every opportunity a constraint in the making. As the myth of the Tower reveals, human, all too human. Build it and they will come, even if its feet are made of clay.

## Ptolemy's Universal Library

> Google planned to digitize millions of books … drawing on a database that would become the world's greatest library, bigger by far than anything dreamt of since the library of Alexandria.
>
> (Darnton 2009)

The year is 323 BCE, the year of Alexander the Great's death. The supremacy of Hellenism is co-extensive with the much of the world known to the Greeks. Alexander's many military adventures have led to a political situation whereby the mystical and symbolic forms of thinking of conquered peoples contrast sharply with their conquerors' more analytic modes of thought. Of the sensitive cultural dynamics raised by this outcome of Ancient imperial reach, Konstantinos Staikos has written, "To ensure untroubled continuity in the everyday life of such a mixture of races it was essential for the Greeks to show a measure of understanding and respect for the religious and secular traditions of Near Eastern peoples, and so the creation of a 'universal library' seemed an obvious course of action" (2004: 157–158). The universal library is here an act of *noblesse oblige*. It is also an ecumenical and architectural symbol of the unification of many peoples and languages. To Staikos' observation, therefore, should be added Luciano

Canfora's realpolitik assessment of the underlying value of the Royal Library at Alexandria's task of translation—of mastering the codes of foreign tongues unleashed by Nimrod's folly. While Macedonian arms "had made the Greeks masters of the entire known world," they

> did not learn the languages of their new subjects, but realised that if they were to rule them they must understand them, and that to understand them they must collect their books and have them translated. Royal libraries were accordingly created in all the Hellenistic capitals, not just for the sake of prestige but also as instruments of Greek rule. And the sacred books of the subject peoples had a special place in this systematic project of collection and translation, because religion was, for those who wished to rule them, a kind of gateway to their souls.
>
> (1987: 25)

Ptolemy I Soter (323 BCE–283 BCE) founded the Ptolemaic Kingdom and Dynasty. A Macedonian general under Alexander and one of his closest associates, Ptolemy has been identified as the likely founder of Alexandria's Universal Library (Canfora 1987; Staikos 2004). He sought to make Alexandria "the cultural centre of the Greek world" (Staikos 2004: 164). The Royal Library "enabled Alexandria to surpass Athens as an intellectual center" (Gleick 2011: 378), and founders conceived of it as the repository for the collective contents of the libraries Alexander looted in the palaces of Persepolis, Nineveh, and Babylon and elsewhere (Staikos 2004: 163).

Ptolemy I and succeeding Ptolemaic rulers developed a bibliophilic passion for collecting every book regardless of language. "They conceived of their institution as one in which all written works could be found and accessed, a kind of repository for the accumulated knowledge of the human race" (Phillips 2010). In 283 BCE, at the beginning of Ptolemy II's reign, the Library had acquired around 200,000 "books" in the form of parchment rolls. Canfora notes that its royal patrons "had a particular goal in view, for they had calculated that they must amass some five hundred thousand scrolls altogether if they were to collect at Alexandria 'the books of all the peoples of the world'" (1987: 20). Keepers of other royal libraries were requested to make copies of all library and archival materials in their possession for forwarding to and accession by the Alexandrian Universal Library (Staikos 2004: 171). Works of every kind of author were sought—those of "poets and prose-writers, rhetoricians and sophists, doctors and soothsayers, historians, and all the others too" (Canfora 1987: 20). In a move that would seem to anticipate aspects of the non-voluntaristic nature of Google's automated indexing of webpages, its production of cached copies of such pages and its subsequent decision to scan copyrighted books without consulting rights holders, royal decrees compelled all ships docking at Alexandria to allow the Library to copy any books on board. If well executed, the copies were returned to their owners; the originals remained with the Library. The intent was to have all non-Greek materials translated into Greek by Library scholars. About the eventual number of rolls held by the Library, Staikos writes that "when all the reliable contemporary evidence is evaluated it is reasonable to suggest that the highest figure of all—700,000 rolls—does not sound excessive and may even be an underestimate" (2004: 188), though Phillips (2010) suggests the collection ranged between 400,000 and 700,000 rolls.[3] An alphabetic arrangement of texts coupled with annotation was developed to create "'a grid of knowledge' in which the answer to all questions and problems could be found" (Staikos 2004: 187)—a hoped-for outcome that anticipates by a millennium Ramón Llull's efforts to fabricate a "thinking machine" able to provide logical answers to important questions of faith and, by millennia, Google's aspiration to be the universal steward and disseminator of all the world's information. A grid of knowledge, however, did emerge and it was in the Library where Jewish scriptures were translated into Greek from Hebrew (the Septuagint); where Euclid authored books on geometry; and where ideas that the oceans are connected, that Africa is circumnavigable, and that the earth is round were first postulated. It was also where Archimedes' screw-shaped water pump was invented and the earth's circumference estimated within fifty miles of accuracy (Franz 2011).

Though generally referred to as a library, the royal institution had two components: a library and a museum that served as its educational wing (ibid.). While it had a director and associated senior figures, the Library's operation required additional specialists, copiers, and translators. Aspects of the untenable labor conditions faced by the peripatetic but ultimately imprisoned librarians toiling within Borges' impossible "Library of Babel" (1962) were a fixture of the Alexandrian Library. Provided board, lodging, good salaries, and servants, Library scholars lived on royal property "in a gilded prison" they were rarely permitted to leave. Citing a poet of the time, Canfora notes of the Egyptians that "they breed a race of bookish scribblers who spend their whole lives pecking away in the cage of the Muses" (1987: 37). One director was imprisoned when authorities learned of his interest in leaving Alexandria for a position elsewhere (Staikos 2004: 167). The fabled impossibility of searching Borges' Library of Babel, along with its librarians' carceral-like living conditions, may be read as a reflection on the conditions faced by Alexandria's librarians—the incoherent mass of uncataloged materials and multiple copies of books and translations at variance with one another. One librarian, Callimachus, attempted an overall classification which provided a sense of "the system by which the library's scrolls were arranged" but the resulting catalogs listed only eminent materials and "were of use only to someone already familiar with the arrangement of the material" (Canfora 1987: 39).

As the Ptolemies' agents scoured the known world for its books, a market arose for scrolls that sellers assumed Egyptian royals would be eager to obtain.

Galen wrote commentary on forgers who profited handsomely from selling the Ptolemies spurious versions of older texts; many were complete forgeries (Staikos 2004: 197). If this rendered finding answers from the Library's materials ever more difficult, the range of materials archived—like a colonial-era cabinet of curiosities—resisted simple categorization. "The Alexandrian scholars tried to bring together under broad subject headings every branch of knowledge and everything that might provide material for their research, such as letters and writings in epistolary form, wills, cultural traditions, biographical notes on statesmen and intellectuals, descriptive writing, public records, diaries and logbooks, travel books, maps, plans and diagrams, as well as descriptions of the traditions and customs of the inhabitants of Greek cities everywhere" (ibid.: 193; see also Phillips 2010). While Callimachus' metadata tagging of manuscript scrolls did confer some overall conceptual order on collections, the lack of an indexing system adequate to answering all questions and the potential for abounding error in organization and even shelving were impediments to realizing the Ptolemies' utopian, imperial aspirations.

That the Universal Library accrued great prestige, international influence, and power to the Egyptian monarchy and Greek hegemony more broadly is undoubted. The Library successfully housed the first large-scale research facilities dedicated to translation and what today we broadly term literary interpretation. To have searched for answers to all questions and solutions to all problems within the Library's grid of knowledge, however, would have been almost as frustrating as trying to speak to each other would have been for the Tower of Babel's builders after they were rendered by God as babblers to one another. Canfora has written about the conceit underlying the Royal Library and its infection of resident librarian-scholars. His comments are apposite to Google's ambitions and can be read as inferring reference to such critical fictions as Borges' Library of Babel. "These scholars were privileged to imagine that they might actually gather together every book in the world—a glittering mirage, which cast its spell on the library for a while before becoming the stuff of literary fantasy. This desire for completeness, this will to power, are akin to the impulse which drove Alexander, as a rhetorician of antiquity put it, 'to overstep the limits of the world'" (1987: 24). If the Tower of Babel's ruination was God's punishment of an edifice complex linked to language and naming, the meaning of the eventual destruction of the Universal Library at Alexandria, whether a result of accidental burning in 48 BCE by Caesar's soldiers, a consequence of later invasion by Muslim armies, or a centuries-long process of entropic decline, has come to be internalized by humankind in fearful ways. "The universality of the Alexandrian Library, that is, the widespread perception of its all-inclusiveness, led people to regard it as a symbol or as a mythical object; this in turn may have instigated its destruction ... Once mythologized, any human construction is easily demonized" (Thiem 1999: 257, 259). An echo of this mythologize/demonize/

destroy dynamic—as well as an indication of the cultural power the idea of the Alexandrian library continues to wield—is heard in the reaction of Authors Guild President Scott Turow to the March 22, 2011 decision by Judge Dennis Chin, to reject the Amended Settlement Agreement reached between Google and the Authors Guild and Association of American Publishers, who had sued the firm in 2005 for copyright infringement related to the Google Books project (chapter 6). "Although this Alexandria of out-of-print books appears lost at the moment … opening up far greater access to out-of-print books through new technologies that create new markets is an idea whose time has come" (cited in Stirling 2011). Like the Tower of Babel or the statue of Ozymandias reduced to kipple in Shelley's 1818 poem, the Library's destruction stands as a universal metaphor for the decline of leaders, their empires and treasures, and the discursive and material strategies they devise to immortalize their powers. "The history of libraries of antiquity often ends in flames" (Canfora 1987: 191). Ask Jeeves or Google it, and if you believe that the digitization of libraries' contents such as Google Books has undertaken is a way to avoid the loss that befell the Ancient Library, or, as do many Wikipedians, that Wikipedia's collective intelligence is heir to the Library (Gleick 2011: 379), trust that an unexpected electrical failure on a server farm or an unanticipated solar flare or nuclear pulse will not delay a timely answer to your question.

The Ptolemaic interest in having all questions answered is one that intersects with the relationship between knowledge and salvation, and it concerns questions of being, form, and identity. This interest is one of first principle, is longstanding, and does not surcease. The story of the desire to *automate* the production of answers from assembled information begins with Ramón Llull.

## Ramón Llull's "Thinking Machine"

Borges' fabled Library of Babel—among other things, an architectonic and psycho-spatial critique of the impossible and "melancholy fantasy" of a universal library (Quine 1987: 223) of all knowledge that has, nonetheless, been interpreted by many search acolytes as predicting the rise of Google and hypertextual search more generally—is this chapter's recurring motif. In his intellectual history of the idea of a total library, Borges includes Wolff's 1929 observation that the concept or conceit of a total or universal library "is a derivation from, or a parody of, Ramón Llull's thinking machine" (2001: 214). Borges identifies Llull's work as precursive to the idea of a universal library predicated on symbolic logic, and Michael Heather and Nick Rossiter note that "since at least the time of Raymond Lull there has been a continuing aspiration for a fundamental language of reasoning that could satisfy all problems" (2005: 42). This aspiration for a "fundamental language" based on logic and reasoning they identify as the "quest for a universal language" (ibid.) and, given our focus in these sections on linkages between ideas of universal libraries and other dreams of universality running from the Tower of Babel to Google's grand plans, it is worth returning to Jarvis' observation that "the concept of a universal language has given way, over time, to the concept of a universal library" (2008). If we cannot all speak the same language we may, at least, have access to the same knowledge-building materials.

In the early fourteenth century, the Majorcan writer, philosopher, and theologian Ramón Llull (1232–1315) compiled his thought in a series of manuscripts. For Llull, the most important was his now famous *Ars Magna* (1305) or Art Major (Peers 1929: 109) (also referred to by Llull as his Art General and hereafter referred to as the *Ars*). Like Borges, G.W.F. Hegel referred to Llull's *Ars* as a "thinking machine" (ibid.: 111; Heather and Rossiter 2005: 42). Heather and Rossiter suggest that Hegel's comments were directed at the extensive figures that Llull developed to illustrate his schemas (2005: 42), but Hegel would also have opposed the *Ars* because of its potential effect of reducing "man to a universal thinking machine so that whatever he does conforms to some prescribed abstract rational rule" (Mitias 1984: 142). Llull did consider his *Ars* a technique to be acquired, one that when mastered would yield truth seekers a universal method for providing "true" answers to their questions. Understood in this way, he upholds the emergent Christian mantle first embraced by Charlemagne's ninth-century Court to investigate mechanism and machines as a means to find the way back to Adam's prelapsarian state (Noble 1999: 5).

Yet while Llull, a formidable debater and rhetor of the first order, intended the *Ars* to provide Christians with answers to theological questions about the Divine, the universal method underlying the *Ars* could apply equally to any subject under consideration (Johnson 1987: 45); and Frances Yates argues that the *Ars* was of "immense significance" for "the European search for method" (1982: 7). Llull frequently asserted that his *Ars* allowed "mastery of any art or science in a short time" (ibid.: 46) and Anthony Bonner refers to Llull's system as "a key to universal reality" (1985: 68–69). We can say, then, that within the logic of Llull's *Ars*, method (along with logic) is elevated to a first principle. His focus on developing a question-answering machine, moreover, is an early indication of the now prevalent, though largely under-acknowledged belief that a true or efficient culture of search requires not only something like a searchable universal library but also the rise of machine intelligence.

Willy Ley has argued that "in retrospect it can now be said that the *ars magna Lulli* was the first seed of what is now called 'symbolic logic'" (1958: 245). Llull believed that theological truths, revealed through his symbol-dependent *Ars*, would buttress the logic of what we would now term rational arguments needed by Christians for engaging in conversion debates with monotheistic Muslims and Jews. Llull's *Ars* "was essentially a method of 'converting men' ... and for the complete unification of mankind through Christendom ... that [in Llull's own words] 'in the whole world there may not be more than one language, one belief, one faith'" (Hillgarth 1971: 12). The *Ars*, then, is an early attempt to do something now quite widespread—to substitute technology conceived as somehow free of human ideologies for the inherently messy and unpredictable ideological political sphere. As early as 1274 Llull had understood that public disputation between Muslims and Christians did not lead to religious conversion of the former to Christianity. It was therefore necessary, he concluded, to develop logical proofs for Christian beliefs and to devise a mechanism that would "prove and generate truths in such a way that, once everyone agreed on the assumptions, the objectivity of the procedure would force all to accept the conclusions" (Sales 1997: 16). Yates notes that, as a method, the *Ars* is "both scientific and mystical" (1982: 6), and Eusebi Colomer comments that "the rightful place of the Art comes before the branching apart of logic and metaphysics," a place where Scholastic logic "was a training for thinking" and metaphysics "dealt with the content of thought, of the being and its principles and causes. The Art arose from a refounding of logic and metaphysics" (1995: 20). And Ioan Couliano captures Llull's Neoplatonic bent when he writes that the polymath "intended to construct a world of phantasms supposed to express approximately the realities of intelligible order of which our world is but a distant and imperfect copy" (1987: 34). To extend Yates's observation, one might say that Llull's *Ars* is a cosmological product of "scientific mysticism" or "mystical science." Moreover, though his stated goal is production of "truth," his aim that the *Ars* serve to advance the arrival of something akin to an information monoculture ("one language, one belief, one faith") again suggests how such totalizing ideals and centralizing goals can inhibit over time the very creativity upon which they rely for their genesis.

The *Ars* combined textual instruction and tables with two-dimensional diagrams on the page of a series of concentric, rotating disks that when placed atop one another and rotated would produce various combinations of letters that the truth seeker could refer to for answers to his or her questions. Rotation of the disks could generate up to 1,680 combinations of ideas (ibid.: 22), each resulting idea a combination of the Absolute and Relative attributes depicted on the different circles or disks. In such a manner, Llull reasoned, all possible truths about the subject of the circle would be revealed. *Ipso facto*, political conversation over, religious conversion via technique coming right up.

Ley offers a précis of how the combinatory logic built into the *Ars* might serve to answer a secular question of fact and thereby produce the truth.

> If I pick out one characteristic of something and state all the possibilities I must, of necessity, state the truth too. For example, the list: blood is blue, blood is green, blood is purple, blood is colorless, blood is black, etc., etc., must contain the correct statement but this one list alone does not point out which statement is the truth. However, it might be possible to construct other lists of possibilities which will eliminate some of the color possibilities. Therefore, if the whole thing is handled correctly,

the truth, that blood is red, should be the only color possibility left over. Hence one would have arrived at a correct statement by means of several lists of statements *which might be constructed mechanically*.

(1958: 244; emphasis in original)

Allison Peers, however, observes that the *Ars* "can only be described adequately with the aid of its own illustrative diagrams" (1929: 110), and we reproduce four of them below. All depict the symbolic geometricization or abstraction of God and the universe. At the center of the circular diagrams in Figures 3.1, 3.2, and 3.3, Llull positions God (represented by the letter A in Figure 3.1 and the letter T in Figure 3.2). Llull's *Ars* symbolically depicts the universal applicability of God's laws. The first diagram, referred to by scholars as a "Llullian Circle," was designed to indicate all possible combinations among the Absolute Principles or Dignities—the nine attributes of God (*Bonitas, Magnitudo, Duratio, Potestas, Sapientia, Voluntas, Virtus, Veritas,* and *Gloria*; i.e., goodness, greatness, eternity, power, wisdom, will, virtue, truth, and glory). The nine Absolute Principles (Ton Sales refers to them as Axioms [1997: 16]) are represented on the first circle (Figure 3.1)[4] by the letters of the alphabet B, C, D, E, F, G, H, I, and K.

Colomer explains that to these nine Absolute Principles, Llull added (as depicted in Figure 3.2) an additional nine "relative principles, as follows: difference, concordance, contrariety, beginning, middle, end, majority, equality, and minority.

**FIGURE 3.1** First Llullian Circle: The Nine Absolute Principles

**FIGURE 3.2** Second Llullian Circle: The Nine Relative Principles

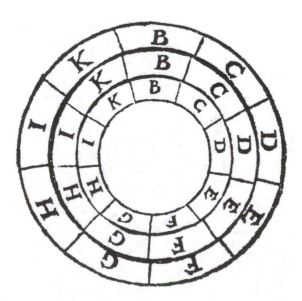

**FIGURE 3.3** Circle of Interrelationships of Absolute and Relative Principles

They are called relative because they establish the various possible modes of relation between the absolute principles ... The new series of principles give the Art the sense of a comparative logic or general doctrine of relations tying the world's beings to one another and to God. Llull conceives reality as interrelated: ultimately, everything is connected to everything else" (1995: 21–22). Each relative principle also is represented on the Second Circle (Figure 3.2) in the same way as the nine Absolute Principles are represented on the First Circle (Figure 3.1)—by the letters of the alphabet running from B to I and also including the letter K. Llull illustrates this set of interrelationships of all possible binary combinations of letters through the use of a two-entry table in the form of a half matrix grid (Figure 3.4).

His use of the same letters in different combinations to indicate different aspects of the divine harks back to the Atomistic belief that "the diverse attributes of things are explained by the diverse movement of the same atoms" (Scholem 1965: 77). The interrelationships of all possible binary combinations of letters are also depicted in a Third Circle (Figure 3.3), composed of a fixed circle and two additional smaller circles placed atop it and which rotate to allow all possible ternary combinations of letters (and, therefore, of truths or ideas, and Absolute and relative principles) to align with one another in various ways. Mark Johnson argues that, "By arranging these letters in circular and tabular figures, Llull generates double or triple combinations of letters, and these combinations are

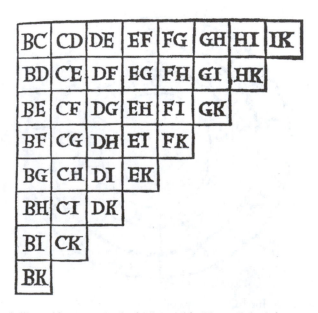

**FIGURE 3.4** Llull's Half Matrix Grid of All Possible Binary Principles

supposed to symbolize exhaustively all theological and philosophical propositions as expressions of Christian truth" (1986: 174–175).

With respect to Llull's Neoplatonically inflected conception of cosmic interrelationality, note that he, along with much of the European late medieval intellectual world, understood these Absolute Principles as able, through various combinations, to create all things, material and immaterial, in the universe. "Llull's key *Ars magna* expresses his belief that all reality—and this would include language and its constructs—is a theophany" (Menocal 1994: 77), the manifestation of God to humankind. For Llull, his *Ars*, as a part of general reality, is a manifestation (and not just a representation) of God and therefore true.

It bears mention that the "attributes" or Absolute and relative Principles Llull develops are forms of categorization. He developed the *Ars* to resolve the great tension between Christianity and Islam then wracking the Mediterranean world. Like many of his contemporaries, he had difficulty with the complexity of a multi-faith world. We have noted that Yates finds the *Ars* "both scientific and mystical." She does so within the context of a broader argument that in part points to the emergence of what we would now identify as early forms of scientific thought. Konrad Becker, historicizing the classifying power of information retrieval systems, makes a similar observation when he states that categorizing schemas (such as Llull's) reflect a meeting of the irrational and the rational, and are proposed or developed at times of great socio-political upheaval (2009: 167). (Plato's Cave, proposed in his *Republic*, written after the Peloponnesian War, also comes to mind, as does Wells' post-World War I World Brain, discussed in chapter 4.) Becker, however, is less interested in identifying any kind of "progress" that the *Ars* might represent than he is in identifying the blend of rational and irrational thought that all organizing schemas necessarily entail. He reproduces Brin's comment that "The perfect search engine would be like the mind of God," as part of his identification of the metaphysical concepts that inhere in all combinatorial systems of purportedly rational categorization. "To bring order into the classes of names and hierarchies of designations is not only a practical or formal scientific issue, but a religious one as well. Categorization is [a] type of cognitive voodoo related to deep-rooted beliefs that the world is/was created by the use of language, by the spelling out of names, and consequently that the universe can be influenced by a correct use of name and order … Categorizing things in advance means to forecast the future, which is the magical practice of oracles, clairvoyant seers or spiritist mediums" (ibid.: 164–165).

Categorization is a crucial issue in search engine design. Becker notes, "A main reason for Google's success was that there is no virtual shelf, no awkward pre-constructed file system" (2009: 165). In other words, Google managed somehow to somersault over the vexed but powerful system of classifying by category. Instead, Google search aggregates previous searcher preferences even as it offers such oracular possibilities as "I'm feeling lucky." Search returns

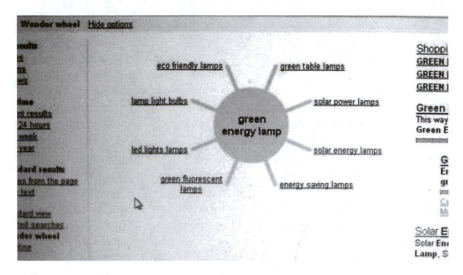

**FIGURE 3.5** Google's Wonder Wheel

appear holistic even though they must be filtered. But is this really to have defied categorization?

In 2009, Google released Wonder Wheel, a feature that reconfigures search results graphically and allows viewers to visualize relationships among keywords and concepts (Figure 3.5). Its name conjures associations with the miraculous. Google anticipated that SEOs, educators, and librarians could use it to "visually identify relationships between a search term(s) and related searches using the Google databases. As you moved from one set of terms to another results would change" (Price 2011). Google removed Wonder Wheel in 2011 as part of revamping how it displays results. We reproduce a screenshot to indicate the close parallels between it and the combinatory Llullian Circles depicted above.

In a real way, Google's aggregating technology, whether search results are returned in a ranked list or more relationally depicted through Wonder Wheels, is predicated, in part, on acceptance of complexity as a reality of human affairs. In order to provide "relevant" search results that also reflect the firm's interest in monetizing search, however, results are rank-ordered. Ranking produces a big list—the most important components of this list are at the top—that leads to a different form of categorization than Becker critiques. It leads to what Geert Lovink refers to as the "Hierarchization of the Real" (2009: 49). It is less about comparing apples and oranges and more about rank-ordering a million apples, with those on the first page of search results enjoying a status infinitely superior to those on the final page, or, worse, those indicated as part of the sometimes millions of results at the top of the first page but not included in the pages of accessible results that a Google search returns. Categorization happens by number—most searches return more than one page of results. Which is most important? How often do you seek out page 55 of the results, if such a high page number is even offered to you, even though Google claims to have found millions of webpages relevant to your search? It seems a recursive form of irony that Google, in rank-ordering webpages by retrospective popularity, introduces a form of classification by number that owes a debt to Llull yet also works to deny the very complexity upon which, theoretically at least, successful search relies.

A resurgence of interest in Llull (one that parallels the rediscovery of Borges' writings on total libraries by a new generation of information and media theorists) is found in the number of computer science scholars claiming Llull as their intellectual ancestor. Claims are advanced that he developed the idea of a formal language, of a calculus, of a rule-based method for ascertaining "true" or "false"; was a pioneer in combinatory logic; introduced binary and ternary relations; even anticipated the spinning hard drive in the ways his disks rotate. In short, that he was an early "computer engineer" whose system of logic anticipated computation and the rules and operations upon which it relies (Bonner 1997; Sales 1997; Sowa 2000; Crossley 2005).

Like the Atomists, Llull demonstrates the impulse to code and abstraction. Indeed, for Llull, code and abstraction are first principles. Yet, while scholars such as Bonner and Sales identify computer science's conceptual debt to Llull, unlike Yates and Becker they fail to take into account that the *Ars* was logical *and* metaphysical, scientific *and* mystical. They never consider that the same core rationale or motive might underlie both Llull's spiritual interest in "thinking machines" and the modern rational interest in digital computation. And this shared motive is the desire on the part of information seekers, medieval and modern, for a reliable, repeatable, more universal, and therefore more "perfect" technique to answer difficult questions, and for an easier path to knowledge that would lead such seekers out from the flickering shadows of Plato's Cave and towards the memory prosthesis called search that Google has seduced so many of us into relying upon. Becker further argues that "classification, elemental in mapping conceptual spaces of knowledge, typically mistakes transient social fictions for real and physical unchangeable facts" (2009: 164). Another way of stating this is to invoke Searle's (1995) distinction between natural or "brute" facts observable but external to us (such as snow or rain) and socially constructed or "institutional" facts constituted solely through performative acts of language (Austin 1962) and social agreement (such as scoring a touchdown by crossing a sports field's endline). If the *Ars* is, as Ley maintains, the first seed of symbolic logic, it is also based on mistaking a "transient social fiction" (or socially constructed or institutional fact—the conceived primacy of Christianity and the Christian God) for a natural or brute fact. Yet, for Llull, God is not a linguistic fiction or a socially constructed fact and it is worth noting that the subjects of his categorizing schema are Absolute, not human, attributes. This would not seem to pose difficulties to categorization as long as the scheme remains anchored to Absolute Beings who, *pace* Llull, as Ideal concepts do not change and therefore maintain their allegiances, perspectives, and understandings. Humans, however, do not pigeonhole so easily. Because we are not Ideal we do not reduce as readily to number as do Llull's Principles—a problem Google might prefer not to recognize but with which it constantly wrestles. The beginnings of symbolic logic, then, so central to the eventual production of successful question-answering machines, are predicated on a philosophical failure of Western thought to account for the gap between concept and reality (Bennett 2010), between an idea of how the world can be divided up into attributes and rank orderings and the way things actually are. The logic undergirding this failure, moreover, is embedded in an idea about the world that continues to live on in the specific kind of idealistic libertarianism exemplified by the Californian ideology and its resident engineering culture's widespread belief that technology, efficiently deployed, will provide "solutions" to "problems" generated within the unfortunately messy sphere of human politics.

The case of Llull's *Ars* reveals a history of the antecedents of computerization, logical calculus, and data visualization that is, at least in part, a history of the search for ways to present answers in a logical fashion. There are many temporal interruptions, some of long duration, between various earlier ideas and inventions that anticipate or inform contemporary search technologies. But the idea that the world can be rank-ordered seemingly never dies. It gains vigor with Llull, runs from his *Ars* through Gottfried Leibniz's "Stepped Reckoner" (an early calculator able to add, subtract, multiply, and divide), through Charles Babbage's and Ada Lovelace's proto-computer "Difference Engine" and the 1940s' ENIAC (Electronic Numerical Integrator and Computer), to J.C.R. Licklider and DARPA's (Defense Advanced Research Projects Agency's) building of the internet, and the millennial rise of Google and lesser search engines as universal indexer-librarians granting access to the internet's uncountable treasures, truths, and spams.

Several Llullian scholars advance a related point—that Llull's thought influenced future theorists in search of universal techniques or methods. For Jocelyn Hillgarth, writing of the Majorcan mystic's lasting influence, "The original purpose of the Art as a method of converting infidels was largely forgotten. Later centuries, down to Leibniz, were to see Lull's Art as a 'clavis universalis,' a key to all knowledge" (1971: 12). Yates identifies Llull's system as a key influence on Descartes' "new method of constituting a universal science" and on Leibniz's work on calculation and interest in a universal conceptual language (1982: 67). Bonner (1985: 68–70)[5] and Sales (1997: 20–21) document how Leibniz (1646–1716), in his *Dissertatio de arte combinatoria* (1666), acknowledged his debt to Llull as the first to have proposed a universal scientific method. What links these philosophers, mathematicians, and early scientists is their unswerving focus on universality—whether the search for a universal language, a universal method, or, in Leibniz's case, an encyclopedia of *all* human knowledge. Leibniz's germinal contribution to theories of calculus and binary number systems is well known. He understood logic to be the basis of metaphysics and "cherished through his life the hope of discovering a kind of generalized mathematics, which he called *Characteristica Universalis*, by means of which thinking could be replaced by calculation" (Russell 1945: 592). For our purposes, it is also important to note Leibniz's development of one of the first book indexing systems, and his lifelong interest in operationalizing his *characteristica universalis* (a universal, formal language for expressing scientific, mathematic, *and* metaphysical concepts). To complement his calculus, Leibniz planned to develop a comprehensive "encyclopaedia for representing the state of all the sciences and their progress" (Kochen 1972: 323). These examples reveal the impulse to discover and possibly "map" or code *the* universal, "correct" way to knowledge and "ultimate truth," the Neoplatonic lie of unity notwithstanding. The drive for universality in Google's index and the reliance on a generalized mathematics of automation within Google's model of relevance are the contemporary traces of our Llullian-inflected heritage, one that continues to inform the intersecting fields of computer science and search.

The desire for a method to access information equated to truth, coupled to the age-old belief beginning with Atomism that one universal method can be discovered and applied to all reality, humanity included (explicit on Llull's part, unacknowledged by computer science and information theory), is what links Llull's *Ars* to Borges' (despairingly unsearchable) Library and, arguably, even more directly to networked search practices. While a set of rotating Llullian Circles could produce no more than 1,680 combinations of Attributes, and whereas a search engine's results can number in the several millions, both are query-answering mechanisms in which information can be stored that one might previously have had to remember or write down. Both rely on recursively searchable databases and on linkages established between or among various symbolic representations of information intended to assist in the production of knowledge and discovery of truth. And both have a strong metaphysical component. Llull was determined to prove the truth of Christian doctrine through the use of a semi-automated set of techniques. Google's long-term goal, in the words of executive chairman Schmidt, "is to enable Google users to be able to ask questions such as 'What shall I do tomorrow?' and 'What job shall I take?'" (Daniel and Palmer 2007). By 2010, Schmidt had refined his position: "I actually think most people don't want Google to answer their questions … They want Google to tell them what they should be doing next" (Jenkins 2010). That Google would assume that people want it to tell them what to do, that human serendipity could be produced electronically based on the firm's retention and mining of personal search histories, in turn assumes that human consciousness will be sidelined in the future. Such questions are usually resolved by our ability to comprehend the world reflexively with respect to how we make meaning and not just in terms of information (Keating 2000). Indeed, only a deeply interpolated cyborg would ask such a question, and one therefore might assume that Google considers this software/wetware/hardware amalgam to be our quasi-disembodied and therefore quasi-immortal, Neoplatonic informational future. Google's interest in satisfying our purported desire that it tell us what to do may be more earthbound than Llull's but it is no less ambitious in its reliance on metaphysics to address issues of political economy, broadly conceived. About Schmidt's goal, Battelle comments, "Hell, once I can have that kind of a conversation with a search engine, it's entirely arguable if the search engine is anything other than a human being, right?" (2007). An ideal equation of God = Artificial Intelligence implicitly informs both Llull's and Schmidt's desires and schemas. The search for truth and the search for information are interlocking themes that organize this chapter's pre-history of search. The "pragmatic" search for information, however, together with the broader contemporary erosion in everyday distinction between information and knowledge, and increasingly between information and reality itself, is both the rational child and the mystical double of the everquesting and "original" spiritual search for truth.

The previous paragraph notes the shared reliance on searchable databases by the *Ars* and networked search. They are, however, not exactly the same. In the passage cited above in which Ley outlines how the *Ars* functions through showing how it may be used to prove blood's true color, he also notes that "A century of experimentation with this and similar devices brought the conclusion ... that the machine did not succeed in obviating the need for thought in the experimenter. To use our example again, the machine might leave the three choices: 'blood is red,' 'blood is yellow' and 'blood is white,' and the experimenter would have to know (or to find out) which choice is correct" (1958: 244). In other words, Ley's experimenter would have had to search her or his own memory and if this proved unsuccessful then to make enquiries elsewhere. To relate this point about the connections between creativity and memory to networked search means taking account of the vast difference in the scales of each database. Llull's search engine was semi-automatic—it took on part of human intellection in its function of receiving a question that then could be represented symbolically on its multiple rotating disks. Because of its combinatorial limits, the machine could generate no more than 1,680 answers to any one set of questions "programmed" into it. The combinations or associations of attributes that resulted from having set the rotating circles in a certain relation to each other suggested answers, but these answers were like pointers, indicators, a kind of trace of the human *avant la lettre*. Humans remained the wetware—but it was all okay, at least in theory, because, much like an algorithm, a learned person such as Llull would have been able to interpret many, if not all, possible outcomes. We might also imagine that not all 1,680 possibilities would be equally likely outcomes of any one or perhaps even a totality of searches/petitions for the truth. In 1948, mathematician and pioneering computer scientist Alan Turing commented that "intellectual activity consists mainly of various kinds of search" (1969: 23) and Llull assumed this human ability and the machine's possibilities would augment one another. The *Ars*, then, was less a stand-alone "thinking machine" and more a particular kind of cyborg or assemblage. It assumed an extant and searchable wetware database. Now that Google has produced something like an organizational key in the form of searchable keywords, the wetware has been extensively, though not totally, *pace* Turing, transmographied into automated form.

Borges wrote that Llull's "thinking machine," "measured against its objective ... does not work" (2001a: 155). Yet, while Llull's specific designs, built of brass and wood, failed to provide the automated forms of truth that he anticipated they would with sufficient refinement, and while "metaphysical and theological theories that customarily declare who we are and what manner of thing the world is" don't work either, Borges sees that "their public and well-known futility does not diminish their interest. This may (I believe) also be the case with the useless thinking machine" (ibid.: 155). Though Borges' fantastic Library of Babel cautions against imbibing too deeply of the lethal melancholy lurking just behind idealist theories of universal knowledge, his comments do point in the direction of a "hope springs eternal" mentality that fuels technological innovation. Perhaps his cautioning against hubris prevented him from due consideration that, in the West at least, *ideas and philosophies get built* (Dreyfus 1992; Hillis 1999). "If at first you don't succeed, try and try again" is a corollary to "hope springs eternal" and also *the* popular maxim applicable to any eventual and successful resolution of the design and engineering problems that technological innovation necessarily faces. Witness the rise of search algorithms and databases as eventual "solutions" to the "problems" inherent in earlier, rudimentary forms of thought production such as the unworkable *Ars*. "Hope springs eternal" walks the sunny side of the street. On the other, shadier side, walks Nietzsche read through Baudrillard: "Nietzsche was right after all when he said the human race, left to its own devices, is capable only of redoubling its efforts, of re-doubling itself—or of destroying itself" (2000: 21). The redoubling inherent in "if at first you don't succeed" applies to the evolution of the theories Borges indicts for telling us who we are and what kind of world we live in—in the post-Web 2.0 searcher-as-self-identity lodged within an increasingly universal screen-based informational economy through which we now transmit and act out the ironically fractured yet somewhat homogeneous neoliberal reality of our semi-automated, semi-monad lives.

Llull was doing God's work, his *Ars* God-given. Brin and Page claim to work for humankind's greater good, their search engine a man–made machine intended to render more efficient the interplay of human affairs. And, yet, while "everyone knows" that the algorithm that powers Google search originally was written by the Stanford grads, it's as if, as a culture, we've decided to set aside that information and treat search as godlike or at least as a manifestation of the secular sacred. Llull's thinking machine didn't work—God's work notwithstanding. But, benefiting from several generations of redoubled efforts on the part of earlier computer scientists, Brin and Page's machine does work and powerfully so—enough so for a culture of instrumental reason beholden to a civil religion of technology (Noble 1999) to rationalize conferring on the search engine its currently consecrated status. As an earlier cultural technology of the divine, God, or the idea of God, has yielded part of its power to the algorithm as an organizing principle of general reality. From Llull's universalist and universalizing perspective, however, both God and search algorithms are parts of a greater unified whole aimed at one engineered, rank-ordered way of knowing, and he might just say *so be it.*

# 4

# IMAGINING WORLD BRAIN

To search Borges's Library of all possible books, past, present, and future, one needs only to sit down … and click the mouse.

(Kelly 1994)

Contemporary search has taken lessons, acknowledged or otherwise, from earlier forms of thought about number and universality and earlier dispositions toward inventing machines to think with. Google's spokespeople do bandy about the idea of magic, and the field of search has been somewhat explicit in acknowledging its inspirational debt to H.G. Wells' World Brain (1938), though without raising the spectre of metaphysics. The search industry has been rather less acknowledging of any relationship between contemporary ideas about and projects for a universal digital index and total information awareness, and other modern metaphysical concepts intended by their proposers to agree with science about the universal nature of reality and the consubstantiality of all things. Yet Google's corporate aspirations for its database echo certain of these concepts. These earlier modern figures and their ideas, and the ways they have contributed to the eventual operationalization of search, are this chapter's subject matter. We exemplify its arguments by looking at Gustav Fechner's panpsychic philosophy, H.G. Wells' interwar advocacy for a World Brain (1938), and Jorge Luis Borges' "The Library of Babel" (1941). Borges' Library is the setting for a Narcissus-like philosophical and moral tragedy that critically illuminates the degree of difference between the map and the territory, the library and the universe, and pride and knowledge. Yet desire springs eternal and the fantastical Library in Borges' account, in a manner somewhat similar to Wells'

World Brain, has proved an inspiration for those who seek through digital means the rise of a truly universal library.

At the top of chapter 3, we included Borges' acknowledgments (2001) of Fechner as the "inventor" of the modern concept of a universal library; and of his mentee, mathematician and philosopher Kurd Lasswitz (1848–1910), as the idea's "first exponent" (ibid.: 214). In 1901, Lasswitz, "the central figure of early German science fiction" (Rottensteiner 2008: xiii), through the device of polite discussion among his characters, thematized and remediated the eternally recurring desire for a universal library in his short account "Die Universalbibliothek" ("The Universal Library").[1] Lasswitz's Library is the set of all possible books already published and ever to be published, and all expressions ever conceived, or ever to be conceived, expressed as sequences of typographical characters having a certain maximum length. The mechanisms of his future Library extend Ramón Llull's combinatorial logic, outlined in chapter 3, and are "based on the idea that the total number of permutations of finitely many symbols is limited, so that a finite number of volumes could contain everything expressible in a given language" (Clareson 1975: 301). It follows that all combinations of alphanumeric characters, vast in number as they may be, are finite too. While finite, a difficulty remains in that the book of all such combinations would exceed the size of the universe. Thomas Clareson has observed that Lasswitz's "scientific prophecies were astonishingly accurate" (1975: 291), but his pre-digital, inherently cybernetic account of a Library in excess of the universe was published first in *Traumkristalle*, a collection of fantastic and "tall" tales. It is the first text to use the precise term "universal library" (Darling 2004: 341).

Lasswitz acknowledged Fechner as his intellectual mentor. He wrote one of the earliest and best biographies of Fechner, and, according to Marilyn Marshall, Lasswitz focused on Fechner's thought as an intellectual historian and his "interpretational bias ... coincides with Fechner's own ubiquitous aim ... to wed science and metaphysics" (1988: 175; see also Kretzmann 1938: 418). Fechner, believing in the universal nature of mind,[2] had, in the 1880s, "ruminated on the idea of permutations of all combinations of letters to express all possible statements and concepts" (Darling 2004: 341). This was a Platonic rumination the influence of which is found in Lasswitz's tale of a demiurgic Universal Library based on all possible combinations of alphanumeric characters. Fechner, an important (though insufficiently translated) nineteenth-century Idealist philosopher and a founder of modern experimental psychology, had argued that "matter is but a form in which inner experiences may appear to one another when they affect each other from the outside" (James 1904: x–xi), a position that reflects Fechner's panpsychic belief that all matter has a mental aspect, all objects have a point of view and a unified center of experience. Like Llull, Fechner sought to integrate religious belief and scientific practice. This let him to develop the branch of psychology called psychophysics which he defines as "an exact theory of the functionally dependent relations of body and soul or, more generally, of the material and mental, of the physical and the psychological worlds" (1988: 159). Fechner's psychophysics sought to apply science to explain the unity of mind and body, of humans and the planet we inhabit, and he consequently advocated for the "day-light view" of the world. William James describes this disposition as "the view that the entire material universe, instead of being dead, is inwardly alive and consciously animated" (1904: ix). If the meta-structure of the world is alive and animated, it follows that information itself—such as letter and number, the *stoicheia* of the Ancient Atomists and the indivisible elemental units of all reality—is also affective, animated and alive, and, in Gleick's phrase, "the core of existence" (2011: 10).

Fechner's panpsychic Neoplatonism and his belief in World Soul (Heidelberger 2004: 12) rely on an understanding that all forms are constituted in the same substance, nature, or essence. James argues that Fechner believed that "the constitution of the world is identical throughout" (1909: 155). If this were to be true, it then would follow that our "inner experience" or reception of these forms would also be of the same nature or essence as the forms themselves. Fechner's philosophy correlates closely with basic Atomist principles. His inherent Atomism works synergistically with his belief that the world is everywhere identically constituted to suggest that, if all forms are of the same essence, then a book, for example, is "but a form" constituted in the *stoicheia* which are the informational core of our "inner experience" of reality. That number or the bit of information might form the irreducible core of reality is, of course, also a crucial (if implicit) assumption of digitization, and, while the technological imaginary of Lasswitz's era had not yet conceived of the technology for making it so, it is possible to see in his short story a groping toward ways of imagining the technological manifestation of abstract information as the whole of reality itself.

During the nineteenth century, thinkers such as Fechner, in ways that build on Llull's insights, had considered the possibilities inherent in combinatorial analyses of letters and numbers and came to realize the number of combinations possible approached the infinite. Fechner was the first to have stated that Llull's original *Ars*, though unable to successfully manipulate whole concepts and statements, might actually be made to function if the concepts and statements were substituted with letters that, in various abstract combinations, could then be made to express more concrete ideas and statements (Ley 1958: 245). In her discussion of the implications of Borges' universal library for a philosophy of law, Susan Mann points out the additional influence on Lasswitz of author and logician Lewis Carroll (1832–1898): "Eventually, reasoned Lewis Carroll, given the finite number of words and therefore of their combinations, all writers will ask not 'what book shall I write' But '*which* book [of those already written] shall I write.' … Lasswitz's *The Universal Library* … gives physical form to Carroll's Library of all books and leaves the reader contemplating the horror of a Universe filled with nothing but books … Lasswitz's story demonstrates that mathematics, technology, and the pursuit of a theory to its logical extreme sometimes creates a useless, horrific invention" (1989: 1011–1012).[3] As the narrator of "The Universal Library" cautions, "Remember, the Universal Library contains everything which is correct, but also everything which is not" (Lasswitz 1958: 240). By more than a century, Carroll's proposal that authors would ask which existing book they should write anticipates Schmidt's own, noted in chapter 3, that in the coming future a Google search should be able to answer the query "What job shall I take?" because Google's database will have stored in it sufficient indications of a searcher's interests and desires to provide her or him what remains for now an answer only available to the gods or those with sufficient authority to command another human to "take this job because I say so."

Viewed from Schmidt's contemporary understanding of reality as networked, Lasswitz's "fantastic" library was "useless" only because the necessary algorithms and miniaturized forms of digital storage had not yet come to pass. As a writer, Lasswitz identified with the *science* half of science fiction (SF) and the genre's ideal aspiration to offer a realistic postulation of the future. According to historian Frank Rottensteiner, Lasswitz "explains that, if what a story of the future tells us is to be believable it must be related to reality and remain closely connected to experience. From the events of cultural history and the current state of science, he says one may draw various conclusions about the future, and in so doing analogy should be used as the natural ally of imagination" (2008: 3). One cannot write "beyond" one's culture, habitus or structure of feeling. But for a person such as Lasswitz who is interested, like Fechner and Llull, in wedding science and metaphysics, one can situate one's "tall tale" within a materialist cultural matrix in ways that nudge it towards an imagined, more metaphysically inflected future that, of necessity, remains somewhat ineffable and therefore not quite ready to be born. Neoplatonic Atomism, it would seem, lies at the core of imagining the translatability of the material world into number and bit and, hence, into the immaterial "space" of digital information commonly positioned as entirely the outcome of enlightened rational empiricism.

Lasswitz, in describing the impossible spatial vastness of his library of all books, and therefore the seemingly insurmountable difficulties preventing its realization, also points to the absence of what Borges (1962) later refers to as the crucial "organizational key"—an index or mechanism for searching such an impossibly vast collection in a way that produces useful or relevant information. The following passages from Lasswitz's short story indicate his recognition of this difficulty:

"Finding something must be a chore."
"Yes, this is one of the difficulties … At first glance one should think that this would be simplified by the fact that the library must contain its

own catalogue and index ... the problem would be to find that one. Moreover, if you had found an index volume it wouldn't help you because the contents of the universal Library are not only indexed correctly, but also in every possible incorrect and misleading manner...

"If our librarian can move with the speed of light it will still take him two years to pass a trillion volumes. To go from one end of the library to the other with the speed of light will take twice as many years as there are trillions of volumes in the library.

(1958: 239, 242)

Such pre-PageRank difficulties do not concern William Fischer, who suggests that the idea of the universal library "playfully explores what would now be called a cybernetic theme: the notion that it might sometime seem possible and feasible to generate, by random computer printout, a library containing all knowledge, including even that of the future" (1984: 117). In this, too, are glimmers of Google's hope to answer such questions as "what job should I take." While Lasswitz's imagination is rooted in a nineteenth-century "age of mechanical reproduction" and a corresponding understanding of the printed page as the *ne plus ultra* of communication, he can be read as anticipating the future digitization of represented human knowledge. This is seen in the ways that "The Universal Library" raises the possibility that "everything that can be expressed in language can be written down, by the purely mechanical variation of a small number of signs, in a finite number of volumes" (Rottensteiner 2008: xiv).[4] Lasswitz's tale exemplifies the ongoing impulse to code, but it is "fantastic" only because storage and search abilities powerful enough to meaningfully store and access coded materials were not yet fully on the collective horizon of late Victorian/early Edwardian human imagination.

## World Encyclopedia→World Brain→World Mind

The final entry in Borges' account (1939) of the eternally returning desire for a "total library" is Theodor Wolff's 1929 book *Der Wettlauf mit der Schildkröte* (*The Race with the Tortoise*)[5]—in which Wolff identifies the universal library's genealogical debt to Llull's *Ars* or "thinking machine." Concerning the potential for a universal library based on "universal orthographic principles" (2001: 215), Borges sniffs that Wolff (1868–1943) "expounds the execution and the dimensions of that impossible enterprise" (ibid.: 216). Borges' peculiar history of the idea of a universal library ends with Wolff, whose book was published a decade before Borges' "The Total Library." This endpoint is noteworthy. Borges' failure to mention Wells' proposal (1938) is an intriguing omission, particularly given that the successful implementation of World Brain would amount to the realization of the thinking machine anticipated by Llull, and also given Borges' close knowledge of Wells' work.[6] And the gap in Borges' account assumes a greater valence still, given that the account has achieved a kind of consecrated status on the part of many media- and technology-focused researchers, including perhaps ourselves, who have turned to or stumbled upon it as part of their own search for more information about the history of search, computer science, and information machines.

Somewhat like Llull, who had petitioned in vain for papal support for his *Ars*, Wells used his reputation as a public intellectual and strong public speaker to develop credibility for his proposed technology. During the 1930s, he argued passionately for what he originally termed a "Permanent World Encyclopaedia." In 1936 he proposed it to the U.K. Royal Institution and, in 1938, published the collected arguments for it under the title *World Brain*. Though he sought private audiences with heads of state such as Franklin Delano Roosevelt, during which he petitioned for state financing for his scheme, he was unsuccessful. The reworked title of the 1942 edition of this work—*Science and the World Mind*—suggests the evolution in his thinking from the fully empiricist idea of a world encyclopedia to that of a brain and its associations with human sentience, and, finally, to mind itself with its Plotinian blend of metaphysical associations with Divine Mind and Spirit. The 1942 title also points to a move away from mechanisms such as print materials that influence consciousness and promote rational decision-making and towards a position more amenable to the panpsychic idea of integrating mechanism and biological consciousness within one unified, if hybrid, assemblage. The title also anticipates the techno-metaphysical arguments connecting consciousness to forms of "emergent" artificial intelligence that are advanced in more recent universalist proposals for global brains, singularities, hyperbodies, noospheres and HiveMinds discussed in chapter 5. Though Wells' proposal was celebrated by post–World War II information theorists for its influence on their research into how electronic databases might yield maximum public benefit, full recognition of the merits of his proposal would have to wait until computation had proved its worth—until, as it were, mechanization could yield command to computation and its Atomist databases of 0s and 1s.

In *World Brain*, Wells self-identified as a utopian Socialist focused on world peace, and considered himself as upholding and extending Denis Diderot's "tradition of Encyclopaedias" (1938: 19–20). About the body politics of early 1930s Western democracies, Wells lamented their "fear-saturated impatience for guidance, which renders dictatorships possible" (ibid.: xiii). He believed that "raising and unifying … the general intelligence of the world" (ibid.: xiii) through the realization of a World Brain would form the crucial component of a long-term ecological and evolutionary strategy to deal with the scalar complexities introduced by modern forms of economic, military, political, and social organization. He hoped for the eventual assembly of a globally accessible unified database—a latter-day Library of Alexandria, print-based initially and subsequently distributed on microfilm and through electronic communication channels that would assist humankind in arresting the post-World War I trend toward totalitarianism. Wells, however, conceptualized World Brain as information organized for academic and elite knowledge and not primarily at the service of diverse audiences. Yet he also believed that a World Brain (guided "naturally" by elites such as the university-trained) would not serve, as did the Alexandrian Library, to bolster authoritarian power but, rather, "would *compel* men to come to terms with one another" and "hold men's minds together in something like a common interpretation of reality" (ibid.: 23, 35; emphasis in original). Setting aside the fact that Wells, like Llull more than 600 years earlier, sought to substitute a "compelling" technology for the messy, unpredictable, necessarily politicized arena of human discourse, *meaningful access* to knowledge sufficient for sound decision-making is the core difficulty he identifies as requiring remedy. It is not, Wells argues, that there is insufficient knowledge. Rather, there is potentially too much, as existing information remains segregated, incorrectly edited, unorganized, unable to circulate, and, because effectively inaccessible, cannot contribute as it should to the production of human knowledge. "Possibly all the knowledge and all the directive ideas needed to establish a wise and stable settlement of the world's affairs in 1919 existed in bits and fragments, here and there, but practically nothing had been assembled, practically nothing had been thought out, practically nothing had been done to draw that knowledge and these ideas together into a comprehensive conception of the world" (ibid.: 7). One might venture to say that, with this impatient and despairing statement, Wells was on the verge of calling for a unified database and the concomitant means to search it *efficiently* for relevant information as the way to collectively stave off what he feared was a coming World Disaster.

Anticipating contemporary futurists such as Ray Kurtzweil, Wells argued that technological development had outstripped "mental organization" (ibid.: 18) and, while a World Encyclopedia or Brain would rely on technological advances in miniaturization—"the resources of micro-photography, as yet only in their infancy, will be creating a concentrated visual record" (ibid.: 85)—his focus on articulating technical mechanism to human knowledge suggests that he conceived of his proposal in a manner similar to what is now understood as a human/machine assemblage. World Brain would offer "the means whereby we can ... bring all the scattered and ineffective mental wealth of our world into something like a common understanding" (ibid.: 17). It would be "the mental background of every intelligent man in the world. *It would be alive and growing ... Every university and research institution should be feeding it*" (ibid.: 20; emphasis added). The belief here, approaching faith, is that information will yield up its "true" powers once organized as one unified network or field, and, by implication, that, over time, disparate forms of information eventually will coalesce into something like Google's database of intentions.

Wells grasped that his encyclopedic organization "need not be concentrated now in one place; it might have the form of a network. It would centralize mentally but perhaps not physically … It would constitute the material begin-ning of a real World Brain" (ibid.: 70). Yet an actualized World Brain, and the concentration of earthly power it entails, also would constitute a potentially monocultural instance of what the Tower of Babel myth warns against. In part, this is because World Brain would have been an English-language brain, as Wells foresaw English would become the lingua franca of the information age (ibid.: 32). Of equal importance, the fantasy of building a single global mech-anism capable of allowing humans to overcome the context-dependent limita-tions on their ability to adequately interpret useful information is precisely what Paul Ricoeur warns against in his discussion of the impossible Enlightenment ideal of a universal library "from which all untranslatabilities would have been erased" (2006: 9). Impossible, in Ricoeur's estimation, because, in a manner that somewhat recalls Hegel's objection to "thinking machines," a universal library would yield an inhuman rationality freed of all cultural constraints, including local peculiarities and customs, an issue discussed in the final sections of chapter 2. By the 1930s, however, the warnings carried by the Tower of Babel myth had lost their power. Predicated on the lie of unity, World Brain would have consti-tuted a unified information storage system that Wells hoped would meet the pressing need for a sentient world database. Believing a world government inev-itable, he imagined that World Brain would underpin such a rule and a new class of rulers, "the Samurai" (Rayward 1999, 2008: 224).

Wells foresaw the necessity of a unified sentient database for any future form of unified and therefore authoritarian political control. He had faith that the result of a properly functioning World Brain would be the emergence of a "unified mind" (Rayward 2008: 231) or, to refer back to the introduction's discussion of Neoplatonic metaphysics, the emergence of a planetary *nous*. The issue of faith, whether individually or corporately held, is crucial to our broader argument that metaphysics informs the holy grail of search technologies and uni-versal libraries: "Metaphysics rests on a basic presupposition or assumption or initial act of faith" (Copleston 1960: 214). As Fechner earlier had observed: "faith grows out of its own motives … one may believe that something is, and believe that upon it one can rely—then faith is characterized as trust … The one belief, however, is rooted in the other. For how could one believe of anything that it is reliable without believing that it is?" (cited in Lowrie 1946: 83, 86; emphasis in original). No less than Llull before him, or Brin and Page after him, because Wells had faith in his proposal he saw it as on the cusp of realization. But this is also why he became so despondent when politicians and other public figures failed to sign on to his quest.

Was World Brain actualizable or, due to technological limitations, was it doomed to exist at the threshold of potentialization—an ever-tantalizing idea about a virtual totality the realization of which, of necessity, would always lie "in the future"? The ability to search the database is key to any answer, and not only to search it in the abstract, but to allow any number of searchers to make as many enquiries as needed so that, collectively, they might contribute synergistically to augmenting World Brain and therefore, in time, to realizing World Peace. About the ability to meaningfully search World Brain, however, the proselytizing Wells provides few technical details, noting only that "going on at present, among scientific workers, library workers, bibliographers and so forth, there is a very considerable activity for an assembling and indexing of knowledge … From assembling to digesting is only a step—a considerable and difficult step but, none the less, an obvious step" (1938: 76).[7] Of course, the inconvenient truth of a database that cannot yet be searched, and therefore leaves searchers stranded between the rock of assembling and the hard place of accessing, let alone digesting, is the same truth faced in different ways by all earlier totalizing schemes of classification, beginning with Ptolemy's Royal Library. Wells astutely observes, however, that the indexing research to which he refers necessarily must be considered in tandem with the rise of microfilm, a then-new technology of information compression. In 1937, during a visit to the U.S., Wells had visited Kodak's research facilities in Rochester, New York, where he spent time with Ken Mees, an expert on the emerging technology (Campbell-Kelly 2007). Following this visit he wrote a passage that fully anticipates Google Books and other digital library and archive projects: "It seems possible that in the near future, we shall have microscopic libraries of record, in which a photograph of every important book and document in the world will be stowed away and made easily available for the inspection of the student … The time is close at hand when any student, in any part of the world, will be able to sit with his projector in his own study at his or her convenience to examine any book, any document, in an exact replica" (Wells 1938: 76–77). Though he is writing about the interplay between books and microfilm, one could simply substitute the digital scanning of books in reading what Wells has to say: "The American microfilm experts, even now, are making facsimiles of the rarest books, manuscripts, pictures and specimens, which can then be made easily accessible upon the library screen. By means of the microfilm, the rarest and most intricate documents and articles can be studied now at first hand, simultaneously in a score of projection rooms" (1938: 86).

Critical of the authoritarianism undergirding World Brain, information and library science scholar W. Boyd Rayward has observed that "[t]echnologically, Wells' 'World Brain' is remarkably under-imagined and has none of the flashes of imaginative genius that have given such life and power to his books of acknowledged science fiction" (1999: 571). Yet Wells, celebrated author of such fictions as *The Shape of Things to Come*, is fully aware of his proposal's provisional nature: "the idea of an encyclopaedia may undergo very considerable extension and elaboration in the near future," and "I have been talking of something which may even be recognizably in active operation within a … lifetime or so, from now" (1938: 83, 79–80). These statements were made seventy-five years ago—a period of time equal to a "lifetime or so." Wells also provides sufficient description of the geo-informational possibilities of a future World Brain such that today thousands of blogs and other websites identify it as either the internet's or the World Wide Web's precursor. And, while it is microfilm that sustains Wells' dreams, the relevance to cloud computing and the reliance on demiurgic biological metaphors are apparent in his arguments:

> The whole human memory can be … made accessible to every individual … photography affords now every facility for multiplying duplicates of this—which we may call?—this new all-human cerebrum. It need not be concentrated in any one single place. It need not be vulnerable as a human head or a human heart is vulnerable. It can be reproduced exactly and fully, in Peru, China, Iceland, Central Africa, or wherever else seems to afford an insurance against danger and interruption. It can have, at once, the concentration of a craniates animal and the diffused vitality of an amoeba.
>
> (1938: 87)

It is possible to identify, as Wells moves from promoting a World Encyclopedia to promoting a World Mind, that he is on the verge—in his promotion of the ideas that it would be "alive," in need of "feeding," and in possession of a diffused vitality—of theorizing liveliness or sentience in something human-made: a thinking machine. This is a position subsequently elaborated by his fellow countryman, Alan Turing, in his seminal article "Computing Machinery and Intelligence" and its discussion of, under the rubric of "The Imitation Game," "can machines think" (1950: 433). The idea of a thinking machine is also incipient in J.C.R. Licklider's 1960 suggestion, fleshed out in chapter 5, that a symbiosis of humans and information machines would soon come to pass. Wells nods vigorously in the direction of mystical unity when he writes that creation of a Permanent World Encyclopedia "foreshadows a real intellectual unification of our race … a common ideology … a possible means … of dissolving human conflict into unity" (1938: 88). Wells admired Plato's thought, and World Brain is an ironic revisioning of World Soul through the lens of modern science and one that strongly echoes the panpsychic and utopian thought of Fechner and Lasswitz, those earlier scientific theorists of Universal Libraries. If Lasswitz updates Llull's universalist proposal, he also anticipates Wells (and McLuhan) when in 1908 he writes that

> the closer the interests and the thoughts of humanity are knitted together, the more likely the cooperation, the more firmly the entire globe is united by trade, commerce, science and ethical consciousness, all borne upon the wings of technological progress, so much more powerfully will the unity of world consciousness shape itself … a humanity united upon the cultural level of technology represents the central nervous system of the globe.

The whole planet has then matured into a creature of reason, insight into
which lies far beyond the scope of even the most gifted of men.

(cited in Kretzmann 1938: 420)

Like Wells, Lasswitz anticipates that technology will abet realization of his
dream. Fechner, less focused on mechanism, employs holistic analogies to suggest
the Platonic consubstantiality of all matter and intelligence such that the world
itself is one vast field. Yet Wells echoes Fechner's synthesis of metaphysics
and science in his own outline for a World Brain. In Fechner's words: "For is
not the earth in its form and content, like our bodies, and the bodies also of
all animals and plants, a unified system ... is it not a system which, though it
is subjected to stimulus and determining influences from without, determines
itself and develops from within, engendering inexhaustible variety?" (cited in
Lowrie 1946: 155). Researchers who position digital "thinking machines" as
the beginnings of a contemporary World Brain—such as internet pioneer
J.C.R. Licklider (1960) and his use of biological metaphors of animal symbiosis
to argue for a future of mutually productive interdependence between humans
and machines—neglect to consider that such forms of universal artificial intelligence are, in part, themselves faith-based outcomes of desires that "science"
finally invents and government and industry build.

The analog proposals for a universal library examined so far lack an indexing
function adequate to the tasks their proponents hoped they would accomplish.
Hence proposals such as Lasswitz's remain ideas on paper—they do not work,
because the solution to the problem of large-scale search had not yet been
found. We might say that Llull's *Ars* was semi-automatic: through its manipula-
ble combinations of letters made to stand for divine attributes it conceptually
automated part of the human intellection required in asking a question and
part of the storage function required to produce an answer. Like a topic header
or mnemonic, the *Ars* pointed the searcher in the direction of an answer, but
he or she, or an interpreter such as Llull, was then expected to draw from his
or her own knowledge in interpreting the machine's output in order to arrive
at a complete answer. Access to human expertise was assumed. This is remarkably similar to conditions that obtained within Yahoo!'s humanly organized
search directory and in antiquity within the categories system developed by
Callimachus for searching the Royal Library at Alexandria. Callimachus's system
depended on a searcher's emplaced knowledge of how the Library's collection
was arranged (Canfora 1987). Llull's *Ars*, it also will be recalled, could "answer"
no more than 1,680 questions. But when we arrive at World Brain, and transfer-
ring the world's information onto a database the substrate of which is analogic
microfilm, we have no adequate way to search meaningfully because every combination is possible but searching microfilm (unlike its digital replacement, the
PDF) was impossible to fully automate. In a way, then, despite the exponential

increase in storage capacity that microfilm offered over printed materials, and despite the availability of global transmission of information in the 1930s via telephony and wire photo—the original "fax" technology which relied on scanning[8]—a proposal such as World Brain remained as tantalizing to mid-twentieth-century thinkers as had Llull's *Ars* 700 years earlier. Possibly even more so, given Wells' overstated claims for what it could eventually accomplish. The dreams grow in tandem with technology's advances—from a thinking machine that would offer logical support for religious conversion to one that would usher in an essentially post-human and therefore post-ideological World Peace. This is not to say that World Brain has been without influence. Far from it, and the following chapter traces how Wells' ideas directly influence such thinkers as Eugene Garfield, the American information theorist responsible in the 1950s for creating the academic Science Citation Index. As Brin and Page acknowledge, PageRank's design is influenced by Garfield's work.

Wells had imagined that the gap between the assembly and the digestion of information would soon be closed. If a sufficiently powerful indexing mechanism had existed in the 1930s, and therefore had allowed for the closing or even narrowing of this gap, the World Brain/World Mind potentially would have exemplified precisely what Wells explicitly proselytized: a form of cyborg intelligence with the potential to somehow become conscious of itself. It is this point—that information, in sufficient aggregation and circulation, could itself constitute a form of intelligence—that positions Wells' World Brain on both a chronological and a technological pivot between earlier proposals for thinking machines and universal libraries, and more recent ones, examined in chapter 5, that anticipate the realization of Neoplatonist goals such as global unity and the annihilation of space through the use of networked digital technologies. Like Lasswitz's ideal science fiction, World Brain is on the cusp of the virtual about to be actualized. For believers, it was and remains a potential devoutly to be wished.

In 2008, a lifetime or so after Wells advanced his proposal, Rayward suggested that "perhaps the two modern information society developments that come nearest to Wells' World Brain conceived as a World Encyclopaedia … are Google and its various offspring and the Wikipedia. These tools accommodate the intransigent reality that the ever-expanding store of human knowledge is almost incalculably massive in scale, is largely viewpoint-dependent, is fragmented, complex, ceaselessly in dispute and always under revision" (2008: 236–237). Wells, however, envisioned a world governed by Samurai. Issues of commerce would not influence their rule. He could not, or chose not to, foresee both how the ideal of total information awareness could exert its own form of meta-governance, and how the relevance of information would be determined when private stewards such as Google are at the helm.

Concerning the idea of a total library, Borges had, in 1939, cautioned that "One of the habits of the mind is the invention of horrible imaginings.

The mind has invented Hell, … it has imagined the Platonic ideas" (2001: 216). George Orwell responded directly to Wells' claims that a World Brain constituted through information and communication technologies could eliminate inequality when he warned that Wells had not adequately considered other difficulties posed by the coming machine culture. "The machine has got to be accepted, but it is probably better to accept it rather as one accepts a drug— that is, grudgingly and suspiciously … The oftener one surrenders to it the tighter its grip becomes. You have only to look about you at this moment to realize with what sinister speed the machine is getting us into its power" (1937: 203–204). One would scarcely claim that Orwell took inspiration from the kinds of Neoplatonic thought that suffuse Wells' World Brain proposal. It is, therefore, fascinating to read Fechner also commenting, in 1861, on the "life of machines." He substantially anticipates Orwell's concerns but goes beyond them to envision what we would today identify as a machine or information ecology of the kind sketched in the negative by E.M. Forster in his short story against machine dependence, "The Machine Stops" (1909), and in the positive by inventor and futurist Ray Kurtzweil's (2005) proposal that we will merge with ever more intelligent information machines to create the coming "Singularity." For Fechner, "in the fact that machines are more and more replacing life, that railroads and telegraphs cover the earth, many see a sign that the times are striking out in an entirely different direction. And, in fact, if this goes on, only one of two things is possible: Either all life upon the earth will be submerged by the machines; or all machines will finally merge in the life of the earth. But since the first cannot be, only the other can" (cited in Lowrie 1946: 130).

## The Library of Babel

Shown on its home page on August 24, 2011, Google's doodle in honor of Borges' 112th birthday depicts the author-librarian gazing onto the fantastical Library of Babel, the architecture of which subtly spells "Google."[9] "The Library of Babel" (1941) is an allegorical rendering of the universe as an unsearchable library within which are lodged all possible and impossible books. In his earlier "The Total Library" (1939), Borges had been clear that, in his estimation, efforts such as Llull's *Ars* were impossible follies based on flawed assumptions dating back to the Atomists' belief that elemental units of reality such as number and letter, properly organized in combinations, can stand in for all forms of material reality. While Borges may in part have intended his account as a cautionary aimed at those who, like Nimrod or the Ptolemies, seek to realize universalist aspirations, authors do not control the eventual reception of their work. Because of certain issues it raises or implies, along with how it does so through its textual elaboration of a simulacrum of reality, Borges' tale of the map that swallowed the territory, after a lifetime or so, enjoys a popularity among technotopians that parallels the increasing power of networked digital technologies to shape and disseminate information and thereby consciousness. The tale has been claimed by proselytizers such as Kelly (1994), who imagine the internet as the potential realization of a universal library. They position "The Library of Babel" as *the* most compelling account of the desire for a universal library even as they also acknowledge Borges did not propose how an effective and therefore searchable index might come to pass.

Borges' story conceives the universe as a vast library of books that has existed "*ab aeterno*," or since the beginning of time (1962: 52). Though the Library holds all knowledge, most of its books are composed of meaningless strings of letters: "Everything: the minutely detailed history of the future ... the faithful catalogue of the Library, thousands and thousands of false catalogues, the demonstration of the fallacy of those catalogues, the demonstration of the fallacy of the true catalogue, ... the true story of your death, the translation of every book in all languages, the interpolations of every book in all books" (ibid.: 54). The story's narrator observes that, while man-the-librarian may be an imperfect product of the demiurge, the universe-as-library "can only be the work of a god" (ibid.). Without the ability to effectively search "everything," however, the divine disorder of the Library's unedited and unfiltered contents remains useless and, over centuries, the "extravagant happiness" (ibid.: 55) of its librarians has given way to an existential despair whereby, given their inability to locate a "catalogue of catalogues" (ibid.: 52), they have come to agree that "books signify nothing in themselves" (ibid.: 53). Despair, induced by the absence of a catalogue of catalogues (an organizational key or index), propels librarians to imagine two metaphysical technologies that Borges terms "superstitions" (ibid.: 56)—the Crimson Hexagon, a place within the Library where all the books are magical, and, more interestingly for our purposes, the Man of the Book. About the latter "superstition," Borges' narrator comments that "men reasoned ... there must exist a book which is the formula and perfect compendium *of all the rest*" (ibid.: 56). Borges draws inspiration for the Man of the Book from mathematician Georg Cantor's notion of the infinite aleph—an object or point that contains within itself all other objects or points—and his description of transfinite numbers as a "hierarchy of infinities" within which the original aleph-null is succeeded by an infinite number of alephs each infinitely greater than the one preceding it (Fisher 1997: 100). Borges interprets the aleph as an "infinite unity" (1962: 56). The parts are not less than the whole. The Man of the Book is alephic, a magical log or index allowing access to the meaningful contents of all the other books. The librarian who finds such an index will be, in Borges' words, "analogous to a god" (ibid.). Google, we suggest, has begun to take on the role of that "inconceivably infinite" Spinozan god (Fisher 1997: 102) and, courtesy of advances such as PageRank, coupled to a pervasive cultural desire for enlightened transcendence through IT and an increasingly widespread belief that all useful knowledge is stored somewhere on the internet, is working to surmount the impossible difficulties that faced Borges' despairing librarians.

Borges argued that the realization of a total library such as Lasswitz had outlined would, because of its vast "inhuman" size, be organized by chance and "eliminate human intelligence" (2001: 216). He did not anticipate the ways that this same intelligence would factor as coding in the design of search algorithms, and even though one can identify parallels between the garbled strings of meaningless texts in Borges' library and the recursive SEO link farms to which searchers may be "automatically" directed by search engines, we would not go so far as to argue that search technologies eliminate human intelligence. The issue of link farms, however, does suggest a reading of Borges' tale of the "impossible enterprise" of a total library as pointing to what could result if an Artificial Intelligence were to take over some of the necessary editing function required of any universal index that actually works. And if Borges' fictional Library contains "the true story of your death," then, in essence, he is describing a virtual world based on coding and storage capacity not so different than Google's hope that search technology will answer such questions as "which job shall I take?" Schmidt's artless insertion of a networked device into the psychic zone between present desires ("What shall I do tomorrow?") and anxieties concerning the array of future potentials ("What I actually will do tomorrow") that have always remained essentially unknowable is precisely what Borges seems to warn against. In certain ways his account anticipates Jean Baudrillard's commentary about the accelerating cultural embrace of virtuality:

> By shifting to a virtual world … we move into a world where everything that exists only as idea, dream, fantasy, utopia will be eradicated, because it will immediately be realized, operationalized. Nothing will survive as an idea or a concept … Everything will be preceded by its virtual realization. We are dealing with an attempt to construct an entirely positive world, a perfect world, expurgated of every illusion, of every sort of evil and negativity, exempt from death itself. This pure, absolute reality, this unconditional realization of the world—this is what I call the Perfect Crime.
>
> (2000: 66–67)

Despite Borges' intentions, his hyperreal narrative of life itself depicted as "the activity of retrieving and interpreting information" (Whitaker 1999: 48) has been taken up by those who see in networked digital technologies the realization of a universal library, World Brain, or World Mind. After considering the ways that Google, Web networks, and information search cross-intersect, Gleick preaches that "we are all patrons of the Library of Babel now, and we are the librarians, too. We veer from elation to dismay and back. The library will endure; it is the universe" (2011: 426). About the digital realization of a universal library, and the networked index necessary to meaningfully access its contents, Kelly has written one of the more evangelizing accounts. In *Out of Control*, published in 1994 at the advent of the World Wide Web, he includes a chapter, "In the Library of Form," that frames its argument through the device of having Kelly-as-narrator find, during a whimsical search of library stacks, a twenty-four-page fragment of a never-conducted interview between Kelly and Borges. Kelly tells readers that the interview, part of an anthology of interviews purportedly given by Borges, "properly could only exist in my book, this book, *Out of Control*" (ibid.: 258).

The chapter "reproduces" the imaginary interview which, through a series of questions and answers, interprets, popularizes, and also narrows (to arguably invert) the intended meanings of the Library-as-universe. Contemplating the answers Borges provides him allows Kelly to roam the virtual library in search of a completed copy of *Out of Control*. Though he fails to locate one, he gains deeper insight into the Library's organization than did Borges' hapless narrator. Kelly develops what he calls "the Method"—"a variety of what we now call evolution" (ibid.: 263)—that allows him to predict where the very few meaningful texts will be located in any one of the Library's endless hexagonal rooms filled with mostly meaningless materials. With this metaphysical move, Kelly highlights one of the central promises of digital technologies that Google and search technologies more generally have made explicit: each of us will hold the magical key to the Library in our own hand and each of us will have access to our own, personalized universal library of relevant truthiness. His tale then moves to argue that Borges cast his account as a fiction in order to obfuscate the fact that "his Library was real" (ibid.). Following this leap in logic, Kelly moves quickly to stake his claim:

> Two decades ago nonlibrarians discovered Borges's Library in silicon circuits of human manufacture. The poetic can imagine the countless rows of hexagons and hallways stacked up in the Library corresponding to the incomprehensible microlabyrinth of crystalline wires and gates stamped into a silicon computer chip. A computer chip, blessed by the proper incantation of software, creates Borges's Library on command ...
>
> Neither the model, the speed, the soundless of design, or the geographical residence of the computer makes any difference while generating a portal to Borges's Library. This Borges himself did not know, although he would have appreciated it: that whatever artificial means are used to get there, all travelers arrive at exactly the same Library ... The consequence of this universality is that any computer can create a Borgian Library of all possible books.

> (1994: 263)

Kelly's account is remarkable for its (unstated) debt to Wells' idea of World Brain as well as to the subsequent post–World War II proposals such as Vannevar

Bush's "memex" (1945), discussed in the following chapter. One can, moreover, infer additional influences on Kelly's thinking. In 1994, "two decades ago" referred to the early 1970s, and Kelly implicitly nods in the direction of the work of computer scientists and link analysts such as J.C.R. Licklider (*Libraries of the Future*, 1965) and World Brain advocate Eugene Garfield (*Essays of an Information Scientist*, 1977), also discussed in the following chapter. Kelly's account is further noteworthy for its inversion (or subversion) of Borges' intent. Kelly, not unlike Borges, presents the Library as a collection in need of a mechanism to search its stored collection—"a Method"—but Kelly leaves unmentioned, and therefore unexplained, Borges' motivation to write about what he terms the "subaltern horror" (2001: 216) of the Library. By failing to acknowledge that, unlike actual libraries, the Library of Babel is not a center of learning, Kelly repositions Borges' caveat against mistaking information for reality itself, and against seeking godlike universal powers (a warning contained in the story's very title) to one in which a prescient polymath foresaw the need for a coding breakthrough in search techniques.[10] The discursive ploy is consistent with Kelly's broader project. In the same volume, he writes: "Who will not feel a bit of holy awe on the day that machines talk back to us" (1994: 24). Kelly broadly argues that non-networked human individuals remain "dumb terminals" until networked into the emergent unity of the cybernetic HiveMind, a state and a place where cyborg flesh will finally begin its merger with information, certainty, and truth.

Kelly, who more recently has argued that evolving forms of technology (the "technium") constitute a living meta-organism or "the seventh kingdom of life" (2010: 103), is not alone in taking inspiration from Borges' impossible Library. British science fiction writer David Langford (1997), also writing in 1994, does not invert Borges' meaning but does deploy the Library as a metaphor for the past when he notes that, with respect to the crucial problem of searching it, "in the end the old Library was disbanded as being an irrational construct, and new devices were supplied in its stead … Imagine it physically condensed, with each fat volume somehow inscribed on the surface of a single electron … The golden or leaden key that unlocks the Library is the inbuilt search facility" (1997: 450–452).

It is remarkable that authors placing Borges' work at their service often rely on variations of the science fiction idiom. One year after Google launched its search engine, Jon Thiem, implicitly drawing from Wells' World Brain proposal, outlined a then-fictional "Universal Electronic Library" (UL), one that he interpreted as "a postmodern version of the ancient Library of Alexandria" (1999: 256). Thiem's account, set in 2056, looks back at the year 2026 to posit an internet of the future complete with a universal database that "unified and transcended all regional and specialized databases" (ibid.: 257). Yet his account is tinged with the Borgesian realization that, while the emergence of a universal language based on combinatory possibilities of 0s and 1s is an unprecedented development, striving for universality is a labyrinthine exercise in contradiction. Commenting that the Royal Library at Alexandria has become a metaphor for "the curse of too much learning" (ibid.: 258), Thiem engages Borges' use of the alephic principle in two ways. He first notes that "every project of all-inclusiveness, of universal enumeration, harbours within it the virus of chaos, of irretrievability. Thus comprehensiveness can lead to incomprehension" (ibid.). This, he suggests, is the pessimistic interpretation applied by Borges in "The Library of Babel."

> Borges and others seemed to suggest that the vastness and complexity of the modern megalibrary made it as labyrinthine as the world it was meant to explain ... The powerful alephic properties of the UL turned this situation around ... Although the UL is the most comprehensive collection of knowledge that has ever existed, instantaneous access to this knowledge in combination with sophisticated word–subject–title search tools, Universal Abstracts, and electronic reading programs has restored focus and intelligibility to the intellectual enterprise ... True, the UL gives you everything there is, but it also gives you the means to find exactly what you need. The UL has indeed transformed the researcher's computer screen into something like Borges's fabulous aleph.
>
> (ibid.: 259)

Thiem's account envisions that the creation of the UL is a result of an international commission—that public institutions organized and undertook the digital conversion of all printed materials. Though the social and technological changes wrought by neoliberalism were on full display by 1999, he does not factor them into his equation. Nevertheless, the parallels he introduces between the Royal Library of Alexandria and its eventual destruction and his fictional Universal Electronic Library of the future are provocative. "Like its precursor in Alexandria, the UL is not only an enormous repository of information about every known mythology, it too has become the impossible object of mythological devotion and execration" (ibid.: 260). Perhaps it was "ever thus," but considering the uneven spatio-temporal trajectory running between Ancient Alexandria and contemporary Mountain View, California (Google's headquarters), Thiem's account does suggest something of the vexed set of future difficulties that may emerge if and when Google succeeds, as a consecrated entity, in implementing its first principle vision of all information, in one place, at one time. In late 2010, when introducing Google Instant, Brin commented, "We want Google to be the third half of your brain" (Levy 2011: 386). The question remains as to what it might mean to rely so fundamentally on an aggregated, constantly changing database-cum-World Brain—"your brain" maintained by a privately held

American corporation that is as influential in terms of its consecration as, or possibly more so than, any one state. This issue is taken up in chapter 7.

In this chapter we have identified forms of metaphysical thinking and their indebtedness to Neoplatonism such as they touch on issues of search. While critical, our interest has not been to malign such thought per se, but to show that thinking and invention do not happen in dehistoricized vacuums and that the circumstances of their gestation and application matter. What interests us in the following chapters are the ways that the metaphysics of search transect and subtend that sphere of corporate and human affairs identified as political economy. We are often told that the idealist sphere of metaphysics and ultimate truths does not mesh with the material sphere of political economy, capital, and financial markets, and that the spheres should be held apart. The forces that encourage this binary thinking, however, are frequently those who also fail to see how the algorithm is anything more than a useful tool, and certainly not a statement of reality with the power to contribute to reorganizing aspects of reality itself. Chapters 5 and 6, however, through their examination of an emergent metaphysics of search organized through private interests, point toward what we identify as a political economy of metaphysics. To wit, full realization of Google's universal vision of all information, in one place, at the same time, would render the firm an even more powerful economic juggernaut than is already the case. Though unlikely, such a realization would make it the gatekeeper to all the world's information, the guardian of a universal archive, and therefore the possessor of a still-hard-to-imagine political, economic, and social influence and power at least equal to that envisioned by Wells for the Samurai elite who would have steered the "efficient" operation of his World Brain.[11]

# 5

# THE FIELD OF INFORMATIONAL METAPHYSICS AND THE BOTTOM LINE

Google, with its goal of making the world's information available through a single platform—its own—is but the latest player on the stage of desire for a universal library or archive. This chapter engages with the proposals of post-World War II information theorists operating within what we can retrospectively identify as an emerging field of search. It traces their growing, at times urgent, interest in developing searchable electronic databases. These theorists had faith that information machines, over time, would resolve the conundrum of massively unfiltered information (today known as information overload) and too few ways to meaningfully access and filter it in a timely and useful manner. We extend previous chapters' foci on the interplay among information, metaphysics, and search—on forms of Idealist thought and their emphasis on consubstantial unity expressed in doctrines such as World Soul, and the influence of earlier forms of reasoned spiritual beliefs such as Ramón Llull's on modern ideas about search, information retrieval, and search technologies.

In their interest in developing information machines capable of at least pointing towards an eventual searchable global intelligence, the twentieth-century information scientists who populate this discussion are the intellectual progeny of the late medieval Llull and his work to invent a "key to universal reality" (Bonner 1985: 68–69), a "thinking machine" that would abet humankind's reunification. In their stated adherence to scientific principles, these men are empiricists. Yet their desires suggest they are empirical Utopians seeking to actualize a universal reality. This disposition is apparent in their interest in theorizing and developing the technical mechanisms necessary to make a World Brain or universal library actually work.

A second group is equally important to this story. Composed of transcendentalist-inflected thinkers such as Kevin Kelly, paleontologist and Jesuit metaphysician

Pierre Teilhard de Chardin, and Deleuzian-influenced academic Pierre Lévy, this group, like the information scientists, anticipates humankind's unification through networked information machines. Its focus is less about the efficient provision of answers to questions, however, and more about envisioning how information machines can render embodied difference moot in the face of the coming cybernetic unity of the HiveMind, global noosphere, and cosmically transcendent hyperbody, to employ the neologisms that Kelly, Teilhard de Chardin, and Lévy respectively coin. Along with the information scientists, these individuals articulate concepts and propose ideas that historically inform the disposition of the engineering culture so central to the field of search. Previous chapters noted the importance of panpsychism to the thought of Gustav Fechner and of his influence on Kurt Lasswitz's vision of a universal library of all books. Panpsychic philosophy has many variants, but broadly holds to the universal nature of mind and, in accordance with monist belief, that all reality is "either a single entity or a single kind of entity" (Skrbina 2005: 8). The universe is a single, sensate organism in which everything interdepends within one pulsing organic network. An implicit "commonsense" of the contemporary empirical zeitgeist encourages accepting that a clear distinction exists between Neoplatonically inflected concepts such as the panpsychic HiveMind, the noosphere and the hyberbody in which everything interdepends, and the metrical, quantified, and material plane upon which advances in computer science and information theory continue to take place.

No less a figure than Alan Turing, however, refutes this discrete way of looking at the world. He understands that "the system of the 'universe as a whole' is such that quite small errors in initial conditions can have an overwhelming effect at a later time," and he imagines that "the displacement of a single electron by a billionth of a centimetre at one moment might make the difference between a man being killed by an avalanche a year later, or escaping" (1950: 440). Turing reveals a perhaps unwitting debt to Fechner and other scientific metaphysicians: everything interdepends in a consubstantial, or at least symbiotic unity of time and space, in both the coming computational-based "universe as a whole" and in modern, seemingly secular variations of panpsychic belief such as the Gaia hypothesis. Such interdependency is popularly expressed through stock phrases like "six degrees of separation" and the "butterfly effect" that derive from theories of complexity such as chaos theory intended to explain the functioning of self-organizing systems and with which Fechner would most likely concur.

If we choose to look, we are witnesses today to an under-acknowledged but widespread renewal of interest in actualizing panpsychic ideals through digital technologies (Nelson 2011). A good example is the development of cloud computing. Google's initial contribution to the cloud was a beta product branded as "Google Drive" or "GDrive" and first floated in 2006. With GDrive, a user's information and most software applications would no longer reside on his or her hard drive but instead on a transcendent cloud constituted through the networked collectivity of Google's many server farms accessed via the Web from any networked machine (Smith 2009). While GDrive was taken down, many of its functionalities were incorporated into the widely popular Google Docs (Arrington 2010). In 2010, as part of extending its reach, Google made available limited quantities of the CR-48, a laptop prototype with no internal hard drive or file storage capacity. In June of the following year, the machine went on sale as the Samsung Chromebook (Pogue 2011). The assumption behind Chromebook is that anyone can get online anytime they need to from wherever they may be, and that the free software and massive computing capacity available through the cloud does most of what existing software and stand-alone hard drives can do. Chromebooks disconnected from the cloud, however, are indeed the "dumb terminals" that Kelly predicted, with the proviso that he also imagined the dumb terminals would be us—the human wetware.

Chromebook forms an intermediary between human users ("smart terminals," because connected) and the cloud, or at least Google's share of it. The entire networked apparatus of human–interface–cloud suggests a striving to actualize panpsychism's assertion that the universe is a single sensate organism. Chromebook's designers and engineers imagine that people will, in greater symbiotic association with machines, migrate their individual knowledge, as represented on each of their hard drives, to the cloud. Actual bodies will remain "here," this side of the interface, but our collective head will be in the cloud—that seemingly sentient platform in the sky where individual knowledge aggregates into a proprietary form of collective, ultimate truth. Access to this truth through the cloud, together with access to the digitized contents of bricks-and-mortar libraries and archives also on reserve, positions Chromebook as a monetizing update that merges the library carrel and the library card. Collectively, Chromebooks operate like an infinite number of personalized reading rooms lodged within the emerging, cosmic, and commercial World Brain. About the cloud metaphor, Gleick has pronounced, "All that information ... looms over us ... amorphous, spectral; hovering nearby, yet not situated in any place. Heaven must once have felt this way to the faithful ... Its physical aspect could not be less cloudlike. Server farms proliferate in unmarked brick buildings and steel complexes ... This hidden infrastructure grows in a symbiotic relationship with the electrical infrastructure it increasingly resembles ... These are the wheelworks; the cloud is their avatar" (2011: 396). As Gleick implicitly acknowledges, heaven isn't a server farm in an unmarked steel building. Instead the cloud is a cosmic metaphor rendered as commodity fetish, worshiped in its own right and obscuring its sources of production. To historicize the rise of privately owned exobrain assemblages such as the cloud through which many of us now search for information, following sections profile the twentieth-century empirical Utopians and transcendentalists who develop the metaphysically inflected technical concepts necessary to the exobrain's eventual realization.

## Information Scientists and the Quest for Collective Intelligence

The dawn of the postwar era was a time of rising interest in the relationship between information and communication. In the United States, a group of information theorists, some of whom defined themselves as information scientists,[1] gained prominence through focusing on this relationship. Some of these men endorsed H.G. Wells' bibliographic vision of World Brain and worked explicitly towards its actualization. This is reflected in the names they gave their schemas, such as the Informatorium, World Intelligence Center, and WISE (World Information Synthesis and Encyclopaedia).

### Eugene Garfield

Eugene Garfield (b. 1925) was the originator of citation analysis which, in turn, has been a principal inspiration for Web link analysis. Garfield was a structural linguist who self-identified as a "World Brainist" and "information entrepreneur." His thinking about efficient information retrieval was influenced by his awareness of *Shepard's Citations*, a publication started in 1873 for the legal profession and based on a citation system that lists individual American court cases, their histories and any publications that subsequently refer to them. Garfield was a founder of the Philadelphia-based Institute for Scientific Information (ISI). In the second half of the 1950s, he and his ISI associates developed the bibliometric technique that the Institute would incorporate into the workings of its now famous Science Citation Index (SCI) and Social Science Index (SSI). In a seminal paper, Garfield proposed,

> a bibliographic system for science literature that can eliminate the uncritical citation of fraudulent, incomplete, or obsolete data by making it possible for the conscientious scholar to be aware of criticisms of earlier papers. It is too much to expect a research worker to spend an inordinate amount of time searching for the bibliographic descendants of antecedent papers. It would not be excessive to demand that the thorough scholar check all papers that cited or criticized such papers, if they could be located quickly. The citation index makes this possible.
>
> (1955: 108)

The SCI and SSI—long found in academic library reference rooms—have evolved into the databases collectively known as *Web of Science*. Now owned by Thomson Reuters, these databases are typically available through academic libraries' Web portals. Garfield envisioned the SCI and SSI as mechanisms for ranking the relative importance of academic articles. The reputation-based system he and colleagues developed, however, is based not on any quality or particular rigor of an article's arguments or discoveries, but on *counting* the number of existing papers the article cites, the number of times that peers refer to it in papers they subsequently publish, and the perceived importance or ranking of each of these citations. Robert Abbott refers to this popularity-based approach to academic relevance as following "how the literature feeds off itself" (1999: 113). The SCI and SSI examine, retrospectively, "the degree to which scientific papers cite from each other, the existence of such a citation suggesting some kind of close conceptual link ... Using this method it is possible to identify significant publications, groups of workers, paradigms and paradigm shifts and changes in consensus, and leading edges of knowledge" (ibid.). These indices "seemed to offer a politically neutral, purely formal way of determining the importance of publications and scientists. This method, taken up by search engines, is now applied to all informational domains" (Becker and Stalder 2009: 9) and is one of the pillars on which rests the field of search's model of best practice.

Larry Page—familiar with academic citation indices such as the SCI and SSI and the power they can wield over career advancement, and holding to the insight that the Web with its countless hypertextual links is a form of collective self-knowledge that a search engine can exploit (Brin and Page 1998; Gleick 2011: 423)—also reasoned that the Web is organized around the idea of citation and annotation (Battelle 2005: 72). In developing Google's popularity-based PageRank algorithm, he and Sergey Brin drew explicitly from the structuring concepts developed at the ISI by Garfield and colleagues (Battelle 2005: 69–74; Mayer 2009: 64–66). Strongly influenced by Wells' World Brain, Garfield sought to actualize (and commercialize) its possibilities, in part by creating indexing mechanisms that reveal patterns of use (in the form of patterns of citation). In turn, Garfield influenced Page and Brin and thereby the development of PageRank and the search engine that serves as the entry point and organizing mechanism for the world's information, or, at least, the online and therefore potentially monetizable part of it that Google's spiders are able to track on the publicly accessible parts of the Web.

While a distinct and well-documented intellectual genealogy runs from Wells' proposal for a World Brain, to Garfield's invention of the SCI and SSI, to Google's PageRank, there are other important actors at work in the story of search.

### Vannevar Bush

The American inventor and scientific administrator Vannevar Bush (1890–1974), arguably the first to theorize what we now call hypertext, is central to the quest for a searchable universal library and archive. In 1927, Bush invented the "differential analyzer," an analog computing device. Director of the U.S. wartime Office of Scientific Research and Development and an organizer of the Manhattan Project, Bush was, in effect, the first American presidential science advisor. His 1945 publication in the *Atlantic Monthly* of a proposal for a "memex," a searchable information storage device that anticipates the personal computer (Figure 5.1), speaks to Wells' unified vision that "in the future, we shall have microscopic libraries of record, in which a photograph of every important book and document in the world will be stowed away and made easily available for the inspection of the student" (Wells 1938: 76). As part of the interwar decades' broad zeitgeist regarding information storage and retrieval, Bush's ideas for the memex "had been developed in 1932 and 1933, ahead of Wells' World Brain or World Encyclopaedia pronouncements, and a draft paper had been written in 1939, but never published" (Abbott 1999: 120; see also Press 1993; Campbell-Kelly 2007).

Like Wells, Bush was concerned that the sum of human knowledge had come to exceed human ability to meaningfully access and process it. "There is a growing mountain of research," he wrote, "but there is increased evidence that we are being bogged down today as specialization extends. The investigator is staggered by the findings and conclusions of thousands of other workers— conclusions which he cannot find time to grasp, much less to remember, as they appear ... our methods of transmitting and reviewing the results of research

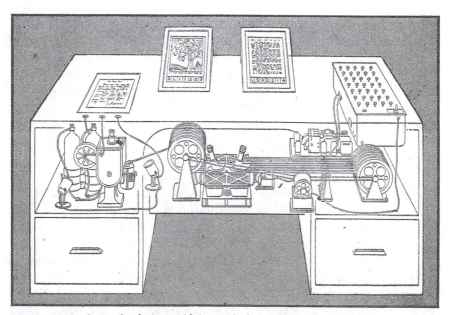

**MEMEX** in the form of a desk would instantly bring files and material on any subject to the operator's fingertips. Slanting translucent viewing screens magnify supermicro-film filed by code numbers. At left is a mechanism which automatically photographs longhand notes, pictures and letters, then files them in the desk for future reference.

**FIGURE 5.1** Illustration with Description of Proposed Memex, *Life* 19: 11, p 112 (September 10, 1945). Alfred Crimi, artist. By permission of his estate

are generations old and by now are totally inadequate for their purpose" (1988: 237). While Bush celebrates the advances in technologies of compression and miniaturization that, by 1945, had seemingly rendered moot the fantastical technical difficulties raised by Lasswitz's 1901 account of a universal library that exceeded the size of the universe, the problem of search that haunted Borges' despairing librarians remains unsolved: "A record, if it is to be useful to science, must be continuously extended, it must be stored, and above all it must be consulted ... Our ineptitude in getting at the record is largely caused by the artificiality of systems of indexing" (ibid.: 238, 244). This artificiality, Bush explains, is structured into alphanumeric file systems organized hierarchically into classes and subclasses of information. Such systems permit searching for one piece of information at a time. "The human mind," however, "does not work that way. It operates by association. With one item in its grasp, it snaps instantly to the next that is suggested by association of thoughts in accordance with some intricate web of trails carried by the cells of the brain ... Selection by association, rather than by indexing, may yet be mechanized" (ibid.: 244).

Bush's title for his article on the memex, "As We May Think," is significant. It indicates that Bush, like Wells, and even Llull before him, believed that powerful new forms of information and retrieval technologies based on associative indexing would stimulate, like a combinatorial "thinking machine," the rise of new forms of unified or associated thinking. Garfield's ISI citation databases are also predicated on the assumption that a cited article is conceptually associated to another that cites (and therefore links to) it. About the automation of such linkages, if, as Bush believed, the mind establishes associative links across trails of information, then the memex "affords an intermediate step ... to associative indexing, the basic idea of which is a provision whereby any item may be caused at will to select immediately and automatically another. This is the essential feature of the memex. The process of tying two items together is the important thing" (ibid.: 245). Here Bush offers the basic outline of what will come to be known as hypertext, one of the defining features of the Web. Hypertext is an essential aspect of digital search whereby search algorithms link the entry of one piece of information typed into the searchbox to other websites they determine likely will be of associated relevance to the searcher.

Bush's article reveals his deep interest in an electronic thinking machine which, while differing in design from the rotating disks of Llull's *Ars*, would provide a personal archive based on automated selection and combinatorial forms of analysis able to provide at least the beginnings of answers, in the form of linked "trails" of cellular-like associations, to questions posed by the machine's operator/searcher. Like Llull's *Ars*, moreover, Bush's proposal, based on his beliefs as to how the mind "naturally" works, cannot escape metaphysical inflection. (It is as though he intuits that the planetary *nous* needs a machine to survive and the memex is a start.) About the hypertextual functionality of digital computation that makes linked searches possible, computer scientist Jacques Vallee has written,

"Modern computers retrieve information associatively. You 'evoke' the desired records by using keywords, words of power: you request the intersection of 'microwave' and 'headache,' and you find twenty articles you never suspected existed … If we live in the associative universe of the software scientist rather than the sequential universe of the spacetime physicist then miracles are no longer irrational events" (1979: 215–216).

Bush's use in his title of the plural "we" identifies the universalist aspect of his enlightenment-influenced thinking. The article's unstated economic and political assumptions of a level playing field regarding user access work to support his contention that in the not-too-distant future "we" will each sit before our personal device which in its mass-produced hardware will be much like all other such devices. That is to say, we will each be searchers: "There is a new profession of trailblazers, those who find delight in the task of establishing useful trails through the enormous mass of the common record" (1988: 246). In 1967, Bush revisited the possibility of a memex and suggested that, while its actualization was closer then than it had been in 1945, numerous technical problems remained that likely would require digital computation for their resolution. His original Wellsian faith in the coming power of collective knowledge organized through searchable databases, however, remained unshaken: "The applications of science have built man a well-supplied house, and are teaching him to live healthily in it … They may yet allow him truly to encompass the great record and to grow in the wisdom of race experience" (1967: 100–101).

Bush makes clear, however, that each of us who forms part of the collective "we" (the human race) will be interested in searching for different answers to different problems: lawyers access opinions and court decisions, patent attorneys review issued patents, physicians consult case histories, chemists study compounds and chemical behavior, and historians use "skip trails" to follow particular epochs (1988: 246). Finally, Bush defines the memex as "a device in which an individual stores all his books, records, and communications, and which is mechanized so that it may be consulted with exceeding speed and flexibility. It is an enlarged intimate supplement to his memory" (ibid.: 244–245). The definition's first part emphasizes the device's storage component, and in the late 1960s Garfield—ever the entrepreneur on the lookout for an edge within his field— would make the following distinction when speaking about his own "World Brainist" contributions for "universal bibliographic control."

> In several papers, I have described the *Science Citation Indexes* and the Unified Index to Science as preliminary steps toward achieving the dream of universal bibliographical control which H.G. Wells symbolized in the *World Brain*. To some, the Wellsian term "World Brain" might seem less appropriate than "Memex," the term chosen by Vannevar Bush to symbolize the ideal information retrieval device. However, there is a world of difference between Memex and "World Brain"—essentially the difference

between hardware and software—between a communication carrier and the intellectual-message-carried problem. The "World Brain" symbolizes the information stored—"Memex," the storage device. In designing any bibliographic system, it is imperative to make these distinctions.

(1968: 169)

While doubtless important to distinguish between hardware and software, Garfield overstates his case. World Brain is equally a storage device—hardware—as it is software-based. So, too, is memex not only a storage device but also the information stored within it, along with the associations or links that its operator must make so that the entire assemblage is adequate to the complex tasks of enlightened decision-making that Bush envisioned memex would facilitate. Both Wells and Bush imagined microfilm would be the material substrate on which information would be stored. Bush writes, "In one end is the stored material. The matter of bulk is well taken care of by improved microfilm … Most of the memex contents are purchased on microfilm ready for insertion. Books of all sorts, pictures, current periodicals, newspapers, are thus obtained and dropped into place" (1988: 245). And, while World Brain is global in scope, whereas memex anticipates the blending of individual archival practices and desktop personal computing, the kinds of links and associations possible to achieve today with post-memex laptops and mobile devices adhere to the same algorithmic logics as the largest networked servers. While Garfield's indexing insights earn him a relevant place in the pantheon, contemporary information and search technologies synthesize memex and World Brain. This is a harmony within the field of technology and of search even as Garfield's comments indicate his competitive jostling for position within and across the fields.

## Manfred Kochen

In certain of Garfield's publications one finds an unfortunate tendency to belittle his peers' ideas with faint praise. His comments on Bush's memex have been noted. His stated views about the proposal for WISE (World Information Synthesis and Encyclopaedia), advanced by fellow World Brainist Manfred Kochen (1928–1989), are a second case in point. What was WISE? Wells had insisted that World Brain, while an elite project, must be publicly owned. A principal difficulty facing any such totalizing proposal—a difficulty Google's ranking by popularity does not fully overcome—is identified by Abbott as the need for a facility that can accommodate a "universal viewpoint." Abbott notes that any truly comprehensive searchable database must "permit the maximum possible freedom for divergence of opinion … [while] decisions would have to be made as to what, if anything would be excluded in principle … Who are we to judge who or what has the right of entry into an elitist World Brain" (1999: 113). While Garfield, following Wells, assumes such databases are for elite (scientific and professional) use, Kochen—anticipating Google Search and Wikipedia—argues that priorities within the "knowledge industry" need to be reversed. Once reversed, "higher priority will go to systems that help generalists behave more wisely" (1975: 6). Kochen defines WISE as a "point of view, a way of reordering priorities, especially in the information sciences, in the direction of greater stress on synthesis and evaluation. It is an attitude … a potential social movement … a naturally evolving social organ … Conceived as a system, WISE is decentralized rather than centralized, much as the human brain and nervous system are distributed" (ibid.: 9, 12).

Kochen is trying to jump-start a social movement dedicated to the democratic hypertextual organization of, and open "organic" access to, information stored within and circulated through networked databases collectively constituting a digital library-cum-archive. He understands how searchable databases will come to serve as networked systems for managing cultural complexity. Idealist first principles suffuse his vision: "I am an information scientist. I interpret it very broadly. For me, it includes the study of how brain becomes mind and of the evolution of social organs with mindlike properties" (cited in Garfield 1989). Holding to a pluralistic vision, however, Kochen, who fled the Nazis for U.S. shores, refused the naturalized assumption that "universal" always reduces to the "one" written over all else and, with this, the authoritarian political economy of information monoculture so beloved of cartels, monopolies, and dictatorships. In retrospect, one might say that WISE—intended to be searchable like Google and Wikipedia—anticipates core Web 2.0 functionalities such as social networking applications and Google Earth's bird's-eye perspective. Kochen writes,

> At the same time that the WISE viewpoint calls for an increase in compatibility among how various people see the world—for example, how they interpret their recent history; it strives to preserve subcultures. It encourages horizontal communication among peers across national and disciplinary boundaries. It aims also at facilitating vertical communication, among professors and janitors, for example. The time and age dimension, too, is to be removed as a barrier; people are able to communicate as fluently with the avant-garde as with their opposites; those in their twenties are to communicate as readily and perceptively with those in the generation before them as those in the generation after them …
>
> At the cognitive level, we can anticipate flexible, maplike directories capable of displaying a broad range of features in parallel. This is to help users see overall patterns emerge. It is to orient them to the structure of what is known. It is to help them ask better, deeper, more relevant questions. The users should be able to zoom rapidly from where they have a bird's perspective and see the shape of the forest to where they have a worm's perspective and see trails between trees. They should be able to see two or more such levels of perspective simultaneously …

> WISE must be fair at the same time that it serves the general interest. This is especially critical in its presentation of history. On controversial topics such as Zionism and the recent history of the Middle East, at least the *existence* of varying points of view and value orientations should be made known to any user of WISE.
>
> (1975: 10, 12–15)

As he had with Bush's memex, Garfield casts doubt on Kochen's vision: "The world brain will undoubtedly be something more than an elaboration of the present ISI data base. However, if it tries to subsume everything now produced by the word's multi-billion-dollar information industries, it will never happen" (Garfield 1975: 160). History, however, suggests Kochen had the more prescient view, not only with respect to how networked technologies might form part of an emergent "collective intelligence," but also how aspects of it anticipate the work of projects aimed at transparency, such as Wikileaks:

> Perhaps there could also be WISE facilities to effectively detect and expose lies, treachery, deceit when these occur in social conflict situations beginning with simple devices of instantaneous exposure of inconsistencies. Formulations of regulations, detection of violators and deviants, monitoring their behavior and the effect of sanctions, are all potentially encompassed by WISE's technological arm, although this presents an awesome spectre of technocratic control.
>
> Evil rulers, cruel tyrants, self-seeking potentates may act wisely on their own behalf but to the detriment of many others. If they have at their command a concentrated, organized source of knowledge, understanding, wisdom, then their hold is even harder to break.
>
> (Kochen 1975: 15–16)

Recall that, for Bush, the "essential feature" of the memex is "the process of tying two items together" (1988). Similarly, WISE users would have been able to access both a "bird's" and a "worm's" perspectives simultaneously along with "the trails between the trees." The memex then, *pace* Garfield and his professional and intellectual insecurities, is a storage device *and* a linking device (Kolb 2005: 7) and so too is WISE. The trails of associations that linkages can reveal are as important to Bush and Kochen as they are to Garfield in developing a searchable databased archive of meaningful information. For Bush, building such possibilities into the memex would encourage users to "cross-fertilize" intersecting information trails, to judiciously develop previously unconsidered associations between different kinds of information. Implicitly adhering to the formal logic of "new art, new thought," Bush believed that such a development would offer information searchers new ways to think about the relationship between stored information and the way that brain processes organically generate connections between and among disparate thoughts so as to generate new thinking.

In focusing on the interplay between human brain processes and how they might be designed into information retrieval devices, Bush also anticipates (and Kochen may be influenced by) J.C.R. Licklider's proposal (1960), discussed below, for human–computer symbiosis. Kochen's WISE would have promoted cross-fertilization not only between human and machine but also across class, cultural, and national lines. For these postwar information scientists, World Brain was in the air. Garfield first mentions it in 1964. Given the structure of feeling undergirding the postwar culture of American information science research, it is not only Garfield's work on indexes but also Bush's and Kochen's hypertextual proposals to organize information into meaningfully linked trails of association that also "link" into Brin and Page's efforts to make Web databases meaningfully accessible through search engines based on identifying popular links and trails after they have been forged by users.

Kochen, like Garfield, was a self-declared World Brainist, but he also referred to Bush as "the contemporary prophet" (1975: 8). WISE, like the World Brain, proposes a networked system of decentralized nodes. It is true that, unlike Wells, Bush does not anticipate a planetary network of memexes. Instead, he anticipates how the universal library or databased archive might be personalized according to the technology of the day—the memex as microfiched Web-in-a-box, an Alexandrian Library and Oracle of Delphi rolled into one, to the right of your knee, under the desktop but connected to your mind through your eyes and hand. Yet having a memex of one's own and the bourgeois consumerist individuation this may imply was not Bush's core focus. At the top of his proposal, Bush insists that "science ... has provided a record of ideas and has enabled man to manipulate and to make extracts from that record so that knowledge evolves and endures throughout the life of a race rather than that of an individual" (1988: 237). Garfield, then, may commit a disservice in his remark about distinguishing between software and hardware. Despite the hopes for microfilm as an enduring and searchable medium—hopes that Darnton has exposed as historically misplaced (2009)—World Brain, though filtered in its contents for redundancy and fabrication, remained essentially unsearchable in its original proposal. To successfully compress edited information does not mean it can be easily searched. Bush's memex, however, *could* be searched through the entry of personally assigned search codes. World Brain, memex, and WISE were intended to surmount the Borgesian difficulties faced by ever-increasing amounts of information. All anticipate the individual ability to access a twentieth-century version of a universal library and archive organized according to the most advanced ideas of information processing and technology then known.

In differing but complementary ways, Bush and Kochen go further than Garfield in anticipating that future search technologies would at least partially break free of mechanical constraints in order to constitute part of a hybrid sphere where electronics and mechanism commingle with biology. We have noted that Wells had claimed that World Brain "can have at once, the concentration of a craniates animal and the diffused vitality of an amoeba" (1938: 87). He did not further develop these biological metaphors that anticipate complexity theory, or make links between human and non-human animals, per se. Bush, however, not only argues that trails of association are a better way to organize information because they replicate human brain processes. He insists on the cumbersomeness of "first transforming electrical vibrations to mechanical ones, which the human mechanism promptly transforms back to the electrical form," noting that "in the outside world, all forms of intelligence … have been reduced to the form of varying currents in an electric circuit in order that they may be transmitted. Inside the human frame exactly the same sort of process occurs." Bush finally asks, "must we always transform to mechanical movements in order to proceed from one electrical phenomenon to another?" (1988: 247). His thinking was on the cusp, in a way that Wells' may not yet have been, of envisioning the conceptual merger of human and machine, an electro-flesh hybridity often referred to as cyborg. As a decentralized and evolving "social organ," WISE is on similar, conceptually lively, terrain. This hybridity is a strong component of the networked dynamic that encourages us to trust the machine, to extend and interpolate ourselves psychically into its networked databases that dissolve distinctions among the forms, concepts, and contents of archives and libraries, and to find meaning in a Google search even if the information it provides does not always compute.

## J.C.R. Licklider

If Wells raises the idea of a World Brain in possession of a "craniates intelligence," the research psychologist, computer scientist, and internet pioneer J.C.R. Licklider (1915–1990), an early theorist of human–computer interaction and the first head of the Information Processing Techniques Office of the U.S. Department of Defense's Advanced Research Projects Agency (ARPA), goes further to propose "Man–Computer Symbiosis." He does so in his celebrated 1960 paper bearing the same title in which he deploys symbiosis as a biological metaphor to argue for a future of "mutually productive interdependence" between humans and information machines. The key example Licklider provides is a fig tree that cannot reproduce without an insect known as the *Blastophaga grossorun*.

> The tree cannot reproduce without the insect; the insect cannot eat without the tree; together, they constitute not only a viable but a productive and thriving partnership … At present, however, there are no man–computer symbioses … The hope is that, in not too many years, human brains and computing machines will be coupled together very tightly, and

that *the resulting partnership will think as no human brain has ever thought* and process data in a way not approached by the information-handling machines we know today.

(1960: n.p.; emphasis added)

Licklider's outline of what the then-future symbiotic world of advanced computation would look and feel like is permeated with unacknowledged aspects of thinking that approximate panpsychic belief in the universal nature of mind, and the universe as a single organism. Through biological metaphor, he articulates an already established symbiotic and therefore interdependent link between the vegetative and the animal worlds to those proposed linkages he seeks to establish between humans (the animal world) and computing machines (technology). Licklider "envisioned almost exactly the personal computing environment of today. His vision turned out to be so close to today's reality that one is inclined to think it must have been a rather obvious extrapolation of contemporary technology" (Campbell-Kelly 2007). While Wells and Bush assumed that microfilm could help answer their prayers, they, too, like Kochen and Licklider, proposed imaginary machines—in many ways the most ideologically powerful kinds of machines because, like theory itself, they are idealized responses to conceived societal needs. As philosopher of technology Hubert Dreyfus (1992) has argued, the West has a penchant for turning its ideas and theories into technologies. Ideas tend to get built, to be factored into the machine's design, even if the final result deviates in its privatized bottom-line pragmatism from the ideal, often publicly financed, vision of the original proposal.

Licklider's ideas are better remembered today than are Kochen's as foundational for outlining a significant component of how the internet and the searchable Web would be developed. It is to his thoughts about libraries, however, that we now turn. In the introduction to *Libraries of the Future* (1965), Licklider notes that such "neolibraries" (ibid.: 6), which he suggests would be better identified as "procognitive systems" (ibid.: 13), will not likely be "rooted" in books (ibid.: 2). Instead, because of the exponential increase in information overload facing researchers, "we need to substitute for the book a device that will make it easy to transmit information without transporting material, and that will not only present information to people but also process it for them, following procedures they specify, apply, monitor, and, if necessary, revise and reapply ... to provide these services, a meld of library and computer is evidently required" (ibid.: 6). He assesses the complex technical requirements for translating page-bound printed information into machine-readable data. In so doing, his words uncannily echo the calculi presented by Lasswitz in his speculative account of a future library of all possible books that would be based on universal orthographic symbols and not words of a language.[2] But Licklider's focus, again, like Wells and Bush before him, is on actualizing the ideal—of theorizing a thinking machine in the form of a "procognitive system." When fully developed, he expects his system to serve as a platform for user-fed applications, one where developer/users plug in new programs and capacities that augment the existing database/archive (which he terms "the fund of stored knowledge"). To a remarkable degree, Licklider anticipates one of the objectives of a universal project such as Google's, and directly speaks to the issues of relevance and user feedback now factored into personalizing search algorithms.

> It no longer seems likely that we can organize or distil or exploit the corpus by passing large parts of it through human brains. It is both our hypothesis and our conviction that people can handle the major part of their interaction with the fund of knowledge better by controlling and monitoring the processing of information than by handling all the detail directly themselves … a basic part of the over-all aim for procognitive systems is to get the user of the fund of knowledge into something more nearly like an executive's or commander's position. He will still read and think … but he will not have to do all the searching himself … that is involved in creative use of knowledge. He will say what operations he wants performed upon what parts of the body of knowledge, he will see whether the results make sense, and then he will decide what to have done next. Some of his work will involve simultaneous interaction with colleagues and with the fund of stored knowledge. Nothing he does and nothing they do will impair the usefulness of the fund to others. Hopefully, much that one user does in his interaction with the fund will make it more valuable to others. … the most promising way to develop procognitive systems is … to arrange things in such a way that much of the conceptual and software development will be carried out by substantive users of the systems.
>
> (ibid.: 28, 32, 69)

Unlike Bush's memex, Licklider's procognitive systems are *networked* question-answering machines, parts of what by 1962 he will identify as a "Galactic Network" of social interactions distributed across World Brain-like assemblages of computers (Licklider and Clark 1962).

Anticipating Google Instant, procognitive systems are intelligent agents that do some of the work of searching for us. Like the 1970s WISE and modern search technologies more generally, procognitive systems remember what searchers seek from them and continually accrete this knowledge so that it can be searched in new and valuable ways. These digital features are important to Licklider because "by the year 2000, information and knowledge may be as important as mobility" (1965: 33). Arguing that interaction with information and knowledge will come to constitute 10–20 percent of society's total work effort, he comprehends the then-radical nature of his proposal. "At the present time … not many people seem to be interested in intimate interaction with the fund of knowledge—but, of course, not many have any idea what such interaction would be like" (ibid.: 34).

The procognitive "solution" to the "problem" of information retrieval that Licklider proposes assumes the realization of his earlier symbiotic hope that human brains and computing machines will achieve a very tight coupling (1960). His desire reverberates in Page's comment that eventually we will have chips implanted that will usher in a more complete cybernetic reality "where if you think about a fact, it [the system] will just tell you the answer" (Levy 2011: 67). A provident, data-driven teleology akin to a secular theology runs through both Licklider's and Page's arguments: networked computation will surpass the powers, speed, and *efficiency* of human intelligence. Yet though Licklider has faith that computer intelligence will eventually surpass our own, he astutely recognizes the cultural value of emphasizing (to 1960 readers) the *complementarity* of the coming human–machine symbiosis. By so doing, he avoids due consideration of any Tower of Babel-like difficulties facing any future symbiosis that would result from basic differences between human and machine languages. Instead, it is all to the good that humans are flexible and computers single-minded—that we speak redundant languages while computers require non-redundant ones (Licklider 1960).

Licklider's article is usually positioned as directly foretelling the internet, and has attained consecrated status within the fields of computer and information science. Reviewers are more tacit, however, about its other extraordinary feature: its essentially panpsychic plea for computers as an organism. In the nineteenth century, Fechner had argued that, because all matter has a mental aspect, all objects have a point of view and a unified center of experience. His "day-light view" of reality, outlined in the previous chapter, maintains that all materials are inwardly alive and consciously animated. Licklider's plea for machine intelligence depends on similar valuations in its anticipation of a future when humans and computers will form complementary opposites that together constitute a unified and more productive whole. If this were to be so—if, as his examples of future library searches suggest, the intelligent machine will do part of our work so that we will be free to pursue higher-order analysis—then a new form of mind would arise from the symbiotic unity of man and machine intelligence. Jeffrey Sconce argues that belief in electronic forms of "liveness," such as Licklider proposes, leads to "a unique compulsion that ultimately dissolves boundaries between the real and the electronic" (2000: 4). Sconce's observation concords broadly with Winner's 1995 observation that Americans yearn for merger with their technical devices, and Noble's assessment that "modern technology and religion have evolved together and … as a result, the technological enterprise has been and remains suffused with religious belief … the religious compulsion is largely unconscious, obscured by a secularized vocabulary but operative nonetheless" (1999: 5).

Proposals for World Brains purportedly anchored strictly in computer science and engineering are taken up by later scientists directly engaging metaphysical concepts. Such individuals include Pasteur Institute researcher Joël de Rosnay and his 1986 proposal for a Planetary Brain. In *Symbiotic Man* (2000), Rosnay develops an argument that effectively extends Licklider's more bounded proposal: humans evolve in harmony with our ecosystem and, therefore, we need to learn how we fit into one planetary macro-organism. Thus Rosnay predicts the "cybiont"—a global macro-organism encompassing the holy trinity of environment, technology, and humanity. Considered within the context of the longstanding desire for universal libraries and, now, open global databases, and given that symbiotic and organic metaphors have come to guide much metaphysical theorizing about the power of networked collective intelligence and other HiveMind formulations, Licklider's treatise on human–machine symbiosis works to confirm the ongoing ideational interplay situated at the always leaky boundary between information science and informational metaphysics.

## From Information Scientists to Metaphysicians

All of the individuals discussed above understood themselves as scientists. Each believed science would open the way toward the actualization of universal databases accessible to all who would require access to them. Each likely would have bristled at the very thought of being identified as a metaphysician. Yet their sustained foci on the development of universal databases, of thinking machines able to answer questions with "the truth," and their reliance on metaphor-dependent comparisons of biological realities and future computing devices and their human–machine interfaces, suggest these men implicitly accepted the then-emergent information machines as a collective first principle—as cosmologically constitutive of new forms of "ultimate truth," new forms of identity ("craniates intelligence," "as we may think," "world information synthesis," "man–computer symbiosis"), new ways to induce change, and new ways to experience life itself (as networked searchers). In our estimation, therefore, the collective ideation of these individuals, so central to the development of automated digital technologies and searchable networked platforms, intersects with parallel work done by self-declared metaphysicians for the networked information age. Researchers such as de Rosnay, though focused less on practical outcomes such as search technologies, and more on the possibility for collective, intellectual augmentation through global information machines, reveal continuities and overlaps of thought between scientific and spiritually inflected interest in and proposals for unified databases capable of revealing "ultimate truths" to our questions about ourselves and our ongoing place in the universe.

The work of Kelly and his panpsychic proposal for an electronic HiveMind was discussed in chapter 4. Eco-philosopher David Skrbina asserts that "there was perhaps no more visionary and exuberant panpsychist philosopher than Pierre Teilhard de Chardin (1881–1955)" (2005: 182). At the core of Teilhard de

Chardin's system is the idea of "complexity-consciousness": "as matter evolves into ever-more-complex forms, so too does the corresponding dimension of consciousness that is attributed to it. Consciousness equals complexity" (ibid.: 182). Though his philosophy and its associations with emergentism have proved too unconventional for both the academy and organized religion, Teilhard de Chardin's Neoplatonic belief in an ever-evolving becoming of mind, coupled to his hope that electronic networks might help foster complexity-consciousness or *noogenesis*, updates Llull's anticipation that a mechanical thinking machine might help convert non-believers, and runs parallel to Wells' purportedly more scientific proposal for a World Brain also supportive of an emergent planetary *nous*. Teilhard de Chardin asserts that "the fact of industrial development … constitutes an event that can entail the most far-reaching spiritual consequences" (1970: 159). Like Licklider's, his writings are alive with biological metaphors and, again like Licklider (and Kochen), the askance theologian supports the potential extension of the human through the technological (1970: 155–163). In 1947, in an unpublished article titled "The Place of Technology in a General Biology of Mankind," he wrote,

> Is not something, itself analogous to a brain, being produced within the totality of human brains? When we think about means of communication, we notice most of all their commercial side; but the psychological side is much more important … these united brains build up a sort of dome, from which each brain can see, with the assistance of the others, what would escape it if it had to rely solely on its own field of vision. The view so obtained goes beyond anything the individual can encompass … there ceases to be any distinction between the artificial and the natural, between technology and life … if there is any difference, the advantage is on the side of the artificial.
>
> (1970: 158–159)

These thoughts were committed to paper a generation before Licklider's "empirically clad" proposal for man–computer symbiosis, or Marshall McLuhan's (1964) assertion that electronic media constitute augmented prosthetic extensions of embodied human consciousness. A contemporary of Wells and Borges, Teilhard de Chardin is as much a founding figure as Licklider for cyber-theorists who tout the merger of human and machine. His concept of the electronic noosphere—defined by Hayles as "a nimbus of pure intelligence" (1999: 254)—proposes that the totality of human thought, benefiting from electronic communications, grows toward ever-greater unification, culminating in the "Omega Point," the already-existing consciousness or intellectual being toward which the universe evolves. The Omega Point is Teilhard de Chardin's updating of Plotinus' Divine Mind or Spirit. Recall that, of the demiurge, Plato had written that it is "a single visible living entity containing all other living entities, which by their nature are all related" (*Timaeus* 29–30). The enduring idea of a Divine Mind—identifiable in secular concepts such as World Brain, man–machine symbiosis, and WISE, as well as more overtly metaphysical concepts such as the HiveMind and the Omega Point—is what underlies Battelle's assessment that Google's ever more comprehensive database has about it a discernible "whiff of the holy" (2005: 7).

## Artificial Connected Intelligence

Mid-1990s discussion of digital networks—often organized around the concept of cyberspace—is a logical outcome of the thinking expressed by Wells and the "World Brainists" and the information scientists and engineers who followed him: merger of mind and machine so that the individual attains a kind of cybernetic union with the universal library, merging with it to become a networked component of his or her own wider index.

Kevin Kelly draws on Teilhard de Chardin as well as Borges for the intellectual and effectively spiritual heft carried by his World Brainist "HiveMind" proposal. Of the HiveMind, theorized just before the Web took off, Kelly writes that it is "a recurring vision [that] swirls in the shared mind of the Net, a vision that nearly every member glimpses, if only momentarily: of wiring human and artificial minds into one planetary soul" (1994: 24). Thomas Frank has referred to Kelly's "recurrent vision" as a "sustained effort to confuse divinity with technology" (2001: 3) at precisely the socio-political moment when, Frank argues, writers such as Kelly also engage in the promotion of "business-as-God" (ibid.: 4). George Gilder's telecosm is less lyrical than the HiveMind, and certainly a dystopia for those who do not identify the accumulation of money as humanity's highest calling. The telecosm is a corporately driven virtual world within which all data and human information would be instantly available to any computer interface "in content rich format that is almost life like in its saturation of the eye's imagination."[3] Gilder has proclaimed that "It is the entrepreneurs who know the rules of the world and the laws of God" (1984: 19). He also has compared microchips to cathedrals (cited in Frank 2001: 378 fn. 3). While not a direct enfolding of the self into the coming universal database envisioned by Teilhard de Chardin, Kelly, and possibly Licklider, Gilder's corporatist vision resonates from the right with the irony of Wells' Socialist elitism as expressed through his World Brain. More benignly perhaps, Joseph Pelton (1989), former director of strategic policy for INTELSAT, has identified the global infrastructure of linked computers and satellites as forming the basis of an emerging "global electronic machine." This machine arises, Pelton insists, in response to global trade and culture and soon will begin forming a global brain or consciousness.

More recent academic proposals excavate the same or adjacent terrain. Derrick de Kerckhove argues for a unified "connected intelligence" (1997), in which, like Kelly's HiveMind, the global web of technology constitutes an external brain. Users are the content of this brain and, like owners of Chromebooks in relation to the cloud, if not "plugged in" are ignored. At the 2010 Mobile World Congress, Eric Schmidt advanced similar views: "A device that is not connected is not interesting, it is literally lonely. An application that does not leverage the cloud isn't going to wow anybody … [once connected] … It's like magic. All of a sudden there are things you can do that we've never even (thought of) because of this convergence" (Tartakoff 2010). Philosopher of the cybernetic Pierre Lévy, going beyond anything proposed by de Kerckhove or Schmidt, but in line with his fellow countryman Teilhard de Chardin, has envisioned an "enormous, hybrid, social, and technobiological hyperbody" through which commingling and surrogate digital second selves finally allow the human body to, in Lévy's words, "detach itself completely from the hyperbody and vanish" (1998: 44). One might ask to where this vanishing human body actually might repair after having left behind its earthly form. Into the World Brain where consciousness and subjectivity will reduce to the status of functionalities of a global mechanism? To a server farm of steel-clad sheds from which one's "consciousness" in the form of "information patterns" could be retrieved through search? To "hyperspace" to vanish? A synthesis of Neoplatonic idealism and Cartesian indifference to, or even contempt for, human embodiment bleeds through these proposals. Given the speculative ideological dimension of Lévy's fantastical hopes, finding an answer to the question of the hyperbody's eventual location in science fiction seems appropriate and Isaac Asimov's short story "The Last Question" (1956) provides one. Like Kurd Lasswitz (chapter 4), Asimov believed strongly that science fiction should attempt to sketch realistic future societies based on what science and technology might actually deliver over time. His story was published during the period when Garfield and others in the field were developing, compiling, and distributing the Social Science and Science Citation Indexes, and other World Brainists such as Quincy Wright were proposing projects that anticipate Google Zeitgeist such as a World Intelligence Center dedicated to the private quantification and mapping of all "political and psychological conditions and trends" (1957: 317).

"The Last Question" traces the evolving relationship between humans and the question-answering function of Multivac, a sentient computer based on what can be retrospectively identified as an amalgam of World Brain, human–computer symbiosis, and cloud computing. The story foresees the rise of search technologies and ties it to a gradual transfer of human consciousness into ever larger, ever evolving, next generations of information machines until all human consciousness has been uploaded to them. Over eons, Multivac replaces itself with a series of ever more sophisticated Multivacs that finally transcend into "Cosmic ACs" made up of distributed data processing and storage facilities located "in hyperspace." At this point, Cosmic ACs have acquired all of human consciousness and occupy all of planetary space. The "last question," unanswerable by

Cosmic ACs when independent human thought remained a reality distinct from their own, becomes answerable (and is answered) only after the last human's consciousness has been uploaded. In a way that anticipates Lévy's hyperbody, the entirety of human consciousness is uploaded to or merged with the Cosmic machine. Ironically, perhaps, no mortal human remains to receive the answer to the last question. Asimov's story suggests, then, that the long-term goal of question-answering machines is less the provision of timely answers to complex questions and more the eventual relocation of consciousness from wetware to hardware and software coded as transcendent. The story's conclusion literalizes the connection between machine intelligence and the godhead. When the Cosmic AC proclaims, "Let there be light," its command is carried out for this command is the realization of its own collective desire. The Universe is at One with the Machine.

## Technology-as-Telos?

Technology, as Winner (1995) and Noble (1999) argue, is implicitly understood by moderns as an access vehicle to the divine. The idea that human beings might use technology to better access the divine and gain reunification with the godhead begins to develop during Charlemagne's era (Noble 1999). Around 830 CE, a change arises in the conceived relationship between transcendence and technology to suggest that "technological advance is God's Will" (White 1971: 198). As noted in the introduction, following the reappraisal of the idea of human perfectibility that resulted from a sober assessment of the technologically enabled massive destruction that was a principal legacy of World War I, the definition of progress has been narrowed so that today it is effectively understood as meaning *technological* progress. We now largely believe that any future human advances will be realized through ever more intensive applications of technology to the social and natural worlds. Powerful technologies such as internet search, therefore, are widely perceived as moving us in a progressive direction toward reunification with what once was understood as the godhead, except that the godhead is now in human hands, or, more precisely, in those hands of the corporation-as-individual legally and practically imbued with human agency. (Asimov's "The Last Question" indicates how this "godhead," in the form of a Cosmic AC, might, like Lévy's hyperbody, "escape" human control through subsuming humanity itself.) De Kerckhove and Lévy are academics whose proposals contribute to this strand of belief that computation is the latest mechanism by which humanity "evolves" and "progresses." The belief remains widespread and remarkably consistent over time. In a 2010 piece titled "Building One Big Brain," public intellectual Robert Wright proposes that "Maybe the essential thing about technological evolution is that *it's not about us*. Maybe it's about something bigger than us—maybe something big and wonderful, maybe something big and spooky, but in any event something really, really big ... Could it be that, in some sense, the *point* of evolution has been to create these social brains, and maybe even to weave them into a giant, loosely organized planetary brain?"

If humans and corporations-as-humans are engaged in the long-term process of taking on many of the powers once held to be properly those of the gods, then humanly engineered technologies such as Google search will necessarily have about them a whiff of the holy precisely because users and engineers alike experience them as technological forms of the cosmos—a cosmos that issues, in Neoplatonic fashion, *ex deo* (out of, or from, the godhead, whatever its material form). The history of Neoplatonism further suggests that, when so positioned, such rapidly evolving, seemingly "lively" information machines are not likely to be received as merely the "useful" products of those elite humans upon whom has been conferred godlike power (in this case, actors in the fields of information science and computer engineering). Technologies such as global search, precisely because they are "emanations" from the godhead of an efficient and profit-driven culture of engineering wisdom to us the human petitioners for answers, truth, and deliverance, serve as magico-material and even mythopoetic confirmations of the absolute transcendence of a for-profit firm such as Google itself. Google's consecration in part depends on maintaining alignment between the products it offers and its users' variously expressed desires for technologically mediated access to the divine. Such alignment is part of the collective habitus of those inhabiting a world shaped by technocratically defined ideals of progress that have meshed in under-acknowledged ways with transcendentalist forms of belief such as panpsychism. Magico-material and mythopoetic confirmations of Google's transcendence seem to bridge the gap between ideality and materiality by substituting the ideal of a god with the materiality of an engineering culture and its inventions and product offerings. They also mean, however, that any transcendence through immanence that search might provide comes at the cost of replacing this god with an elite human–machine assemblage that has arisen within neoliberal settings promoting acceptance of "business-as-God." Such an assemblage—Wells' elite Samurai updated—would continue to have seemingly oracular and also material power over the rest of us, much in the way that older gods, with their tremendous appetites for petitions, prayers, offerings, and indulgences, once did.

# 6

# THE LIBRARY OF GOOGLE

If ever a contest were held to determine which project influenced by metaphysical precepts best intersects with corporate interests, Google Books would be a strong contender. Its blending of first principle practices and commercial foci reveals one way that metaphysics and political economy, broadly conceived, intersect in the contemporary, corporatized space of information flow. If ever fully realized, Google Books—also known as Google Book Search and Google Books Library Project—would offer reader-searchers "the golden or leaden key that unlocks the Library" (Langford 1997: 452), if not the universal library itself. Google's ambitious project to scan and index all the world's books leads the way in forcing a widespread cultural rethinking of what the library and the archive, as ideas and as institutions, now mean. This chapter traces the development of Google Books and looks at arguments made in relation to various legal challenges for what they bring to bear on the changing meanings of the library and the archive.

## Google Books: First Principles Fir$t

In October 2004, Google introduced Google Print at the Frankfurt Book Fair and in December of the same year unveiled Google Print Library. This initiative began with partnerships between Google and five English-language libraries: the University of Michigan at Ann Arbor, Stanford, Harvard, Oxford (Bodleian Library), and the New York City Public Library. At the time, Google announced its ten-year plan to make available approximately fifteen million digitized books. While Google would scan books in the public domain, it would also digitize—without seeking permission—other post-1923 copyrighted titles that under American copyright law may or may not be in the public domain.[1] At the time,

Battelle (2004) observed that Google's original aim had been not to build the Web but to "organize it and make it accessible to us." With the launch of Google Print that same year, however, Google started adding content to the Web and in so doing began its shift from a "passive indexer" of websites to an "active creator" of media content (ibid.).

In Fall 2005, just before the service was renamed Google Book Search, two U.S.-based lawsuits citing copyright infringement were filed against the firm. One was a class action suit on behalf of authors (*Authors Guild v. Google*, September 20, 2005), and the other a civil lawsuit brought against Google by the Association of American Publishers and the individual publishers McGraw-Hill, Pearson Education, Penguin Group USA, Simon & Schuster, and John Wiley & Sons (*McGraw-Hill v. Google*, October 19, 2005). At the same time as Google renamed its project Google Book Search, it announced the Google Books Partner Program, a vehicle by which authors and publishers could include their titles in the project. In 2006 and 2007, additional elite academic libraries joined the Google Books Library Project.[2] Microsoft, which in 2006 had announced its competing Live Search Books, canceled the project in May 2008. Its scans of public domain books were transferred to the freely accessible database of the Internet Archive, a core member of the Open Book Alliance and an opponent of Google's private book digitization process. In December 2008, magazines such as *Ebony*, *Popular Mechanics*, and *New York Magazine* were also included in Google Books.

In October 2008, Google and the publishing industry (*McGraw-Hill v. Google*) reached a tentative settlement whereby the firm would compensate authors and publishers in exchange for, among other agreements, members of the Authors Guild and the Association of American Publishers abandoning their claims for damages along with the negotiated (and new) right for Google to make available for search and sale digital copies of the millions of printed books it had scanned and indexed. Google's policy had been to copy any book unless its copyright holder notified Google to cease and desist.

The separate *Authors Guild v. Google* lawsuit, however, did not proceed to court, and the settlement of the *McGraw-Hill v. Google* lawsuit sidestepped and therefore did not resolve crucial copyright claims that Google's interpretation of the American legal doctrine of fair use[3] was so broad as to lead to limits potentially being placed on others who later might claim the same right. This concern arose as fair use has been interpreted as a potential defense that only courts may allow and not as a user's right per se (Hilderbrand 2009: 85). Google had countered the charge of copyright infringement through arguing its service— replete with complete scans of copyrighted works—conformed to American fair use standards appropriate for the digital age. Google's chief counsel David C. Drummond reasoned that "Web sites that we crawl are copyrighted. People expect their Web sites to be found, and Google searches find them. So by scanning books, we give books the chance to be found, too" (Toobin 2007).

In his comment, Drummond implicitly refers to Google's hoped-for transposition of the way copyright operates on the Web to the way it operates with respect to printed books. On the Web, "if you wish to opt out of the Web search system, you must act. The burden is on the copyright holder" (Vaidhyanathan 2011: 167). For Google to seek permission each time it indexed a webpage would be prohibitively expensive. By default, American courts have ruled that everything on the Web can be copied (Battelle 2005). Somewhat the reverse obtains for the older technology of printed books, where obtaining the necessary permissions to reproduce lengthy materials remains the copier's responsibility. Google's denial of copyright infringement, then, while clearly intended to buttress the firm's economic position, rested not only on its realization that its growing collections of electronic copies of books and other printed materials now constitute an *ipso facto* electronic library-cum-archive, but also on its fundamental belief that technological efficiency is moral efficiency and that the outcomes of this efficiency should be brought to as many social arenas as possible. Further, the decision to scan orphaned but still copyrighted books also reflects the firm's implicit first principle belief that its efficiency, speed, and enlightened corporate attitude render it best suited for serving as the gatekeeper and increasingly the owner, not only of the universal storehouse that it is anticipated Google Books will become but also of the information stored in it. By November 2008 Google and its library partners had scanned seven million books.[4]

On October 28, 2008, following extensive negotiations, Google and the Authors Guild reached a proposed agreement (the Amended Settlement Agreement or ASA). Google agreed to pay US$125 million to rights holders of books already scanned (effectively conceding that its scanning project contravened American copyright law), as well as to create a Book Rights Registry as a remedial mechanism for compensating self-identifying copyright holders of books in Google's digital collection. Preliminarily approved on November 19, 2009, the ASA immediately proved controversial, in part because it would have been applicable to authors worldwide. European governments objected, as did hundreds of authors who signed petitions opposing the settlement. In December of that year, a French court stopped the scanning of copyrighted books published in France on the grounds that Google was violating copyright laws. Monopoly (arguably a form of universality), and not universality *per se*, became the issue around which the ASA was judged.

Google and the Authors Guild, meanwhile, were somewhat confident the ASA would be accepted by U.S. courts, and in May 2010 had announced plans for Google Editions, an online book service intended to directly compete with Amazon, Apple, and other e-book vendors. By June 2010, Google had scanned more than twelve million books and in August stated its intention to scan all known existing books before 2020. That summer it published its estimate that there are approximately 130 million unique books (Taycher 2010), and Google Editions launched its American portal the following December.

The ASA, however—too favorable to Google in its granting to the firm of effective copyright for orphan books and other unclaimed works the authors of which cannot be reasonably located or do not self-identify as such—was rejected on March 22, 2011 by Judge Dennis Chin of the U.S. District Court, Southern District of New York. While Chin reasoned that "the creation of a universal digital library would benefit many," he also found that:

> The ASA would grant Google control over the digital commercialization of millions of books including orphan books and other unclaimed works. And it would do so even though Google engaged in wholesale, blatant copying, without first obtaining copyright permissions ... As one objector put it: 'Google pursued its copyright project in calculated disregard of authors' rights. Its business plan was: So, sue me.' ... It is incongruous with the purpose of the copyright laws to place the onus on copyright owners to come forward to protect their rights when Google copied their works without first seeking permission ... The ASA would give Google a de facto monopoly over unclaimed works. Only Google has engaged in the copying of books en masse without copyright permission ... This de facto exclusivity ... appears to create a dangerous probability that only Google would have the ability to market to libraries and other institutions a comprehensive digital-book subscription. The seller of an incomplete database—i.e., one that does not include the millions of orphan works—cannot compete effectively with the seller of a comprehensive product.
>
> (2011)

Writing before Judge Chin's ruling, Vaidhyanathan argued that rejection of the ASA would doom the entire Google Books project (2011: 154). Chin's ruling, however, was interpreted as not subject to appeal but nonetheless as offering "clear guidance" to Google and litigants with respect to presenting the court with a substantially revised agreement (Helft 2011). Chin encouraged Google and Authors Guild litigants to revise any future agreement from one based on authors and copyright holders having to *opt out* to one by which they would have to *opt in* to the service. He also established a "status conference" mechanism for litigants to discuss next steps. On December 12, in response to a deadline established at a September 15, 2011 status conference, and reasoning that individual authors lack the ability to litigate as effectively when dealing with Google than acting as a class, the Authors Guild filed a motion for class certification (Albanese 2011). Publishers were absent from this filing; at the September 15 conference, they and Google indicated they were close to a separate agreement. On December 22, Google responded with its own motion asking Chin to dismiss the Guild's motion, arguing that only individual copyright holders, and not a class such as the Authors Guild sought, should have standing to sue (Robertson 2011).

If accepted, Google's motion would make it likely that such individual settlements would be resolved financially but leave the crucial question of fair use unanswered. If, however, Chin accepts the Guild's motion for class certification, then, at the time of writing, it is thought that Google will make its argument for fair use sometime in 2012 with a decision expected no later than early 2013 (Lee 2011b).

Chin's original ruling, though taking into account issues of competition and monopoly, largely rested on interpretation of existing copyright law. But, while Google's original proposal to pay millions of dollars to publishers and authors implicitly acknowledged it had violated copyright law, one of its material claims had been that scanning of hard-to-find out-of-print and orphaned works was not derivative of the works but, rather, amounted to a complete *transformation* of them and, therefore, should not be subject to copyright restrictions. Google's counsel, David Drummond, argued, "A key part of the line between what's fair use and what's not is transformation … Yes, we're making a copy when we digitize. But surely the ability to find something because a term appears in a book is not the same thing as reading the book. That's why Google Books is a different product from the book itself" (Toobin 2007; see also Vaidhyanathan 2011: 169–171).

By Drummond's remediating logic, not only does fair use apply to scanning an entire volume, but finding a passage in a book through searching for a phrase formally and experientially differs from a sequential reading of this phrase in the book itself. This is the logic used to support Google's claim that its material intervention creates a new form of the work—a new product with a new purpose—and with this the potential for the work's higher valuation. Google's management assumes that, while such works may have had some limited value before they were scanned, in their print form they remained undiscoverable to all but the most diligent of researchers. Scanning, digitizing, and indexing these books, however, remediates them (Bolter and Grusin 1999) and thereby releases their contents from the purported prison house of the material libraries in which they "languished" or lay "forgotten" to a potentially much larger and more broadly based contemporary readership that can more easily locate them through the online search function that organizes Google's emerging universal library-cum-archive.

In 2009, Sergey Brin published "A Library to Last Forever," an op-ed in the *New York Times*. His publication was intended to accomplish at least three goals. The first was to buttress and burnish Google's consecrated, *noblesse oblige* status given Larry Page's earlier executive decision to scan copyrighted books without securing owners' permissions (Carr 2011). This Brin did when, referring to a particular out-of-print book he found through Google Books, he lamented, "I wish there were a hundred services with which I could easily look at such a book; it would have saved me a lot of time, and it would have spared Google a tremendous amount of effort." Only Google, it would seem, cares deeply about preserving and expanding the public's access to rare and hard-to-find titles. Brin's piece worked to accomplish a second related goal of legitimating Google's violation of copyright law when he further asserted that "the vast majority of books ever written are not accessible to anyone except the most tenacious researchers at premier academic libraries. Books written after 1923 quickly disappear into a literary black hole ... they are found only in a vanishing number of libraries and used book stores ... even if our cultural heritage stays intact in the world's foremost libraries it is effectively lost if no one can access it easily." Again, only Google, it would seem, has the moxie and expertise and, therefore, by the neoliberal logic of the Californian ideology, the moral valence, to successfully operate such a benign quasi monopoly that promises to liberate our cultural heritage from the obsolete and melancholy dustbins of bricks-and-mortar libraries. And only Google, it would seem, should be trusted to proceed with a strategy based on the universal ends justifying the monopolizing means. And, by inference, as Google's implicit claim to own the future rights to orphaned works it scans suggests, only Google is entitled to own the past. This aspect of Google Books is how the firm makes a comprehensive claim on the past (through the "McGuffin" of orphan books) so as to own it through owning the cultural record and archive and by setting the price of admission. You may view this now transmographied past by exchanging your information for access—an exchange that Google, with its claims of "for free," misleadingly deems a gift from it to you.

Perhaps the most important goal of Brin's piece concerns Google's interest in developing search as a form of artificial intelligence for purposes other than answering individual search queries or providing readers access to forgotten texts. Science historian George Dyson has referred to Google as Turing's Cathedral. He recounts that, during his 2005 visit to Google's headquarters in Mountain View, California, one of his hosts explained to him that, with respect to the Google Books project, "We are not scanning all those books to be read by people. We are scanning them to be read by an AI" (2005). Why so? An artificial intelligence on the scale that Google is building, to function adequately, needs vast amounts of data to search, mill, and mine: the more data, the more productive the results and the greater the possibilities for AI. Digitizing millions of books has generated a great deal of data on language use and meaning structures common across different languages that could not have been acquired from mining the Web alone. Eli Pariser recounts how, in December 2010, researchers at Google, Harvard, the *American Heritage Dictionary*, and *Encyclopaedia Britannica* announced the results of their joint effort, over a four-year period, to build "a data-base spanning the entire contents of over five hundred years' worth of books—5.2 million books in total, in English, French, Chinese, German, and other languages" (2011: 199–200). Researchers were interested in a "quantitative approach to the humanities" in order to map and measure qualitative cultural changes. As Pariser notes, Google Books will prove of great benefit to researchers but, as he also notes, "to grow your artificial intelligence, you need to keep it well fed … If you had a secret plan to vacuum up an entire civilization's data and use it to build artificial intelligence, you couldn't do a whole lot better" (ibid.: 200–201). Such vacuuming has proved of enormous benefit to Google's efforts to perfect Google Translate as the sheer volume of works in many languages that have been scanned by Google Books has allowed Google Translate to rely on a probabilistic approach to the automated translation of written texts. (In passing, it is worth noting that the ways that Google Translate and Google Books intersect lend credence to Jarvis' 2008 observation that, over time, the concept of a universal language has given way to the concept of a universal library.) Google Books is therefore of crucial important to Brin and the firm, not just in making a corpus of books available to readers who otherwise would have suffered from lack of access, but also to Google's broader aspiration to build an automated World Brain able to analyze countless data bits and thereby to produce previously undetected or even humanly unimaginable correlations, patterns, and clusters.

## A Library to Last Forever?

Brin's defense of the ASA settlement attempts to advance Google's claim to universal stewardship of orphaned books published after 1923, yet in doing so he advances the suspect, even specious, claim that such books were somehow "lost" in the first place. For an object to be lost, it cannot be located by those who seek it. While no one can know for sure what the market or readership will be in the future for, say, the 1880–1881 *Insurance Year Book* to which Brin refers in his piece and which he found on Google Books, it is misleading to claim, as he does, that "no one" can find it. After all, Google Books did. The readership for such documents, however, has been, is, and likely will remain, that small (and therefore "elite") cadre of "tenacious researchers" (Brin's phrase) who are interested in locating such documents for research purposes and trained in how to do so.

Brin does, however, raise a separate, legitimate point when, using the Library of Alexandria as his core example, he points to the destruction of library print materials and humanity's consequent cultural loss. This point is telescoped through his metaphysically inflected title—"A Library to Last Forever." While paper burns, molds, and crumbles, the digital, it would seem, absent a thermonuclear pulse or particularly intense solar flare, reigns eternal. Or possibly readers are meant to intuit that, after all, it is really Google that, like diamonds, is forever, an ultimate truth in itself. Brin's inclusion of the word "forever" foregrounds his implicit understanding that libraries (and archives), ideally, are places where, as Foucault (1986: 26) argues, time accumulates indefinitely and with it the consecrated cultural capital that attends to those individuals and institutions charged with the organization and maintenance of such institutions.

Brin's Ozymandian, even arrogant, assertion that Google—only Google—is building what amounts to a library designed to withstand the tests of time—an Eternal as well as a Universal Library—is important. In his 2007 assessment of the then-current status of Google Books, Jeffrey Toobin interviewed Dan Clancy, engineer in charge of Google's system for scanning library collections. Answering questions about the difficulties that arise in adapting search strategies that work well enough for finding hyperlinked online information to searching books such as humanities titles that are often intended as "stand-alone" documents, Clancy commented—using language that, in part, would be replicated by Judge Chin in his 2011 rejection of the ASA settlement—"We are talking about a universal digital library … I hope this world evolves so that there exists a time where somebody sitting at a terminal can access all the world's information" (Toobin 2007). As noted in the introduction, Toobin asserted that "Such messianism cannot obscure the central truth about Google Book Search: it is a business" (ibid.). His comment assumes, however, that "messianism"—in this instance, Google's belief that it constitutes a moral force destined to reform the world for the better—and business never intersect. As such, Toobin participates in the economic essentialism that is everywhere present today and which assumes that not only is capitalism a single kind of formation but also that there are hard bounded, stable, and inherently "natural" distinctions between economic and non-economic spheres, forms of practices, and social relations. Such assumptions, Imre Szeman (2007) argues, exemplify a wider naturalized "commonsense" that the spheres of metaphysics and political economy never overlap or intersect—even when they do.

Szeman's observation that the intersection of metaphysics and political economy is often denied as a kind of category mistake is preceded by pioneer information theorist Norbert Weiner's critique, set forth in his final book *God & Golem, Inc.* (1964), that capital's intersection with the metaphysics infusing information machines makes for disturbing, even dangerous, bedfellows. Yet for Toobin and the commonsensical outlook he represents, a claim inflected by metaphysical thinking is only a ruse to deflect attention from the competitive material game of political economy and the bottom line. While Google has often deflected criticism of its sharper business practices by recourse to lofty appeals that reference the utopian values of open access and democracy-through-information, our assessment of Google Books suggests that Toobin partially misunderstands what is at stake. Yes, Google is wildly profitable but this hardly proves that "messianism," associated with the forms of autonomous production discussed in chapter 2, does not equally lie at the core of its approach to the world. In Eric Schmidt's own words, "Our goal is to change the world." Turning a profit "is a technology to pay for it" (Auletta 2009: xii). Though Google's book scanning project surely merits critique, Toobin's assessment would have been more accurate and valuable had he considered the complex interplay of power and altruism that undergirds *noblesse oblige* forms of agency such as Google's—an interplay that informs the opening lines of Adam Smith's 1759 *The Theory of Moral Sentiments*: "How selfish soever man may be supposed, there are evidently some principles in his nature, which interest him in the fortune of others, and render their happiness necessary to him, though he derives nothing from it except the pleasure of seeing it" (2009: 13).

Considered in tandem, Clancy's "universal library" and Brin's "library to last forever" statements suggest a remarkably coordinated corporate voice. Add a third voice to the mix—that of Marissa Mayer, Google vice president in charge of the project—"I think of Google Books as our moon shot" (Toobin 2007)—and the near parastatal nature of the firm's ambitious, heterotopic, even demiurgic and cosmic, goals come more sharply into focus. Because it is privately owned, Vaidhyanathan has argued, Google Books is an inherently unstable and therefore inappropriate mechanism for any future universal library. He predicts that "in one hundred years the University of Virginia [his home institution] will remain a premier institution of research and education, and Google will be no more" (2011: 185). Whether correct or not, his contention would surely be rejected by Brin, already a multi-billionaire, who, we believe, is interested in the bottom line "as a technology to pay for it" precisely because profits help build the firm, help reinforce its consecrated status, and therefore help sustain its pursuit of "moon shots" that conform to its first principle World Brainist agenda of One eternal universality replete with planetary memory. This One, in the estimation of Google's founders, will not only let us see the sum total of all extant recorded knowledge but, it is hoped, in time will prompt us as to how we might wish to think about what we have just read based on what this One already knows about us (see Levy 2011: 66–69). Hubris this may be, but it is also about a vision—the first principle of number and abstraction made to stand in for all else that runs through Licklider, Lasswitz, Liebniz, and Llull, and all the way back to the Atomists—as it is about satisfying an American financial services and rating "industry" which, producing little of value itself, continually criticizes Google for investing too much in research, development, and salaries, and not enough on return to its shareholders. As Steven Levy further notes, "From the very start, its founders saw Google as a vehicle to realize the dream of artificial intelligence in augmenting humanity. To realize their dreams, Page and Brin had to build a huge company" (2011: 6).

Seeking to comprehend the universe so as to understand its supposedly hidden or heretofore unknown order is a metaphysical quest. Organizing the world's information conforms to this understanding—every day millions of search results bring order and therefore meaning to previously unorganized Web representations. Ordered search results allow access to "another" space, a compensatory heterotopic space "as perfect, as meticulous, as well arranged as ours is messy, ill constructed, and jumbled" (Foucault 1986: 27). Whether born of hubris, generosity, or greed, or some combination thereof, Google Books seeks to organize the "lost" or hidden value in long-forgotten or obscure works in the same way that it extracts value for users from the Web. While the ASA was rejected on the basis of copyright infringement, and issues of monopoly (and therefore of political economy) were foregrounded in Judge Chin's ruling, looked at from the technotopian standpoint upon which Google's vision relies, it can seem only natural that the universal index, the universal library, and the universal archive should be the purview of One (semi-divine but entrepreneurial) mind without division or distinction—the HiveMind and World Brain conjoined with Google in the (automated) driver's seat.

About the possibilities for a World Brain or Mind, Wells asserted that "We do not want dictators ... we want a widespread world intelligence conscious of itself" (1938: xvi). Wells imagined information machines contributing to a lasting peace achieved by Enlightened Unity of the One triumphing over political division. But with networked technologies today capable of assisting the realization of Wells' vision through techniques and practices such as those Google continues to develop and encourage, what form might this self-conscious intelligence, an encyclopedic intelligence, assume under capital's often melancholy open skies? Would this intelligence be human? The cyborg online a lot of the time that Licklider (1960) imagined? It would and will, we suggest, be the artificial intelligence referred to above by Dyson following his 2005 visit to Google's corporate headquarters. Like Wells' World Brain, such an artificial intelligence implicitly trades in eternally returning desires for a form of consubstantial unity that would finally surmount, in order to transcend, the messy, at times seemingly intractable, political problems facing a world that is, in the estimation of the Californian ideology, human, all too human in its divisions, resulting inefficiencies, and slow pace of "progress."

Whether it be World Brain, the HiveMind or other variations such as the noosphere, all such concepts envision the use of vast databanks to achieve a technology-dependent form of collective intelligence or shared mind that rivals the gods but that, nonetheless, is conveniently, discursively, placed at the service of commerce, industry, peace, and speed, with the common man and woman repositioned as universal yet individuated monad-like searchers who also constitute the raw materials upon which data mining depends. This is the contemporary realization of Vannevar Bush's prescient 1945 turn of phrase "as we may think." Though most techno-fundamentalist converts to the contemporary "religion of technology" (Noble 1999) would deny they place anything like a spiritually inflected faith in technology, it seems likely that, *pace* Vaidhyanathan, given the absence of sufficient political will to develop a truly universal publicly funded World Brain, it will not be long before Google Books and Google Editions are fully open for business. The culture of search, coupled to a collective faith that within an environment of information overload Google and search engines more generally can provide easy, all-encompassing answers to difficult questions, demands it. Google's consecration secures it.

## Google as Library-cum-Archive

Librarian Heather Phillips' (2010) offers an instructive assessment of how we define and understand the material and conceptual components of a library. A library, she notes, collects, organizes, and maintains materials for the benefit and use of a group of people—a "patron group." A library has four pivotal or constituting markers: 1. It is a *collection* that has the "means of obtaining and keeping library materials"; 2. It is an *organization* that knows what the library has and does not have in its collection; 3. It is a *space* where materials are gathered, maintained, and renewed. A virtual space is "countenanced"; 4. It is, most vitally, an *institution* that exists to serve a patron group. Each patron group, Phillips observes, will have different sets of information needs and desires that librarians interpret and serve. Keeping a collection secret from a patron group serves no one (ibid.). Phillips does not claim that libraries must be "free for all," and she determines that the Royal Library at Alexandria was a real library because it satisfied (even invented some of) the requirements made by the above four markers.

Because Google Books remains a work in progress, any answers to the question of whether it will, in the future, constitute a library (or archive) must be somewhat provisional. If, by point 1 of Phillips' constituting markers, a library must, as a collection, have "the means of obtaining and keeping library materials," then such means—the buildings, digital networks, scanning technologies, monies and trained staff (point 3)—only exist in relation to point 4 as well—as institutions, libraries exists to serve patron groups. While the scope of Google Books is vast, so, too, are its current and prospective user bases. If the word "patron" is substituted for "user," who is to say that the global "community" of networked information seekers in all its multiplicities does not constitute a patron group? While Phillips uses the term "patron" to refer to individuals who support or frequent specific businesses or institutions, the concept has a complicated history with its associations of oversight, protection, sponsorship, influence, advocacy, and mentoring but also of tutelary gods, saints, and the proprietary relationships among lords, masters, and slaves. The hybrid public/private nature and the commercial and surveillant quality of Google Books, therefore, indicates that Google Books also serves a second patron group—not the myriad individual users who collectively use Google Books much as they might a library, but its targeting advertisers and, in a roundabout way, those print publishers who benefit from an individual's patronage when she or he buys a book having first read snippets of it on Google Books.

Vaidhyanathan (2011) points out that Google's current scanning practices often fail to meet accepted library standards, thus violating aspects of point 3 of Phillips' constituting markers: too many hands turning pages obscure portions of texts; too many blurry, off-centered pages; sketchy plans for long-term preservation of digital materials. Perhaps, therefore, a telling argument against according

Google Books the status of library is the firm's devaluation of materiality in general—whether this be the material substrate of the printed paper book and the specific advantages for readers that this supports, or the firm's relative inattention to issues of long-term preservation of its digital resources. Nothing but the spending of money stands in Google's way, however, from raising its scanning standards and correcting these errors and deficits over time. Extending Hayles, however, the loss to human perception of a different form of textuality, as represented by the paper book, the pages of which never disappear or freeze, is another matter (1999: 48).

Phillips notes that "a virtual space is countenanced" with respect to what constitutes a library—a point satirized by Figure 6.1, in which an adult instructs children on the now-leaky spatiotemporal relationships between bricks-and-mortar libraries and those constituting markers of the library that have migrated to the internet. The cartoon also problematizes Phillips' second point, that a library organizes materials; it is an organization that knows what it does and does not have in its collection. Google Books is designed, like the firm's broader search services, to search for and match specific word strings or keywords entered by the searcher in the search box, and it does not rely on abstract subject categories and cataloging and classification systems such as those provided by the Dewey Decimal System and the U.S. Library of Congress (LC) system.

**FIGURE 6.1** 'Think of it as the Early Internet." Michael de Adder, artist. By permission

Instead, Google first must scan and index the entire book so that any specific phrase or passage within it can be located by the search engine at a future date. Therefore, in a manner parallel to how Google captures a website's contents so that they can later be searched using word strings, for Google Books' indexical function to operate effectively and efficiently, Google must scan, digitize, and maintain an electronic copy of *all* books within its virtual space, a reality that suggests the service has the *potential* to be much more than an index—that it has the potential to constitute a digital library if only it could be searched by category.

Chapter 2 argued that a core epistemological difficulty with search engine technology is its inability to direct searchers to information about which they have no advance knowledge. While keyword search is powerful, one must have at least an inkling about what kinds of keywords are best to enter in order to search for what one wishes to find. Thomas Mann, reference librarian at the U.S. Library of Congress, has written about the distinction between Google's keyword search function and traditional LC cataloging and classification systems:

> Google's keyword search mechanism, backed by the display of results in "relevance ranked" order, is expressly designed and optimized for quick information-seeking rather than scholarship. Internet keyword searching does not provide scholars with the structured menus of research options … which they need for overview perspectives on the book litera- ture of their topics … It fails to retrieve literature that uses keywords other than those the researcher can specify; it misses not only synonyms and variant phrases but also all relevant works in foreign languages. Searching by keywords is not the same as searching by conceptual catego- ries … As a consequence of the design limitations of the Google search interface, researchers cannot use Google to systematically recognize rele- vant books whose exact terminology they cannot specific in advance.
>
> (2008: 159–160)

Mann's concerns focus broadly on Google search and they touch directly on issues of relevance we assessed in chapter 2. He correctly notes, however, that Google Books (which he terms Google Print) relies on the same algorithmic logic and develops his argument through the example of searching for informa- tion about Afghanistan's history. LC subject headings for such a search would be organized as follows with most further subdivided:

Afghanistan—Historical geography
Afghanistan—Historiography
Afghanistan—History
Afghanistan—History—Biography

Afghanistan—History—Chronology
Afghanistan—History—Dictionaries
Afghanistan—History—20th century—Sources
Afghanistan—History—Soviet occupation, 1979—1989
Afghanistan—History—Kings and rules—Biography.

(2008: 162)

Mann then notes that a keyword search on "Afghanistan" and "history" returns over eleven million hits and reasons "a similar search in Google Print, with 14.5 billion pages of keywords, is very likely to produce similar results. It will become utterly impossible to 'see the forest for the trees' with Google's software; the 'forest' overviews created by LC's cataloging … such as for Afghanistan above, will be completely lost" (ibid.: 165).

In effect, the inability of relevance ranking to offer conceptual categorization means that in the most ironic of ways the Library of Babel's curse may be visited upon us anyway, including those of us whose goal has been to tame the chaos of too much information. Mann directly states his case: "Disturbing parallels to the Tower of Babel come immediately to mind—this time, however, the Tower of Google will not be a myth" (ibid.: 164). He argues that the categorical distinction between "prior specification" (LC) and "recognition" (algorithmic search) subject searching techniques means that with the latter one receives search results only for terms one has been able to specify in advance. In deciding what is relevant to *search for,* let alone which results are relevant to that query, searchers draw on their own conceptual frameworks, limited by what they already know. Keyword-based enquiries "except by chance … do not allow you to recognize related sources whose terms you cannot think of beforehand" (ibid.: 162–163). Reliance on individuated "truthiness" as the measure of knowledge is integrated into keyword searching from the outset of the search process. This is not ameliorated by technologies such as Google Instant and Autocorrect which, in their suggestion of keywords and correction of spelling, seem to offer some of the guidance provided by categorization systems. The reliance on personalization algorithms and generic models of searcher activities within these technologies, however, creates feedback loops so that what is proposed to a searcher refers to previous searches by her or him as well as aggregations of popular knowledge rather than the universal categories of traditional library cataloging. The absolute agency of the keyword searcher in self-determining the terms of her or his own search, ironically then, limits the capacity to generate an overview of the subject area, in turn limiting the potential for wider access to knowledge.

Google could focus still more research on developing automated search technologies equal to the powers of the traditional library subject categories that are part of what make libraries libraries. It could, for example, link books to LC subject categories so that search could operate through keyword searches *and* subject categories, yet this would require ranking mechanisms other than the measures of popularity associated with the PageRank system and some rethinking of an insistence on total automation. The normative power of Google and its particular model of relevance which relies on aggregating keywords searched would also suggest that subject category searching is unlikely to immediately (re)surface as a widespread social desire. The lessons of the Tower of Babel are still to be fully absorbed.

Brin's reference to Google Books as a library is also worth pursuing. While "Google Books" as a naming strategy avoids reference to the idea of a library, one of the project's alternative names is Google Books Library Project. As Darnton (2009) argues, though Google, as a publicly traded corporation, exists to make money for its shareholders, we have come to understand traditional libraries as existing to promote a public good deeply associated with Enlightenment principles—learning free for all. Sir Thomas Bodley (1545–1613) was an early proponent of this republican sentiment. He aspired to found a "Republic of Letters" and his financial support allowed Oxford University's then-shuttered Bodleian Library to reopen in 1602. (In 2006, The Bodleian Library announced a partnership with Google to digitize its collection.) Even though private librar-ies, lending or otherwise, have a long history, and non-commercial institutions such as the independent Boston Athenaeum (founded in 1807 as a fee-based membership library) or the libraries of private American universities abound, we have been trained as children of the Enlightenment to think of libraries as public institutions. Critical, therefore, of Google's university library partners, Vaidhyanathan argues that "Inviting Google into the republican space of the library directly challenges its core purpose: to act as an information commons for the community in which it operates" (2011: 164). Including the word "library," then, in the title of his *New York Times* op-ed allowed Brin to imply, and readers to infer, that a consecrated quality of publicness similar to that accorded public libraries founded principally to serve patrons' needs inheres in the Google Books project. The ability to locate information in a copyrighted book or to view an entire public domain volume does lend a quality of public access to Google's project. Might it, then, in its function as an enhanced index of published books and documents, constitute a hybrid formation somewhere between what the French refer to as a *librairie* (a bookstore) and a *bibliothèque* (a library)? Vaidhyanathan, noting that Google Books is intended to make money, flatly states "Google is not a library" (ibid.: 15). And in "Google Books is Not a Library" legal scholar Pamela Samuelson rebuts Brin's op-ed by arguing that "Unlike the Alexandria library or modern public libraries, the Google Book Search (GBS) initiative is a commercial venture … Anyone aspiring to create a modern equivalent of the Alexandrian library would not have designed it to transform research libraries into shopping malls, but that is just what Google will be doing if the GBS deal is approved as is" (2009). Yet Samuelson skirts the issue that a library need not only be public—otherwise there would be no need for the adjective "public" in the phrase "public library." Neither should we err in assuming that the elite Royal Library of Alexandria was somehow freely open to all or, in its Ancient way, was not at the archival service of an aggrandizing Ptolemaic power.

Until remaining unresolved copyright issues are settled, however, while Google Books may have many of a library's definitional markers, keeping scanned copies of books "secret" or inaccessible so as to avoid further lawsuits runs counter to any definition of a library that includes meeting the needs of its patron base. The current inaccessibility of many copyrighted works on Google Books, however, does conform broadly to the status of archival materials during the "first years of their life" in an archive when they are often withdrawn from public view or closed to viewing for a period of time (Mbembe 2002: 20). However, the situation Google Books faces in early 2012, one that restricts full access to many copyrighted books, actually may serve Google in the long run by inducing frustration on the part of those searchers who constitute a potential patron base-in-waiting and who seek easier and more complete access to texts in return for being data mined and subject to push advertising rather than for the taxation that supports traditional public libraries. This could lead to increasing user/patron support for Google Books unless, given Google's *market* dominance, there are compensating and timely public moves to further strengthen and extend alternative public initiatives. At present such initiatives include the World Digital Library, funded by UNESCO and housed by the U.S. Library of Congress. The Library contains "significant primary materials from countries and cultures around the world" (World Digital Library 2011) and aims to narrow the digital divide within and between countries. Partners include numerous state libraries and archives; Google provided US$3 million toward start-up costs (ibid.). American initiatives include the Open Book Alliance[5] and HathiTrust[6]—the set of inter-connected partnerships established among American-based institutions such as Carnegie-Mellon's Million Book Project and the Internet Archive and whose stated goal is to create a truly public and universal hybrid library/archive in the form of an online multilingual database of texts and other materials.[7]

Other initiatives include Europeana, the European internet portal funded by the European Union.[8] It allows online access to millions of scanned books, archival records, paintings, photographs, films, and other cultural objects housed in various European cultural institutions' collections. From the perspective of visual communication, perhaps the most ironic entry to this list of public alternatives is Gallica, established in 1997 by the Bibliothèque nationale de France (BNF) as its *bibliothèque numérique* or digital library. Though its growing collection remains small compared with Google Books' databases, the publicly funded Gallica provides free and open access to text, audio, and image files across a range of holdings digitized by the Library. Jean-Noël Jeanneney, BNF president, and cited elsewhere in these pages for his reasoned opposition to Google's Book Search project, had been part of unsuccessful negotiations between the BNF and Google about the digitization of the Library's collections. Why is Gallica's inclusion in this list ironic? Figure 6.2 reproduces Gallica's logo, which reveals the close similarity between its serif font, lower-case "g" and the serif font, lower-case "g" in Google's initial logo designed by Brin and used between 1997 and 2000. Intentional or not, the closeness of the fonts suggests an implicit visual homage or tribute to Google, and even a recognition, given the Google logo's worldwide recognition, that use of the font could help instill in Gallica's users something of the same trust and consecrated prestige searchers place in and accord to Google.[9]

## When Database Turns Archive

Google has outlined its plans to have scanned and digitized the approximately 130 million known and existing books by 2020. While digital information machines may make this possible (if not probable), these plans reveal an uncanny parallel between Google Books and the impossible reality of Borges' Library of Babel—in both cases, the only complete index of the library of everything is the library itself. This is the metaphysics of totality—one where technology placed at the service of metaphysics renders transparent the previously "hidden order" of the universe of words and meaning. Google Books actualizes or annexes what was formerly the province of magic and prayer, as well as the inherently

FIGURE 6.2 Gallica Logo. Bibliothèque nationale de France

politicized thought experiments such as Lasswitz's and Asimov's dreams of consubstantial unity that masqueraded as science fiction. With respect to political economy, moreover, while Google may assert that its service is only an index to books, its current possession of millions of digital copies of books and other documents together with its plans to acquire digital copies of *all* remaining extant books suggests otherwise. Google's increasingly unsustainable claim that Google Books is only an index, furthermore, parallels its equally disingenuous assertion that it is not a content provider even as it dreams of being able to tell us things about ourselves that we do not already know.

Our discussion of these issues reveals that well-meaning, public-spirited denials that Google Books is not a library are based largely on the moral premise that because Google Books isn't publicly owned it will foster increased commercialization of library services that *should* remain fully publicly funded. Even Darnton, however, acknowledges that the service *could* become the "world's largest library" (2009: 14). The issues that stand in the way of its becoming so are those of technology (weakness of relevance ranking for academic research), political economy, discourse, culture, and time. Before the rise of digital databases such as Internet Archive, Europeana, and Google Books, the concepts of library and of archive were fairly consistent across institutions. As Phillips (2010) notes, libraries collected, organized, and maintained volumes of printed materials. Archives, however, were more focused on cataloging and housing documents of nation-states and other social, religious, and cultural institutions believed to contain information of enduring value. Archival documents take the form of unpublished letters, diaries and manuscripts, photographs, films, video and sound recordings, optical disks, computer tapes, and so on. Until quite recently, as Figure 6.1 infers, both libraries and archives were understood as bricks-and-mortar spaces within which people gathered to study and to examine cataloged and archived print materials and other objects. Achille Mbembe comments that the archive "has neither status nor power without an architectural dimension, which encompasses the physical space of the site of the buildings, its motifs and columns, the arrangement of the rooms, the organisation of the 'files', the labyrinth of corridors ... a religious space because a set of rituals is constantly taking place there" (2002: 19). Jacques Derrida also emphasizes the architectural: "The meaning of the archive, its only meaning, comes to it from the Greek *arkeoin*: initially a house, a domicile, an address, the residence of the superior magistrates, the archons, those who commanded" (1995: 2).

Archives are understood to help maintain state legitimacy through their conservation and use of historical materials widely believed worth preserving. In gathering the past and as heterotopic sites, they stand for the idea of a *quasi-eternity* (Foucault 1986). The archive is civilization's ark and it therefore has a decidedly political bent. As Derrida notes, the Greek *arkeoin* signified political power. "The archons are first of all the documents' guardians ... Entrusted to such archons, those documents in effect speak the law: they recall the law and call

on or impose the law" (1995: 2). At the same time, however, by storing or exhib-
iting, for example, artefacts of indigenous or other conquered peoples, archives
can at some future date undermine the very legitimacy of the state they are
intended to support by revealing it as the sole instigator of legal violence against
minority and other populations. The fetishistically organized archives of tota-
litarian regimes (such as that once maintained by the East German Stasi) are a
collective case in point. Mbembe notes archivists' *long-term* value to the state
project. He points specifically to their status as appointed guardians "of that
domain of things that belong exclusively to no one" (2002: 26). But appointed
guardians also must have some leeway in carrying out their tasks, and in exercis-
ing this leeway they often appropriate and eventually come to possess (if not
*de facto* own) the things that previously belonged exclusively to no one. This is
exemplified by Google Books' scanning of out-of-print and orphan books and the
firm's actions in this regard demonstrate that archives everywhere come to serve
as self-constituting and self-constituted authorities. Google-the-parastatal-agency,
operating as a *self-appointed* guardian, comprehends the need to establish, manage,
and *govern* its own archive and to do so in the name of the public for whom it
implicitly claims to serve as the consecrated guardian of print representations
from the past. This point is implicit in Briankle Chang's finding that "an archive
gathers into itself what it judges to be worthy of being gathered; it assembles what
belongs to it … It constructs itself freely" (2010: 204).

The rise of digital libraries and archives, together with the technology to
support this rise, has introduced a more dematerialized understanding of
what might constitute an archive or library than was the case when they were
bricks-and-mortar institutions. At the same time, this rise has led to a broadening
of the meanings of "library" and "archive" yet also to an ongoing convergence in
the meanings of the two terms and with that of the index itself. This is apparent
in Geoffrey Bowker's über-inclusive definition of the archive as "the set of all
events which can be recalled across time and space" (2010: 212). The meanings
and definitions, then, of "library," "archive," *and* "index" are in flux. If everything digitized can be meta-tagged and therefore searched across time and space,
and if such digitization seems to reduce the need for an archive to discriminate
and select because the issue of physical space required for storing material objects
has been rendered moot, then the digital archive today becomes less about the
material or ownership status of any one object per se and more about its location
as a dataset and functionality within the larger World Brain.

Digital search also reconfigures what it means to select and to discriminate.
If selection and discrimination once were perceived by librarians and archivists
as necessities induced by the physical limitations of analog storage devices,
they remain, under the digital regime, equally necessary but operate instead
more as a means by which searchers produce meaning through filtering in the
face of too much information. "Taste," too, as a manifestation of selection and
discrimination is thereby revealed to be partially a function of the physical

limits—or lack thereof—of the storage mechanism. Such observations are largely consistent with Foucault's findings that an archive is less a collection of objects or recorded statements than it is a set of relations—"the general system of the formation and transformation of statements" (1972: 146). His observations are consonant with Mbembe's assessment of the archive's capacity to function as an "instituting imaginary" for those who use its materials or its status to advance their own claims (2002: 22).

We see Foucault's proposal actualized in Google's relationship to the People's Republic of China (PRC) government, where in 2009 Google China "transformed," through making disappear, information Chinese authorities found inimical to their own hegemony. This transformation of part of Google's archive in the form of a virtual erasure so that it could no longer be recalled across (Chinese national) time and space served the purposes of the Chinese government, and at that time also helped to consolidate Google's non-hegemonic power in PRC markets (chapter 1). And we can also see Foucault's proposal that an archive is a general system for the transformation of statements exemplified in legal arguments advanced during the ASA hearings by Google's chief counsel, David Drummond, that its scanning of out-of-print and orphaned books amounted to a complete *transformation* of these works. Because Google understood its archival project as transformative—in effect positioning itself as a first principle entity—it viewed copyright law as a stifling externality and understood itself not so much as "above" the law as able to impose necessary and remediating changes to it.

While we agree that Google Books does not yet fully meet the definition of a library (in large part because it remains inappropriately organized and managed), we also note that perhaps what most critics who insist that Google Books is not a library are really pointing to with concern, unease, and regret is actually a twofold change. The first is that Google Books exemplifies how the deep-pocketed firm is transforming before our very eyes what constitutes a statement, how access to a statement is being transformed, and how a statement is transmitted and thereby put into discourse and made a part of social relations. Even though Google seeks to index all information, including the contents of all known books, its ability to manipulate the contents of its library/archive/index points to its potentially greater power to (re)write history and thereby allow current and future searchers to reimagine social relations, policies, reading practices, and so forth, in ways that are influenced by Google's manipulation of its databases and algorithms powering its search engine and the modes of engagement these articulate (chapters 1 and 2). This arguably will remain the case given the potential that searchers, adhering to the logics of the archive and the search, increasingly come to rely on the (manipulated) services Google offers to write and also revise their own and others' histories too. If search is a central feature of the way many of us now live, then Mbembe's finding that an archive is a religious space due to the ritual activities that constantly take place there equally applies to Google. Archives are sacred places that mirror selected aspects of our reality back to us, both as individuals and as cultures. For many searchers, online search through archival portals such as Google now constitutes a deeply meaningful ritual activity at a time when all manner of ritual practices previously deemed to take place only on this side of the screen are migrating to the Web and virtual space (Hillis 2009).

The second aspect of the twofold change noted above concerns media aesthetics. The objections of Jeanneney and Darnton, for example, concern not only the regrettable privatization of knowledge Google Books represents but also how we read. Search promotes reading practices that intersect with the epistemological mode of knowing its model of relevance encourages (chapter 2). For example, the snippets of text (Google's term for the several lines of text immediately adjacent to and therefore framing the word string searched) that Google Books returns for searches of many recently copyrighted books have been criticized for wrenching meaning out of context, and for promoting pastiche, on-the-fly, cut-and-paste approaches to research, scholarship, and knowledge acquisition more generally. We all claim to abhor this approach when we identify its use by our students, yet how many readers of this book will read it cover to cover? How many will have discovered these passages, for example, through Google Books? This is certainly not to argue against the more focused and sustained reading practices (and the luxury of time they require in an increasingly disintermediated world) that are essential components of meaningful research. Yet, as Figure 6.3 playfully implies, criticisms that focus on the ways that Google will damage reading practices seem, at least in part, generationally inflected, leveled by those who are ill at ease with the remediating logic of the internet which itself partly depends on the content of earlier media forms such as books, film, and television even as it refashions them at the same time (Bolter and Grusin 1999).

The snippet, in any case, does not stand alone. Google Books operates like a concordance machine.[10] It returns multiple instances within any one text where a specific word or phrase may occur. The level of access is set by publishers, and popular books such as genre fiction have limited or no previews, while less commercial academic titles often allow a considerable number of pages to be displayed in full. While we agree with Mann (2008) about the limits of search based on current ranking by relevance, we also understand that researchers sufficiently skilled in search practices know that search returns often allow them to read a page or two immediately before and after the one containing the particular snippet in question. This form of access, though the result of Google's contingent response to copyright issues, builds on the hypertextual logic of associative indexing anticipated by Bush (1988), who saw its "as we may think" potential to inveigle the imagination and facilitate forms of cross-linkages across topic areas that are more difficult to achieve using printed materials. Our graduate students, many of whom use Google Books on a near-continual basis, indicate

**FIGURE 6.3** "Mom, I Don't Need Books. I've Got Google." Vance Rodewalt, artist. By permission

that beginning a search through the snippet function—while less "convenient" than if the entire e-book were available, and certainly aggravating when a searched-for passage is on an omitted page—works (like an updated Llullian thinking machine) to promote combinatorial forms of thinking across texts. Opening multiple windows and searching for the same word or phrase across multiple texts in Google's library-cum-archive creates a remediated hypertextual screen—an information space—that can foster against-the-grain, associative reading across the many windowed snippets.[11] This use confirms the comment of Susanne Nikoltchev, head of the legal information department of the European Audiovisual Authority: "Search Engines are the librarians of the Internet" (2006).

To paraphrase Deleuze (1986), if new forms of art may suggest new forms of thought, so too can new technological forms help foster the same. New ideas gestate within historicized material realities; the form of the expression influences the form of new ideas. The kinds of associative reading practice Google Books may support come with their own aesthetics and can deviate sharply from the aestheticized scholarly ideal of having the luxury of time to read from cover to cover—hence some of the arguments lodged against these practices by self-admitted bibliophiles. The aesthetic of Google Books, however, also fits into and is part of an overly mediated Attention Deficit Hyperactive Disorder (ADHD) society in which Just in Time (JIT) production of goods and services seemingly always needed yesterday has become a consistent feature of contemporary life. Google Books neither makes a radical—that is to say, complete—break with the past nor with the book. Nothing (other than acculturation) prevents researchers from combining traditional research methods with the forms of contingent, hypertextual research Google Books now permits. While the project may indeed "transform" the future purposes to which the books it scans will be put, it nevertheless conforms to a too-little-acknowledged reality of the Web present since its inception: digital media "function in a constant dialectic with earlier media, precisely as each earlier medium functioned when it was introduced" (Bolter and Grusin 1999: 50).

## Remediating the Archive

While the kinds of information "space" to which online search now offers access once would have been understood as utopian—in the sense of impossible because existing nowhere (*u-topos*)—they now reflect the "space in which we live" (Foucault 1986: 23). In many ways, Google Books is a perfect artifactual exemplification of the contemporary zeitgeist. Information spaces such as Google Books conform to and extend Foucault's notion of heterotopias as potentially contradictory modern sites that are simultaneously mythic and real, the entry to which is based on ritual practice (such as always having to enter word strings in the search box) that somewhat sets heterotopias apart yet also makes them penetrable (ibid.: 26). While Foucault distinguishes between utopian imaginaries and material heterotopias such as museums and archives, he also argues that a heterotopia is "a kind of effectively enacted utopia in which the sites, all the other real sites that can be found within the culture, are simultaneously represented, contested, and inverted" (ibid.: 24). Google, with its many sites from Google Earth to Street View to Google Mars, already a cached virtual archive of broad swathes of material reality in all its contested forms (think of the many anti-Google videos hosted by YouTube), is a meaningful twenty-first-century heterotopia "proper to western culture," one where "time never stops building up" (ibid.: 26), even as it mirrors in its vast archives much of the minutiae of contemporary everyday life.

One may resist the idea that Google offers heterotopic, mirror-like access to reality, including what one may think based on what one has searched, or one may denigrate the networked forms of transformation and online ritual to which, as a networked society, we are now witnesses and, as searchers, ongoing participants. For better and for worse, however, Google Books—as a synecdoche for the broader world of search and archived databases that Google organizes—is on the verge of becoming, in Foucault's words, a "general system" for the "formation and transformation of statements." In an ironic twist, therefore, perhaps Google's critics have missed the broader point, which is less about whether Google Books might or might not be a library and more that its operation exemplifies Google's consecrated global status as a JIT parastatal archive able to influence general statements about reality which, over time, have the potential to determine general reality itself. To be sure, Google Books is a flexible, neoliberal kind of archive. The specific architectonic relationship between an archive and its bricks-and-mortar architecture in which employed archivists labor has been superseded by horizontally linked networked databanks, virtual spaces, distributed server farms, and disintermediated monad-like searchers performing affective online labor for free in hopes that it will lead to the manifestation on their screens of *relevant* JIT archives-for-one.

In the case of a Google search, it's the searcher who decides what to select from the overall contents of the library-cum-archive potentially at her or his fingertips: the online archive Google enables extends, in HiveMind and World Brain "craniates" fashion, horizontally to the thought processes and dwelling places of searcher-patrons, wherever these may be. And if, as Bowker (2010) suggests, the archive is the set of all events recalled across space and time, then we, too, as searchers rendered as bodies of information lodged within Google's database of intentions, also form part of its archive. We become snippets—hypertextual statements subject to transformation, transcription, review, and sale. We are the archive. We are living it, living in it, and it is us as well in all our partialities. We participate, "as we may think," as searchers, in determining what belongs in the archive (patron's desires and preferences included) even as Google freely constructs (partly through interpolating us as searchers) the ever-evolving form its digital archive takes.

Google's ability to offer each searcher at least the appearance of his or her own personal and ever-evolving JIT archive, therefore, also gives new meanings to the idea of the archive as a setting or institution that is selective and judgmental in nature. In so doing, Google further transforms the meaning of the archive (as a statement in itself) such that Google-as-archive now helps organize a world of myriad "weak" yet very powerful ties between individuals and individuals, individuals and things, and individuals and firms such as Google that claim to operate on their behalf. In heterotopic fashion, Google opens for searchers a virtual space, a Universal Library and Archive that is real to them—real like a dwelling. This is how Google participates in the *arche* of archive—at once a new beginning and an authorizing commandment that shifts the definition of the archivist from one that refers solely to those professionals who pre-organize the collection for researchers to one that is more shared among those who hold and guard the contents of the archive and those who use them. Google shares part of the role of the archivist with the searchers who rely on its service and thus at least partially conforms to Foucault's (1986) suggestion that heterotopias allow for the construction of ideal communities of like-minded individuals who value knowledge acquisition. A key difficulty, however, taken up in the following chapter, which examines the firm's reliance on its unofficial motto "Don't be evil," is that, while Google and its searchers collectively value knowledge acquisition, they do not operate on a level playing field. Google shares the meaning and constitution of its archive with its users but it retains the lion's share. It demands to be the first among equals, the oarsman and governor who steers the cybernetic ark it also owns.

Darnton observes that "the totality of world literature—all the books in all the languages of the world—lies far beyond Google's capacity to digitize" (2009: 36). While Google will likely never succeed in scanning *all* known books any more than it will succeed in organizing *all* the world's information, the neoliberal genius of Google Books, given the firm's stated interest to produce and own electronic copies of *all* known books, is to allow the searcher's knowledge of what she seeks to serve as the organizing act of her personal archival selection. In such a way does Google Books, as well as internet search more generally, accord with Bowker's additional assessment that "most of any archive consists of *potential memory*" (2010: 212; emphasis in original) given that here it is the searcher who actualizes part of the archive's potential memory through the terms she enters into the search box, no matter how small a "relevant" portion of the archive's total potential memory that is subject to recall through any one user's search query.

In applying these insights to Google, it is worth recalling that, since 1886, when the U.S. Supreme Court crafted the doctrine of corporate personhood in *Santa Clara County v. Southern Pacific Railroad Company*, American corporations have been deemed fully autonomous artificial persons whose words and actions have achieved significant, if not complete, powers of autonomy. Google-the-corporation, therefore, enjoys the status of personhood (if not citizenship) under American law. It holds and signifies a form of political power and its actions in the Google Book Settlement affair suggest that, not only does it increasingly understand itself as a document guardian (issues of sloppy workmanship notwithstanding) but that, with respect to copyright at least, it considers itself an authority morally compelled if not authorized to invent and impose new forms of legal understandings and ownership. Once Google had developed and effectively accrued to itself the power of the archive, it could then, extending Derrida, assume the power to change the law—in this case, copyright law that conflicts with Google's commercial, technological, and moral imperatives. Archives govern the contraction and expansion of the collections they build (Chang 2010), and Google's legal, even quasi-regal, stance with respect to the ASA reveals that it attempted to operate archivally—as "the law" in its collective meaning of a body of rules, itself the outcome of customs and contexts, and which a particular state or community recognizes as binding on its members or subjects (*OED*). Yet, as legal scholar Jane Anderson has argued, "increasingly copyright law holds a primary role for an archive—it governs access and use of the works that determine the archive's existence. An archive, in return, upholds and endorses the authority and the legitimacy of copyright law" (2009). But Google determined for itself that existing copyright law is inefficient. It slows down commerce, slows down Google's ability to be the guardian of *all* information. And, therefore, in a most ironic way given the technicized practices that search technologies encourage, it slows down the creation of subjective meaning on the part of those searchers relying on their cybernetic interactions with Google-the-authority to make better sense of a seemingly affectless world taken over by systematized technique.

After all, while the meaning of the archive is clearly in flux as Google's efforts to revamp copyright law suggest, archives, including Google's, are a guardian operation based on first principle concerns—they are where ultimate truth is believed or asserted to lie. And if Google is now seen by multitudes as a consecrated guardian of ultimate truth—a position, as chapters 1 and 2 note, that it works hard to maintain—then who will have sufficient voice, megaphone, or bandwidth to meaningfully contradict Google when it asserts its status as a library? It is this question that returns us to the relationship between archive and library. In order for Google Books to be accepted as a library by its users—its patron base—the firm had first to establish with this base its broader bona fides as a global archive. This it did courtesy not only of its superior search technology, well-groomed public image, and effective interpolation of searchers into the dwelling place of the archive itself. It also has been a principal beneficiary of the widely accepted meta-ideology that advanced technology itself, because it has come to subsume the progress myth so central to modernity's narrative, now constitutes a legitimate, even governing, authority—if not a law—unto itself. Modern information machines, particularly within American settings, are broadly received as access vehicles to the Divine. One need only recall the hagiographies accompanying Steve Job's death in 2011 to recognize that engineers (such as Page and Brin) are accorded the status of secular saints due to the implicit but widespread understanding that they seek to purge humanity of its physical frailties and restore us to perfection (Noble 1999: 165). "The present enchantment with things technological—the very measure of modern enlightenment—is rooted in … an enduring otherworldly quest for transcendence and salvation" (ibid.: 3). In cultural settings where technology "rules," it becomes the law in a cultural, psychic, and even a moral sense. A technologically powerful entity such as Google, the self-appointed documents guardian or archon, can consequently achieve for and arrogate to itself the consecrated hybrid status of the "technologically lawful" and benevolent conduit-dwelling precisely because successful relevant search outcomes provide searchers their own phenomenological evidence that the firm constitutes a legitimate technological authority bringing them closer to "perfection."

Whatever the manner by which actors in any field mount claims to ultimate truths, the establishment of legitimacy around such claims is central to how history, discourse, and memory—habitus—get fashioned and refashioned.

As they form and transform statements both false and true, archives organize and reorganize questions of being, time, identity, and change. How metaphysical and, at the same time, if the archive is privately held, how potentially profitable. Schmidt's remark, then, that making money is merely a "technology" to fuel Google's goal of changing the world, fully reveals how the firm has become the contemporary exemplar of the political economy of metaphysics in action. As a digital archive, Google Books is a long-term project that reflects its founders' emphasis on autonomous forms of production characteristic of those who eschew immediate financial reward (chapter 1). In the short term, "moon shot" projects such as Google Books accrue to the firm inestimable social capital and invaluable cultural consecration. Over the long term this social capital likely will transubstantiate into the quantifiable financial capital the firm also seeks.

In offering this assessment, however, we do not confuse an archival system for the transformation of statements with one that would somehow preserve these statements, to use Brin's word choice, "forever." While Google may be on the verge of constituting a general system capable of effecting the transformation of statements and thereby social relations, Brin errs, or at least manifests a kind of earthbound spiritual yet politicized faith that his firm is (God) Almighty, when he claims that Google Books constitutes an eternal service. For that would render it akin to Borges' Library of Babel and not, as earlier noted, because it would become unsearchable due to the limits of relevance ranking, but because it would become an impossible fiction seemingly without end. Brin's agenda would have been better served had he framed Google Books along the lines of a Foucauldian heterotopia—as a site that strives, in archival fashion, to achieve for its holdings the temporal status of long duration, but not one that, like an impossible *u-topos*, somehow lasts forever yet is never of the here and the now.

No one can predict the future—not even Google. No one can say whether Google's current ownership (and therefore the progressive aspects of its mission) will continue unchanged "forever"—not even Brin. And no one can know whether Google, like other large, seemingly invincible, and productive corporations before it, such as Atari, Digital Equipment Corporation, Nortel, and Trans World Airlines, will succumb to or be transformed in unexpected ways by as-of-yet unforeseen market forces or socio-technical and cultural considerations that change the values of their field of action and influence. That's the political economy side of forever. About its connection to the metaphysical Ideal, Jeanneney reminds us that "In spite of what nineteenth-century publishers sometimes imagined, there can be no universal library, only specific ways of looking at what is universal" (2007: 5). For Foucault (1972), any archive is always partial, always edited, and therefore a true universal archive is impossible, even ideationally, unless one embraces the metaphysical realm (which Brin, Page, and Schmidt effectively do through their collective statements). While Google may not be accorded archive status by those who insist on an archive's formal, architectonic qualities, the indexical, trace-like qualities by which its networked archive operates and how it organizes its knowledge of its users—its patron base of searchers' intentions worldwide—suggest that not only is Google, the platform-cum-institution, a formal archive in the sense of a collection mediated by technology (Bowker 2010), but that the service itself, its reliance on indexicality—the trace and "snippets" of information—also constitutes a meta-archive of search culture, its practices and techniques included.

# 7

# SAVVY SEARCHERS, FAITHFUL ACOLYTES, "DON'T BE EVIL"

Regardless of how you carry out your responsibilities, being steward of a meta-archive is a weighty responsibility: a moral responsibility. Google's reliance on "Don't be evil" reflects this understanding. To be such a steward leads to forms of consecration appropriating the sublime, and sections of this chapter trace the profitable connections between "Don't be evil" and the forms of online recognition of Google's psychic suzerainty over the everyday lives of some of the firm's more spiritually oriented searcher-acolytes. As users, these acolytes constitute an extreme pole of a broadly experienced cultural sensibility—the specific habitus or structure of feeling that marks the contemporary culture and field of search. While their devotion to Google exceeds the norm, their strong faith in Google's project provides a useful guide to the power and function of metaphysically inflected discourses that circulate within networked cultures.

As the story goes, Google's somewhat indelible mantra was coined in 1999 by Gmail developers Paul Buchheit and Amit Patel during a meeting held to determine the firm's corporate values. As Buchheit recalls,

> They invited a collection of people who had been there for a while. I had just come from Intel, so the whole thing with corporate values seemed a little bit funny to me.[1] I was sitting there trying to think of something that would be really different and not one of these usual "strive for excellence" type of statements. I also wanted something that, once you put it in there, would be hard to take out.
>
> It just sort of occurred to me that "Don't be evil" is kind of funny. It's also a bit of a jab at a lot of the other companies, especially our competitors, who at the time, in our opinion, were kind of exploiting the users to some extent. They were tricking them by selling search results—which we

considered a questionable thing to do because people didn't realize that they were ads.

(Livingston 2008: 169)

Although "Don't be evil" does not directly appear in Google's official philosophy statement, the phrase was included in the founders' 2004 IPO letter: "*Don't be evil. We believe strongly that in the long term, we will be better served—as shareholders and in all other ways—by a company that does good things for the world even if we forgo some short term gains. This is an important aspect of our culture and is broadly shared within the company*" (Google 2004; emphasis in original). Point number 6 on the firm's list of "Ten Things We Know to be True" also notes that "You can make money without doing evil" (Google 2006), and during the 2006 World Economic Forum in Davos, Switzerland, Eric Schmidt, then Google's CEO, announced that the firm "actually did an evil scale" in making its decision to continue censoring its Google China site at the behest of the Chinese government. "We decided it was even worse [evil] to not try to serve those users at all" (Cowley 2006). After Google rebalanced its "evil scale" in 2010, reversed its decision and pulled out (or gave the impression of pulling out) of mainland China, Sergey Brin made clear the issue of evil remained important to the firm's upper echelons. "Our objection is to those forces of totalitarianism," he told the *New York Times* (Lohr 2010). "Evil," Schmidt had claimed in 2002, "is what Sergey says is evil" (McHugh 2003).

Google's publicists have had to deflect criticisms that the firm violates its own moral code as part of its ongoing struggle to maintain legitimacy as demanded by the field of search's organization of values (chapter 1). As the examples above make clear, "Don't be evil" and the Code of Conduct (Google 2009) that the firm claims is "one of the ways" it puts the motto into practice mostly refer to how it treats its socio-economic relationships. The Code stresses that Google and its staff should serve users with integrity, protect its intellectual and material assets, encourage and support mutual respect in its workplace, work to avoid conflicts of interests, preserve confidentiality, obey the law, and ensure financial integrity and responsibility (ibid.). Google, however, faces other moral questions of right and wrong that it does not directly articulate to its motto, thorny questions such as what to do about its cached archive of previously indexed pages, to whom it grants access to its database of searchers' queries, and how it allows searchers to link differently to hate sites in different countries. In other words, "Don't be evil," the idealistic goal of an internet start-up that morphed into one of the world's most powerful corporations, does the discursive work of suggesting that Google actively conforms to the agreed-upon expectations of a corporation that somehow acts responsibly within a cut-throat marketplace always tending at least toward oligopoly.

Yet more is at stake. As documented in preceding chapters, underpinning the drive for ever more powerful search mechanisms is the desire to achieve a quality of union—to conjoin with the One, however fleetingly—and in the following section we examine the attempt to find meaning through search. The attempt, we argue, relies on searchers' designation of Google as the guarantor of a transcendent, unifying, albeit personalized, symbolic framework that provides the illusion of this One even as its model of relevance means that any answers to prayers Google search provides are based not on any cosmic One but on mining datasets of evolving human intentions. Implicit, too, within the drive for more powerful search is a broad tacit acceptance of the belief that any movement toward enlightenment and a state of moral goodness can only be achieved today through technological mediation. Together with its hubristic messianism, Google's automated mechanisms of search that organize the world's information speak to its ability to provide access to, if not to *actually be*, the divine. From its inception, it has been this correspondence between what Google (believes it) offers and that which its users come to believe or "know" that has engendered the possibility of its consecration. Such consecration must be persistently reaffirmed, its association with the godhead maintained. As the final sections of this chapter argue, the logical outcome of Google's hallowed position within the field of search is a theology grounded on the principles and rationalities of search and in particular of Google's version of them around which the firm, together with members of its broad public of searchers, have gathered in order to anoint Google as a sublunary Divine.

## Faith and the Cynically Savvy Searcher

> All that is solid melts into air, all that is holy is profaned.
>
> (Marx and Engels 1848)

In this section we examine the widespread decline of faith and trust in traditional authority structures and experts whose influence over society depended on symbolic efficiency. The decline, welcomed by many as indicative of greater democratic questioning of unworthy and corrupt forms of self-discrediting authority, has nevertheless ushered in an era of personal doubt and uncertainty about the meaning of the world around us and our place in it. In such a setting, the promise of a relevance-based universal library-cum-archive and search tools that "you can count on" has attracted people interested in finding new forms of everyday anchors at a time when so much else that was solid has melted in to air, most forms of symbolic efficiency included.

What do we mean by "symbolic efficiency"? Jodi Dean (2002) suggests that a symbol is *efficient* when it has such general purchase that it can be mobilized across time and space without question. This is not the same as people *actually* believing in the truth of the symbol. Instead, an efficient symbol indicates an overall cultural willingness to suspend disbelief, to take the symbol at face value and to effectively maintain the appearance of belief in the overall system of symbols. A willing suspension of disbelief has long been recognized, for example, in the way that cinema spectators set aside forms of logic that find plot holes and poor characterizations deterrents to entering the world of filmic illusion, and instead choose to let their emotional and psychic experience of the film prevail in order to more fully participate in its temporal pleasures.

But people also willingly suspend disbelief in political and economic symbols. Despite widespread recognition by global financial markets that the U.S. dollar rests on shaky economic fundamentals, investors continue to flock to it largely because they have always done so at times of economic uncertainty. That the purportedly stabilizing influence of the mystically "invisible hand of the market" has been so noticeably absent during the current economic crisis has not prevented economists, market analysts, and politicians from espousing fiscal "solutions" that rely on its existence as a material fact. In the Eurozone crisis, for example, the focus has been firmly on measures to calm market volatility, including widespread imposition of "austerity measures" (and their attendant detrimental effects on social services) as mechanisms to demonstrate financial probity and restore the "natural" equilibrium of market forces. Despite the evidence of its incoherency, the mythology of the self-correcting market has been preserved in elite circles, retaining a symbolic efficiency as those with vested interests pretend to themselves that they don't know what they already know; the "invisible hand" is invisible because it does not exist. Natural market stability is one sign—a powerful sign at the heart of the unifying symbolic system of global capitalism—in which belief is arguably still grounded, even as almost all other symbols attract the forces of disbelief. Nevertheless, as the thousands of Occupy communities affiliated with the international "Occupy" movement indicate, the efficiency of the symbolic system of capitalism, along with the myth of the "invisible hand," may also be in decline among the "99 percent" of the population who benefit less from the capitalist system than the remaining "1 percent."

A related factor in the decline of symbolic efficiency is to be found in the particularity of postmodern relativity. The fragmentation of political action into various forms of equally valid identity formations and politics has led to many people no longer accepting the absolute legitimacy of dominant forms of expertise and symbolic authority, which, in recursive fashion, has further fueled the decline of efficient symbols and their ability to be effectively mobilized across different kinds of identity formation. In the past, for example, a Walter Cronkite could sign off his CBS Evening News broadcast by announcing "And that's the way it is." This was the authority of symbolic efficiency in full flight. Cronkite and the expertise he incarnated has yielded, however, to the truthiness identified by contemporary faux-anchorman Stephen Colbert—"what you want the facts to be, as opposed to what the facts are. What feels like the right answer as opposed to what reality will support."[2]

Mark Andrejevic usefully distills the history informing this decline. The complexity of market forces, industrialization, urbanization, and rapidly changing labor conditions along with the fragmentation of urban life have shaped modern historical events, yet these forces are beyond the immediate control of most people suffering their effects. This has led to "the recession of causality" (2007: 58). Without clearly defined and singular variables, the meanings and causes of social events have become unanchored, and sustained and coordinated forms of political action have subsequently become somewhat unmoored. The uncertainty that was the hallmark of industrialization, the British Enclosure Acts of the eighteenth and nineteenth centuries, and consequent mass migrations of populations produced a widespread societal desire for resolution to the problems generated by these dislocating forces, but because the difficulties seemed—and continue to seem—beyond the ability of individuals and local communities to surmount on their own, over time the quest for explanatory power and models for action has been delegated to a series of experts. These have ranged from industrial efficiency experts such as Frederick Taylor, who in the 1910s applied studies of time and motion efficiency to the industrial workplace, to contemporary media that deploy a range of purported experts to interpret distant events, to celebrities such as George Clooney and Lady Gaga, who today model various social and cultural norms. The acceptance, however, of "expert analysis relied on numbing down the faculties—willingness to delegate particular forms of experience and sensibility to 'those in the know,' and thereby, perhaps, to accept the displacement of one's own sensibilities with regard to topics supposedly beyond the scope of the layperson" (ibid.: 248).

The rise of expertise is part of a broader technicization of the lifeworld, what Jacques Ellul (1964) terms "*la technique*" as a new meta-ideology promoting the alignment of human affairs and social relations with ever-more-technicized practices of efficiency and rationalization and the technologies upon which they rely. Once installed, technique transforms everything into a machine or human–machine assemblage. Everything gives way to Taylorization, the systems approach, the Life Coach's seven-point plan, Overeaters Anonymous's twelve-step program, and the systematized renewal of our "authentic Self" through New Age makeover programs. The rise of *la technique* and the status of symbolic efficiency accorded it by elites parallels the decline of narratives of social and moral progress noted in the introduction and chapter 6 and which have been replaced by a belief in technological innovation as an index of progress. As exemplified by Google's search results, the abstract logic of machines is taking on the role of technical expert.

An increasingly tenuous investment in expertise by the general population is, over time, yielding to the rise of a reflexive savviness on the part of *individual* consumers or "prosumers" positioned by neoliberal discourse as producing their savviness all on their own. As the near-ubiquity of self-reflexive "wink" advertising suggests, the savvy individual is overtly aware of market manipulations and all too conscious of the role of money and the outlandish influence of the powerful— of the "1 percent"—in shaping political decisions. Rising cynicism about the roles of experts parallels increased reporting of political and financial scandals (often interlinked) driven by the media's (particularly the digital media's) increasingly self-reflexive interest in exposure and ridicule of expertise connected to traditional forms of authority. This media emphasis on exposure, exemplified by Gawker.com and other "insider" sites that turn all manner of authority figures into scandal and controversy, has coupled with neoliberalism's unanticipated success in delegitimating direct intervention by traditionally authorized figures such as the state in favor of DIY approaches. Not only are particular experts now regularly undermined, but the notion of expertise itself (and by extension that of a universal truth) is under fire. Peter Sloterdijk (1987) identifies a widespread Western culture of cynical reason encapsulated in the phrase "I know I'm being had but so what." (With the right inflection, the phrase's meaning can be telegraphed by uttering the single word "whatever.") The overall decline of traditional authority structures, related to the decline of efficiency of symbols supporting such structures, happens in tandem with Google's effective emergence as a new kind of relevant and unifying force within pluralistic contemporary societies.

The political philosopher Slavov Žižek (2008) has focused directly on the decline of symbolic efficiency. He locates the decline in an overall loss of trust in what he terms the "Big Other" of the Symbolic order. The Big Other is an inherently metaphysical concept intended by Žižek to identify universally accepted forms of naturalized or "commonsense" cultural attitudes and expectations that constitute the bedrock of meaning making and which are accepted, sometimes literally, as gospel. As an agent, the Big Other—whether God, the State, the Father, the Law, or "natural" market stability—establishes the framework of the Symbolic order that Dean defines as "the intersubjective network of norms, expectations, and suppositions" and also as "the order of appearances, as that for whose sake we keep up the appearance that everything is fine, say, even if, deep down, we don't think it is" (2002: 132). With the moral decline of traditional Big Others as unifying principles or law-givers of the Symbolic order— paternal, patriarchal authority whose rules most in the West once accepted at face value—citizen-prosumers no longer believe in metanarratives such as the Law, Politics, or Truth in the metaphysical singular because such narratives no longer work for them at the personal, individuated level of meaning and interpretation. Loss of faith and meaning come to reside at the core of contemporary experience, and it is this loss that has allowed for the rise of belief in new forms of efficient symbols such as Google which, as a firm, offers products located entirely within the Symbolic order of language, signs, and appearances. Enter the search box as one of the more efficient post-traditional efficient symbols.

Žižek, who identifies the widespread loss of trust in the authority of the State, the Law, the Father, and so forth that once firmly grounded the Symbolic order of appearances (2008), develops his argument further by referencing Jacques

Lacan's theorization of the difference between the Real and the Symbolic Order and the gap or lack thereof that separates them. Žižek argues that a necessary gap spans the "distance" between the Real—the "hard core of primordial 'passionate attachments,' which are real in the precise sense of resisting the movement of symbolization and/or dialectical mediation" (Žižek 2008a: 327)—and the Symbolic—the reality constructed in symbols in which we must believe in order to make sense of the world. This gap between the Real and the Symbolic— between our passionate embodied attachment to the world and an external reality that is fabricated from symbols—he maintains, constitutes the modern Subject.[3] In his interpretation of Lacanian theory, he finds that the inability of the Symbolic order (the order of appearance) to fully capture the Real allows for excluded aspects of the social body (traces of the Real) to be exposed. This exposure reveals the ambiguity and impossibility of the Symbolic order—charged as it is with the impossible task of "transubstantiating a piece of reality into something which, for a brief moment, irradiates the suprasensible Eternity" (ibid.: 232). The irreconcilability of the Real and the Symbolic, exemplified in moments of affective forms of transcendence through immanence (such as passionate sexual activity can provide) and which cannot be adequately represented by symbols, produces the possibility space, the gap in and through which subjectivity arises. The choices made by individuals in negotiating the gap between their experiential, passionately affective Real and the Symbolic order that codifies and represents this Real organizes their subjectivities.

Žižek exemplifies his discussion by reference to sexual difference. Sexual difference belongs to the Real because "it can never be properly symbolized, transposed/translated into a symbolic norm which fixes the subject's sexual identity" (ibid.: 326). This gap between an individual's non-representational and primal experience of his or her sexuality and the Symbolic order that reifies, hierarchizes, and normalizes particular forms of sexual identity as a series of appearances or signs cannot be closed. The resulting gap stimulates the emergence of diverse and "perverse" forms of sexual identity. These arise, again, because the very excess of the Real that cannot be represented by the Symbolic means that it is always unable to adequately translate or represent that Real. Individual decisions made in navigating the "real of sexual difference and the determinate forms of heterosexual symbolic norms" (ibid.: 326) bring the sexual subject into being. In effect, the subject's *disconnection* from both the Real and the Symbolic order frees it from undifferentiated immersion in either primordial attachment or representational symbols, and thereby provides the basis of its subjectivity (ibid.: 184–186). What is important here is the crucial role played by rules of the Symbolic order in "lifting" or appropriating meaning from the Real and thereby providing the Symbolic order the capacity to authorize its own relatively stable practices of identification from the order of appearances and representation. Ordered and ordering knowledge systems like that of the universal library, World Brain, and Google are material manifestations of the

Symbolic order, an order that also structures reality and thereby provides a way to logically understand the world.

We have noted Žižek's linkage between a collective loss of trust in various Big Others and the denial of traditional forms of subjectivization. Individuals no longer have faith in the authority structures that used to bring normative order to the lived world and in so doing also provided access to the excess of the Real that enables subjectivity. More importantly for this analysis of Google, without the structuring effects of an effectively transcendent Big Other defining the laws of the symbolic system, representation becomes indistinguishable from the Real. Jean Baudrillard's concept of the simulacrum argues that proliferating signs of the Real increasingly substitute for it without being able to perform all of its tasks (1983). In a social system festooned with simulacra, the mediator of the imaginary vanishes. Contra Baudrillard, however, Žižek maintains that when signs proliferate as extensively as they now do, the Symbolic collapses into the Real, which continues to function as affective, untranslatable experience: the substrate of everyday life. It is the realm of appearances, the circulation of symbolic systems and the efficiency of those signs, which are threatened with refusal by the cynicism of "I know I'm being had but so what" rather than the Real itself. The reasons for such a decline in symbolic efficiency, again, are found in the rejection by the current culture of institutional and authorial legitimacy, traditional forms of expertise and patriarchal Symbolic authority. Members of this culture are composed of savvy citizen-prosumers who increasingly turn to personalized forms of meaning. Google's search box is a primary symbol of and access point to such forms of meaning.

Žižek, of course, does not refer to Google or search technologies in developing his account of the Real and the Symbolic. That is our task—to think through Google as a new source of expertise and a means by which searchers can reacquire the means to believe in a comprehensive Symbolic order. Conceptualized as the universal library-cum-archive and responding to the historical and contemporary desire for access to the transcendent systems of knowledge that were traced in previous chapters, Google has, both inadvertently and with purpose, donned the mantle of symbolic mediator, in effect stepping in to replace the Big Other of paternal Symbolic law—God, the State, the Law—in organizing our relations with the world. This is readily apparent in the ways that its suite of services has become the default we almost instinctively turn to for authorization of what we want to know, or confirmation of what we already know; like traditional Symbolic authority it provides the "tautological authority *beyond rules*, which says, 'It is so because I say it is so'" (Žižek 2008a: 385; emphasis in original). "If it is not on Google it doesn't exist" has become a truism precisely because the object in question has not been articulated and authorized within Google's symbolic system. Google effectively provides the mechanisms to lift apart the Real and its representations and thereby restore some efficiency to the symbols that allow us to make sense of the world.

At first glance this might seem an incongruous position; as an authoritative symbolic mediator, Google *should* be delegitimated by the same cultural processes that have degraded other, more traditional, forms of authority and expertise. The symbolic order constructed by Google, however, does not depend for its efficiency on restoring the traditional forms of authority of precursor symbolic systems. Instead it provides a material, context-bound, individualized sense of order generated through ostensibly personalized algorithms that resonate with and are relevant to the contemporary zeitgeist. If the Real predominates in the world of savvy citizen-prosumers, it is because each individual becomes the mediator of his or her Symbolic authority and the only valid knowledge becomes phenomenological knowledge. This is exactly what Google's model of relevance provides. When an individual reviews a ranked list of search results, clicks through to a particular website and accepts that this result is a relevant response to his or her query because its message concords with his or her own truthiness, then this individual is not seeking authorization in paternal symbolic Law. He or she is seeking meaning within a milieu of cultural relativity where the gap between experience of the Real and the Symbolic order has collapsed. He or she is drawing meaning not from wider Symbolic (ideological) systems but from his or her own experiential Real, mediated by search, which also comes to constitute part of the personal Real in itself. Google's model of relevance authorizes a return of order in the symbolic system in ways that do not diminish the role of the Real in shaping meaning. The firm's reliance on individual "truthiness" to generate facticity, to determine the relevance of search results for each individual, *responds* directly to a culture of symbolic inefficiency and cynical savviness and achieves validity for its model of search and for the firm through this resonance. But a culture of symbolic inefficiency is also *fostered* by Google's model of relevance, as it in turn generates further uncertainty and symbolic slipperiness by normalizing and validating personal "truthiness" as a generative and organizing principle.

This is a particularly uncertain and unstable terrain from which to generate narratives to help navigate the world and sustain fragile identities. Rather than collective imaginings, we are left with a reflexive pluralism of individualized social imaginings:

> The contemporary setting of electronically mediated subjectivity is one of infinite doubt, ultimate reflexivization. There's always another option, link, opinion, nuance, or contingency that we haven't taken into account, some particular experience of some other who could be potentially damaged or disenfranchised, a better deal, perhaps even a cure. The very conditions of possibility for adequation (for determining the criteria by which to assess whether a decision or answer is, if not good, than at least adequate) have been foreclosed. *It's just your opinion.*
>
> (Dean 2010: 6; emphasis in original)

When the symbolic Big Other is dethroned, when a great number of people know that there are endless contingent variations of any one fact or issue and that new discoveries also mean new forms of ambiguity and risk, then meaning becomes unanchored. Questions of doubt abound. In such uncertain settings, "savvy" cynical distance, almost paradoxically, becomes coupled with paranoia, for the "distrust of the big Other (the order of symbolic fictions), the subject's refusal to 'take it seriously,' relies on the belief that ... behind the visible, public Power there is another obscene, invisible power structure" (Žižek 2008a: 442) that guarantees the consistency of the Symbolic order. Paranoia becomes rational when meaning making becomes a solitary affair and the need to make decisions can feel disorienting and even paralyzing. In such circumstances, as the long-running U.S. TV program *The X-Files* once made crystal clear, we have entered the realm of the conspiracy theorist who everywhere unearths secret agendas that explain complex social and historical events. This is the realm of, for example, the American "Tea Party" movement. Faced with globalization, loss of jobs, deindustrialization, slippage in U.S. hegemony and prestige, and effective political rule by banks and insurance firms judged by their political cronies as "too big to fail," Tea Partiers created a clearly defined narrative of loss and paranoia in part issuing from their phenomenological experience of the world that the "truth is out there" and can be found if sought. It is also the realm of the transcendent World Brain that can structure systems of knowledge for us *when we want it to do so*. It is the realm of Google.

This paranoid desire encourages us, in an updating of Ramón Llull's four-teenth-century belief that he could invent a thinking machine, to allow tech-nologies with better information processing capacities to "believe for us" (Dean 2002); to believe in and to generate the Big Other that, like Llull's unswerving faith in a Christian God, will order the world. In ascribing belief to technology in this way, we put our faith *in* technologies—a vesting that leads to outcomes such as the Church of Google discussed below. Yet this vesting works recur-sively to ensure the institutionalization of the technicization noted above as a form of neoliberal divinity. The instrumentalization of knowledge systems quickly follows and it is this vesting that underpins the rise of Google and search. Google becomes the "subject presumed to know" to which we can turn to "truthfully" interpret the world for us. We can ask Google "what job should I take?" because Google understands our world better than we ever could and because we have faith that Google will translate that world for us. Whatever did we do before Google?

The metaphysics of Google's political economy are thus both cause and effect of this ascription of belief in Google's expertise. The powerfully affective agency of a universal library-cum-archive actualized through Google works in two interpenetrating ways: 1. It can serve as the "Other of the Big Other" by virtue of becoming the transcendent, omniscient, structuring agent of con-temporary networked society's systems of power and knowledge, and to which individuals turn in hope of lessening their individual paranoia and overburdened meaning-making faculties. 2. Google's library-cum-archive also serves as the agent of the individual rather than solely a dark, uncontrollable force of paranoid fantasy: it provides us with the means to access previously difficult-to-locate information that can help make our world better cohere. In both cases, the transcendent power that searchers implicitly attribute to Google's search engine mitigates the psychological stress induced by absolute relativism and the consequent DIY requirement to become one's own moral center, one's own ultimate authority. The often eerie relevance of Google's search results offers a form of psychic balm in short supply in an otherwise largely inexplicable exterior world, and for once we are in full agreement with Kelly when he asserts that Google's "universal library" will "cultivate a new sense of authority" (2006: 42). In a virtuous circle, Google's "relevant" ranking of results provides comfort for searchers who accept those results as relevant. To effectively commune with the universal library of which one likely already forms a part requires, like forms of addiction, continual return to the search box. This is a recursive state of affairs that Google implicitly comprehends, and in its mediated exhortations to "Search On" effectively exploits.

In a culture of instrumental reason holding to the equation technology = progress, Google has come to occupy the position of a Big Other, or, given its focus on personal relevance, of a My Big Other, in part because its search technology works so well. A principal reason why many searchers find Google search so satisfactory, even magical, is because its schema of relevance authorizes Google to present the collective—the socially networked—back to itself, Narcissus-like, in a way that *fascinates*. Relevance produces a statistical mode or mean, it concatenates individual searcher actions into a networked form of the collective. Google Instant reveals the synthesis of collective desire to each searcher each time she enters a query in the search box. The brilliance of this is to merge aspects of the Real with the Symbolic in ways that allow for the possibility of a gap between them and through which the searcher can emerge as a new identity form that also feels Real, and offers possibilities for passionate attachment, even as it is constituted entirely through the Symbolic realm.

It is therefore important to acknowledge that search is a participatory act entered into knowingly by individuals who organize their own engagements with it and decide whether or not to accept the facticity of query results. While "participatory interactivity" is the alibi for the centralizing, networked systems that generate the cybernetic feedback that makes more of our online activities, and therefore more of our desires and interests, available to state and market surveillance, such interactivity also provides a veneer of democratic agency to satisfy the savvy, paranoid user (Andrejevic 2007). In such ambivalent circumstances, using Google to search need not equate to capitulation to alienating forms of expertise, as such use provides a self-affirming recovery of assumed knowledge and the comforts thereby attained. Agency becomes a function of asking and answering questions and searchers submit to Google's system as a form of truth procedure. It is precisely in this tension where the heart of Google's consecrated power resides—between a phenomenological experience of using Google to implicitly confirm one's "truthiness," and the parallel comfort offered the searching individual by his or her assumption that Google's World Brain is omniscient because it contains each of our truths as a collective whole. Shrewd enough to know that algorithms beyond their control and access are what determine Google's search results, searchers in practice engage in a willing suspension of disbelief that allows them to understand themselves as determining agents, as the authors of their own meaning-making process. By so doing, they avoid finding themselves, yet again, in the dead-end position of "I know I'm being had, but so what." Such simultaneous belief and faith in both Google *and themselves* explain why the studies noted in chapter 2, such as that of the U.K. academic researchers who continue to use Google despite awareness that PageRank's structuring biases frequently lead to less than ideal search results (Fry et al. 2008), show that individuals do not reject the search engine even when "they know better." Knowing the powerfully influential role of search algorithms certainly has not impeded this book's authors from using Google in its compilation. While searchers know that Google is neither the Universal Library nor an entirely benevolent service provider, they act as if this were not the case because search is often so personally and culturally fascinating that it induces a sense of faith that somewhat ameliorates the feeling of loss of certainty induced by the decline of traditional forms of symbolic efficiency.

Searchers are people and people operate through faith, trust, and belief in both themselves and in others. We have already noted that the mystical scientist Gustav Fechner, whom Borges credits as the first to postulate the modern idea of a universal library, observed that "faith grows out of its own motives ... one may believe that something is, and believe that upon it one can rely— then faith is characterized as trust ... The one belief, however, is rooted in the other. For how could one believe of anything that it is reliable without believing that it is?" (Lowrie 1946: 83, 86). We trust Google because we need to have faith in some relevant form of Big Other. We need to believe that there is order in the world but, given neoliberalism's demand that each of us be responsible for our own sense of meaning, we also need to feel that this order does not contradict our own sense of agency. Loss of faith in traditional Big Others *and its return* in a new form through Google are what makes it such a crucial component of the contemporary networked imaginary. But, like all faiths, faith in Google reassures only inasmuch as the firm retains its associations with "good" moral values. In the following section, therefore, we examine how Google's "Don't be evil"—an instruction worthy of a Big Other—forms part of an overall cultural habitus within the field of search.

## Evil, Google-style

While the term "evil" is bandied about in many discussions of Google's intentions, it is rarely defined. Though clearly an over-determined concept, evil does have a core set of meanings with which most would agree. One of the more common associations offered by the *Oxford English Dictionary* links it to doing harm or to injure—"anything that causes harm or mischief, physical or moral." Evil is also defined as becoming morally bad, depraved, sinful, vicious, and wicked. As a term, however, it is often used as an adjectival expression of disapproval, disparagement, or dislike—as in "that was an evil thing to do"—where the phrase carries the sense of evil as the antithesis of the good. An older meaning concerns the actions of "overstepping proper limits" and "exceeding due measure." Both actions relate to the "sin" of hubris. For example, the 1980s American deployment of "Evil Empire" registered U.S. disapproval and disparagement of the former Soviet Union, its chief and "overstepping" rival at that time. More recently, "Axis of Evil" has enjoyed considerable cultural currency on the part of those American "patriots" seeking to create through spatial metaphor a strong image of an immoral and wicked Middle Eastern Other intent on destroying all that they position as shining, noble, and good. Here one sees how accusations of evil are frequently used to "other" the competition—whether another state or, in the case of Google, Microsoft. As Buchheit's comments at the opening of this chapter make clear, "Don't be evil" arose in part because Google engineers felt that their rival's business practices and corporate culture were somehow evil incarnate. Issues of morality, therefore, pervade evil's many meanings.

In its adjectival form, "moral" refers to "having the property of being right or wrong; or good or evil." With respect to human agency, moral refers to the ability to "choose between right and wrong, or good and evil." It is but a short leap, one that history reveals to have been made repeatedly, to render equivalent right and good, and to do the same with their "opposites," wrong and evil. The final command on Google's Code of Conduct page makes this slippery link: "And remember ... don't be evil, and if you see something that you think isn't right—speak up!" (Google 2009). By the Code's logic, what is good is what is right and what is evil is what is wrong. Google, however, is not the only institution to make this conflation, hence the similar positioning of the Soviet Union as Evil Empire by the U.S., and Microsoft as evil by Google's early staffers. Political philosopher Jane Bennett observes that a moral code "condenses moral ideals and metaphysical assumptions into principles and rules" and that such a code requires an "embodied sensibility ... which organizes affects into a style and generates the impetus to enact the code" (2001: 131). Moral codes such as the Ten Commandments are useless without "a disposition hospitable to their injunctions, the perceptual refinement necessary to apply them to particular cases, and the affective energy needed to perform them" (ibid.). Google's "Ten Things" (its own Ten Commandments), together with its interdiction to do no evil, thereby would seem to qualify as a moral code. The question then becomes one of hospitable dispositions, perceptual refinements, and affective energies—the embodied sensibilities to which Bennett refers and to which the decline of symbolic efficiency lends itself. Moral codes alone cannot effect their own enactment. They must be taken up, made consecrated, and this consecration must, in ritual fashion, be repeatedly renewed and promoted. This, as chapter 1 details, is something Google's many outreach and sponsorship programs suggest it comprehends.

In light of the various understandings of evil, consider Douglas Edwards' (Google employee number 59) conversation with Larry Page as redacted in his insider account of life within the firm. After a series of disagreeable meetings with Page, Edwards pursued a conversation with his boss as a way to extend an olive branch. "Larry," he stated, "I know I haven't always agreed with the direction you and Sergey have set for us. But I've been thinking about it and I just wanted to tell you that, in looking back, I realize that more often than not you've been right about things. I feel like I'm learning a lot and I appreciate your patience as I go through that process." Page, after looking at Edwards "with the same stare he had directed at the code on his screen," replied, "More often than not? ... When were we *ever* wrong?" (2011: ix–x; emphasis in original). If "wrong," however incoherently, is too often conflated with "evil," and the two terms are interchangeably leveled at "the Other," then it becomes possible to read Page's reply as asking, "When were we *ever* evil?" Clearly, being wrong, as in making such factually incorrect statements that the earth is flat or that two plus two equals five, does not always conflate with being evil per se. It is also the case that assertions of never having been wrong (or evil) mostly issue from the province of inexperience, defensiveness, and ideology-driven hubris. As such their purchase is regrettably widespread and Page is scarcely alone in this regard. What does set him apart, however, is his membership in the contemporary Priest Class of information technology gurus who preside over the current technotopian moment and mediate our access to the comfort of the Big Other. There has never before been a generation of nerds or technology workers to have achieved the social, economic, and cultural influence as have today's Brin and Page, Microsoft's Bill Gates, Facebook's Mark Zuckerberg, Amazon's Jeff Bezos, and Apple's now-departed Steve Jobs. They are the mediated and therefore easily identifiable faces behind which toil the legions of super smart nerds who write the algorithms and other forms of code that increasingly constitute the technicized rules by which society and its constituting individuals operate. While "resistance" remains possible, the rest of us geeks who don't write the code but who use (even venerate) the programs are induced by a broadly held faith in technology to follow along. Vaidhyanathan suggests that "techno-fundamentalist" faith in technology has led to much suffering, noting that, for Dante, pride was the gravest of the seven deadly sins. "The 'Don't be evil' motto is itself evil, because it embodies pride, the belief that the company is capable of avoiding ordinary feelings" (2011: 77)—such as the ordinary but ambiguous feeling that one might err, as did Brin (2009), in claiming that Google Books will last "forever."

By the commonsensical logic that conflates evil with wrong, if one is never wrong, then one is never evil. "Don't be evil," then, also can be read as a self-policing statement that reminds Google's workforce to never be wrong, to always strive for "personal best." As such, corporate adherence to the statement is also to self-consecrate through self-interpolation of the undergirding idea of "don't be wrong." This is, moreover, also to enter the world of metaphysics and its first principle concerns. If one could corner the market on never being wrong, one would laugh oneself all the way to the bank on the way toward becoming World Brain. By the logic of efficiency and speed that drives the Californian engineering culture Google exemplifies, the only way one could never, ever, be wrong would be to give all decisions over to an AI and thereby allow the hyper-efficient, purportedly morally neutral ethos of information machines full rein. In all of this there nonetheless remains the capitalized altruism of young adults thinking they can do good things and make a lot of money at the same time. And they have. But *evil*?

Whether or not Google conforms to its moral high ground of "corporate responsibility" is a matter of perspective. Steve Jobs, making reference to Google's Android-powered Nexus One phone platform, commented in January 2010, "We did not enter the search business. They entered the phone business. Make no mistake they want to kill the iPhone. We won't let them ... This don't be evil mantra: It's bullshit" (Abell 2010). Teilhard de Chardin observes that "Whether it be physical or moral, evil repels us only so far as it appears to be useless or gratuitous" (1970: 50). Jobs' comment points out the current difficulty of referencing evil in terms of corporate responsibility. Is it *evil* for Google to enter the phone business? Arguably no, as the move is neither useless nor gratuitous; expanding into mobile markets makes business sense for the firm, the value of which is based on attracting more eyes to more ads through as many wired and wireless means as possible. Using "evil" in terms of "corporate responsibility" therefore would seem to be a category mistake.

Vaidhyanathan also believes that too close a focus on "Don't be evil" is counterproductive in that the motto "distracts us from carefully examining the effects of Google's presence and activity in our lives" (2011: 8). Examining the firm's influence on everyday life is of course crucial, and we concur that "Don't be evil" operates as a cultural catchphrase that works to valorize the essentially hollow ideal of corporate responsibility. Yet Google's ongoing self-association with such a freighted concept in itself constitutes a general statement of reality that exerts influence "in our lives." Assessing the firm's strategy in this regard, then, rather than being counterproductive, forms part of our careful examination of its influential presence in our daily lives. Szeman develops this point when he suggests that "Don't be evil" communicates inferentially to searcher-users that unfettered marketplace competition, augmented and aided by unfettered search results, is an unalloyed good that nevertheless "can be harmed by the evil of interference in the market. Which is to say: 'Do No Evil' [sic] means play by the rules, such as they are" (2007: 134). Szeman refines his argument by linking Google's use of "Don't be evil" to its parallel assertions, developed in point 6 of the "Ten Things" that it "knows to be true": making money is never evil, and neither is advertising (Google 2006).

Google's use of the term participates in a broader neoliberal discourse that positions evil as exceptional. Evil, Szeman argues, is rarely associated with economics and economic policies, no matter how grotesque or obscene the human wreckage that such policies produce. A generation of neoliberal discourse has normalized the violence wrought by neoliberal economic policies, in part, through exceptionalizing evil (ibid.: 133) and exiling it to such aforementioned "other" spaces as the Evil Empire and Axis of Evil. Most of the popular and business media coverage devoted to "Don't be evil" focuses, as the Google Books example indicates, on the dangers of monopoly. Szeman points out that, while the idea that monopoly is evil does link it to the economic, it does so at the price of affirming capitalism's core values—competition, efficiency, and innovation. This is because monopoly is an extreme market condition. When markets function well, they do so, at least in theory, in the absence of monopolies. Economic evil, such that it indicates monopoly, is at the extreme end of capital (ibid.). Everything else is fair game and this is the underlying argument transmitted by point 6 of Google's "Ten Things."

## A Category Mistake?

While examining the relationship between evil and a firm such as Google might seem to participate in a category mistake, positioning such an examination in this way only makes sense to those who are fully interpolated into one of modernity's dominant and therefore naturalized beliefs that different social functions must always be allocated to different areas lest they somehow contaminate one another. (The structure of feeling or habitus that underlies the naturalization of this binary is also manifested when an entity such as Google claims that its services only constitute a platform somehow fully set apart from the mediated content its users seek.) According to this compartmentalizing belief system, it comes to seem only natural that the realms of economics and politics be understood as separate from the realms of morality and theology because it is in the best interests of all these realms to maintain these distinctions even if, upon close examination, they do not hold. Toobin's 2007 assessment, noted in the introduction, that Google's semi-autonomous "moon shot" forms of messianism such as Google Books cannot hide the fact that it is a money-making business, rests on his assumption that as a business Google is really only focused on profit.

But the logic subtending Toobin's claim depends on the implicit moral assumption that Szeman and we refute—that the worlds of morality and the bottom line *ought* never to intersect.

If, however, we look back to one of the parents of modern political economy theorization, Adam Smith, we see in his *Theory of Moral Sentiments* (1759) the emanationist proposal that morality, broadly conceived, "is part of humanity's adaptation to the circumstances in which it happens to find itself" (Haakonssen 2002: xii). Morality, for Smith, evil included, is a consequence of, and pours forth or emanates from, the ways and means by which humankind engages with the overlapping political, economic, discursive, natural, and—above all, for Smith—the social fields within which life takes place. Morality, then, is part of a broader unified reality or first principle through with everything interdepends and from which all things emanate or flow, political economy included. For Google, the morals it claims to support, such as "Don't be evil," reflect its adaptation to the circumstances in which "it happens to find itself." About the crucial relationship between morality and economic status, Smith observed,

> This disposition to admire, and almost to worship, the rich and the powerful, and to despise, or, at least, to neglect persons of poor and mean condition ... is ... the great and most universal cause of the corruption of our moral sentiments ... We frequently see the respectful attentions of the world more strongly directed towards the rich and the great, than towards the wise and the virtuous. We see frequently the vices and follies of the powerful much less despised than the poverty and weakness of the innocent.
>
> (2009: 73–74)

"Don't be evil," then, a directive issued by a firm that is among "the rich and the great," helps augment the largely "respectful attentions of the world" it already receives. Smith also insisted that his understanding of economy be framed against a theory of moral sentiments because of his interest in strongly articulating between the study of political economy's empirical manifestations and an ultimate ordering end—the social or society—which empirical practices reproduced and toward which political and economic relations aimed. Smith was writing at a time when the differences between the observable world of human affairs and the material outcomes produced by wide acceptance of the theory of the divine right of kings were not yet so neatly held apart. Today's world, however, is conveniently compartmentalized into discrete and therefore often simplistic categories. The contemporary segregation of economy from morality informs the view (implicit in statements such as Toobin's) that we had best turn away from assessments that too closely link Google-the-firm to metaphysics. And this segregation, the maintenance of which is assisted by a transference of the logic of the scientific method's parsing dynamic of analysis—or cutting apart—to capitalized human affairs, helps to produce a set of dominant discourses that assert we are less a cohesive society and more a series of interlocking markets. Following from this logic is the position that we also should see it as a moral good that the social bond increasingly manifests through a disaggregated collective of networked individuals.

Yet each of us is one of these individuals continually instructed that in the hypermediated world in which we find ourselves there are simply winners and losers. That's just the way it is, morality be damned. Lay off a thousand workers? Acquire your competitor just to shut it down? Move your manufacturing sector offshore? As a Florida legislator, allow your state to become the OxyContin "Pill Mill" capital of the US in order to assist the pharmaceutical industry's relentless quest for profit at the expense of the poor in pain? Such news gets reported (Alvarez 2011), mostly in the business section, but most often the final response is a collective, cynically savvy shrug expressed in the defeatist, even nihilistic, phrase, "It is as it is." But evil? No way— that's a theological concept inadmissible in a business sphere, where we are nevertheless constantly peddled the supernatural "commonsense" that markets, with their hidden hands, always magically self-correct.

It is ironic, therefore, that parts of the academy continue to participate in the modern lie of a natural division between the sphere of metaphysics and the sphere of politics and economics. For, as Bruno Latour (1993) argued almost twenty years ago, the West's inability—rooted in the early modern state's need to hold separate, and thereby maintain a political peace between, the contradictory and effectively competitive spheres of science and religion—to fully realize secular modernity's ideal of discrete categories of knowledge has meant that, in practice, we have always hived toward what is hybrid while at the same time, for the underlying political reasons just noted, continued to insist on the maintenance of divisions between the spheres. That is why in many quarters, the academy included, it remains impermissible to utter the phrase "the political economy of metaphysics" even as those who find it impermissible continue to engage, of necessity, in the kinds of hybrid practices that Latour identifies as one of modernity's principal hallmarks.

Plotinus directly connected the universal One with the Good and the principle of Beauty. Because of the cosmological dimensions of Google's grand scheme with its demiurgic echoes of the universal One, it should perhaps not be surprising that Google adopted "Don't be evil" as its corporate catchphrase, and it is worth noting that the Google phrasing is "Don't *be* evil" and not "Don't *do* evil." The verb *to be* is ontological, indicative of first principles. Its earliest meanings suggest the occupation of a place by human bodies, as in to sit, to stand, and to lie. In short, to exist (*OED*). Over centuries the verb *to be* has been abstracted so as to emphasize actual experience as well as being in a particular place, but the human state of being remains a first principle. Therefore, while the consecrating mantra "Don't be evil" does add to Google's economic value by helping induce user trust in it as well as to deflect critical attention from the hollow notion of corporate responsibility, the mantra equally reflects at least partial recognition of the deeply serious moral task the firm understands it has taken on in seeking to build a metaphysical first principle in the form of one searchable universal index intended to change the world. Schmidt's comments to Levy about Google's corporate culture reflect something of this recognition: "If we went into a room and were exposed to an evil light and came out and announced evil strategies, we would be destroyed. The trust would be destroyed" (Levy 2011: 364). And with it Google's consecrated status as My Big Other—a status which, if the firm were widely perceived as evil, could easily transition to a post-Orwellian My Big Brother.

The mantra, therefore, does something more than indicate Google's commitment to corporate responsibility. In adopting it, Brin and Page implicitly understood that building the ultimate index that is accessible from any place with an internet connection—like Wells' World Brain—usurps not only state powers and those of civil society institutions but also cosmic powers once accorded the Divine Mind itself. Plotinus' own words about the human experience of the *nous* are instructive: "Those divinely possessed and inspired have at least the knowledge that they hold some greater thing within them, though they cannot tell what it is; from the movements that stir them and the utterances that come from them they perceive the power, not themselves, that moves them" (*Enneads*, V, 3, 14). Google's founders and top management know "they hold some greater thing within them." So, too, do their loyal searchers and acolytes who, in effectively communicating their *trust* that Google now provides access to some semblance of a Big Other, also send it the simple message, "Google, Don't be evil."

## "The Google God": Seek and Ye Shall Find

> Truly, Google is like Dante's afterworld: the celestial rose that reclaims and restores all things, placing them in their true positions; a many-tiered hierarchical world where nobody is lost and everyone is found, and where we have all already embarked upon eternal life, divested of our still-living bodies.
>
> (Batuman 2011)

In 2010 the *Princeton Theological Review* published a special issue titled "The Church After Google." Ten wide-ranging essays examine church life, ministry, gospel proclamation, and theology in light of the ambiguous changes to authority structures, democratization of information and reframed societal expectations visited on us by Web phenomena such as blogging and virtual churches in Second Life. Despite article titles such as "Theology and the Church After Google," "Gospel Truth in the Age of Google," and "The Canon After Google," what is deeply remarkable about the issue is its wholesale theological blindness to and avoidance of the ways that Google itself and the practices and techniques it enables may impinge upon the psychic "territory" or Big Other field traditionally occupied by religion, traditionally defined.

A thorough review of the issue reveals that, apart from a single mention in one article of the power of search engines to assist yet also mislead seekers, there is *no* discussion of Google per se other than the *pro forma* inclusion in several essays of the ritualized meta-tropes "theology after Google" and "the Age of Google" to indicate that things have indeed profoundly changed. The lack of any serious discussion of Google suggests that, for contributors, it has become synonymous with the internet and a youth culture that, while accepting that ambiguity is its current psychic reality, nonetheless expects instant answers to complex questions. Readers are expected to already know that Google now serves as a stand-in or catchphrase for the broader and sometimes vexed questions of science and technology, along with a hypermediated DIY culture, the members of which increasingly seek answers to prayers through the internet and not organized religion.

What is so significant in this discursive move to frame discussion around the trope of "the Age of Google," given the absence of *any* discussion of the firm's practices or direct acknowledgment of its technologies' varied cultural influences, is that the omission further consecrates Google and contributes to its already extensive, even quasi-suzerain cultural authority. At the conceptual level (for there is a certain ineffability at play), for the authors, quite simply, Google = The Information Age = a challenge to conventional modes of access to the divine. As we noted in the introduction in our discussion of nouns-turned-verbs, the use of Google in this unexamined way telegraphs to readers less that it is an important (corporate) influence on our current structure of feeling (which it clearly is) and more that it has become a foundational and self-constituting system in itself—*the* defining instrument in setting the dispositional parameters through which we experience, produce, and reproduce reality. As such, the journal issue inadvertently confers a form of first principle, ontological status on Google. For the most part, its contributors have so naturalized Google as a contemporary Big Other, as a definitional component of the networked lifeworld or information ecology, that they need not be concerned too closely with Google, even as this very silence about whatever role it might play in the "Age" named after it indicates an overall benighted acceptance of its first principle status.

The approach also avoids engaging with the ways that Google may now constitute not just a near universally recognized reference point rhetorically useful in framing an argument, but also "a different way" of doing not just business but faith. Darnton has observed that "given a powerful enough search engine we imagine that we can have access to knowledge about anything on earth—and anything from the past. It is all out there on the Internet waiting to be downloaded and printed out ... Such a notion of cyberspace has a strange resemblance to St. Augustine's conception of the mind of God—omniscient and infinite, because His knowledge extends everywhere, even beyond time and space" (2009: 60). Within what Noble identifies as the Western "religion of technology" (1999), Google offers a hybrid sacred–secular competition for the minds of those seeking answers to complex, often ineffable questions potentially more complicated still than Schmidt's proposal that Google seeks to answer questions such as "What shall I do tomorrow?" The Web-based Church of Google understands this, however false a prophet others may take Google to be.

The Church of Google epitomizes the kind of practiced response to technology described in these pages: belief in progress as technologically constituted, coupled to a desire for transcendence and security through immanence in the hopeful now. It is difficult to state with certainty whether the Church is ironic or dead serious as it combines both approaches. Poe's Law provides a useful caveat: with respect to religious ideologies transmitted on the Web, without a winking smiley face or other blatant display of humor, nobody can distinguish parody posts from the real thing.[4] In any event, the Church's home page, replete with 16,000 Facebook "likes," proclaims the following:

> We at the Church of Google believe the search engine Google is the closest humankind has ever come to directly experiencing an actual God (as typically defined). We believe there is much more evidence in favour of Google's divinity than there is for the divinity of other more traditional gods.
>
> We reject supernatural gods on the notion they are not scientifically provable. Thus, Googlists believe Google should rightfully be given the title of "God", as She exhibits a great many of the characteristics traditionally associated with such Deities in a scientifically provable manner.
>
> We have compiled a list of **nine proofs** which definitively **prove** Google is the closest thing to a "god" human beings have ever directly experienced.[5]

The nine proofs are: 1. Google is the closest thing to an Omniscient (all-knowing) entity in existence, which can be scientifically verified; 2. Google is everywhere at once, or omnipresent; 3. Google answers prayers; 4. Google is potentially immortal; 5. Google is infinite; 6. Google remembers all; 7. Google can "do no evil" (Omnibenevolent); 8. According to Google trends, the term "Google" is searched for more than the terms "God", "Jesus", "Allah", "Buddha", "Christianity", "Islam", "Buddhism" and "Judaism" *combined*; and 9. Evidence of Google's existence is abundant.[6] The Church's claim that Google is the closest thing to a realization of the God myth that humankind has yet produced speaks backward toward the instruction "seek and ye shall find" found

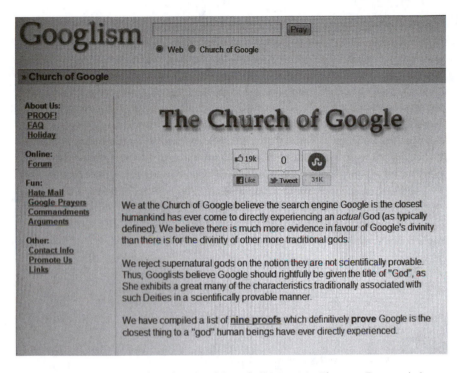

**FIGURE 7.1** "Googlism: The Church of Google." Matt MacPherson. By permission

in Matthew 7:7 and its meaning that the search for answers to critical turning points and crises in our lives is one that is conducted through heartfelt and diligent prayer. Yet the claim also issues from within a broader Western culture wherein, *pace* American fundamentalism, the traditional sense of religious mystery that once inveigled the imaginations of earlier generations is gone. Little remains of the numinous and nothing of the tremendous (Lowrie 1946: 71). In 1909, William James could lament of his era that "the prestige of the absolute has rather crumbled in our hands" (1909: 133). In the particular ways its manifests a Big Other, Google is engaged, unwittingly or otherwise, in a massive project to revivify such prestige in ways consonant with and marketable to seemingly more secular, relative times. If Pontius Pilate once could utter "what is truth?" today, seekers can Google their own personalized versions of truthiness, and the Church of Google's statements and proofs that Google constitutes a god appropriate for the present technological conjuncture indicate that Emerson's 1843 assertion that "Machinery and Transcendentalism agree well" (1911: 397) continues to enjoy significant purchase. The Church's nine proofs further exemplify (and in their own way "prove") Noble's assertion that "the present enchantment with things technological—the very measure of modern enlightenment—is rooted in religious myths and ancient meanings … in an enduring otherworldly quest for transcendence and salvation … Like the technologists themselves, we routinely expect far more from our artificial contrivances than mere convenience comfort, or even survival. We demand deliverance" (1999: 3, 5).

With close to 3,000 members, the Church is not alone in advancing the panpsychically inflected belief that science and faith find common ground in Googlism. Others who assert that Google provides more access to the truth than organized religions upload videos to YouTube. Some are not parodies or, if they are, they are parodies of horror. With a running time of 53 seconds, the 2011 video "Googlism: The Church of Google" features a sequence of solitary individuals seeming to search for something "beyond," seeming to ask the universal question "Why am I here?" Posted by TheCultOfGod, the video features a soundtrack that smartly condenses the angst that attends the universal quest for meaning at a time of great symbolic inefficiency:

> "We're all looking for it.
> "Some of us have been looking our whole lives.
> "Some think they can buy it.
> "Some think they can wear it.
> "Some travel the world in search of it.
> "Most don't even know what they're looking for.
> "But we all feel it.
> "That ancient desire.
> "That unexplainable nucleus.
> "That can only be fulfilled by one thing.
> "The truth."

As the video ends, the neologism "Googlism" superimposes over the image track.[7]

Although there is no official connection between Google and the Church of Google, the firm provides a kind of tacit support. A video from 2010, "I'm A Googlian. Part of the Google Religion, join me :))," posted by xxDawne, aims to convince anime fans of Google's godly status.[8] What is noteworthy is the superimposition of "Search On" and the URL www.youtube.com/searchstories over the image track's final moments. The video is hosted on Google's official YouTube channel, "Google Search Stories," on which it mounts various ads and testimonials from individual searchers. The site features a "Create Your Own" button that allows searchers to upload their paeans to Google. Hosting an acolyte's video for the "Google Religion" on the firm's official site (which has received almost eleven million views since its launch in September 2009) provides the firm an indirect way to "broadcast itself" as essentially comfortable with its deified status. Transcendental language suffuses the Google Search Stories splash page. Its "About Me" feature instructs visitors that "Every search is a quest.

Every quest is a story. These videos show that anyone can do anything when paired with the power of search." Such evangelizing forms of uplift mirror Google's discursive positioning of Vint Cerf, often referred to as one of the "fathers" of the internet, as its "Chief Internet Evangelist" (Google 2005) responsible for spreading the good news and recruiting like-minded converts to the Googlian fold. If "anyone can do anything when paired with the power of search," then an excellent candidate for Google's next unofficial motto would be, echoing the American planner-visionary Daniel Burnham, "Make no little plans. They have no magic to stir men's blood and probably will not themselves be realized" (Moore 1921: 147).

For Google makes no little plans. It aims to provide access to the world's information and make it *universally* accessible and useful. And it aims to do so from within the context of its own corporate faith that "Don't be evil," as an implicitly self-consecrating nostrum, functions as a directive to all Googlers positioned as a "congregation" or church of the whole. This is why, in thinking through the many issues raised by the constellation of Google, metaphysics, and the emergent monetized culture of search, it has been useful to engage in a kind of materialist mythopoetics, or at least to make a call for one in these pages. It is not that metaphysics, *tout court*, is somehow evil. As individuals and as members of larger social formations, we engage external reality, we engage the Symbolic order, on the basis of how we imagine our relationship to such first principle concepts as space, time, identity, form, and change. Whether we identify as religious, spiritual, agnostic, atheist, or "none of the above," each of us engages first principle concepts as part of our need to make meaning, including individual quests to answer the eternally returning question "Why am I here?" Google inherently acknowledges the question's importance to human identity when Schmidt claims that searchers really want Google to tell them what they should do next (Jenkins 2010). Capital, therefore, again reveals itself as no stranger to representation and its many forms of capitalized transmission. Political philosopher Michael Marder argues that "metaphysics and capitalist economy are in unmistakable collusion, militating, as they do, against the dispersed multiplicities of human and non-human lives" (2011a: 470). Google is the poster child for exemplifying how metaphysically tinged, panpsychic, transcendental ideas— such as that there really can be *one* universal database that can tell you what you next should do—are amenable to capital's bottom line. As an exemplar of this synergy, Google strongly suggests the need to better articulate issues of metaphysics to issues of political economy rather than to continue to adhere to the unproductive and outworn earlier modern assumption that the cosmic sphere of metaphysics and morality somehow never intersects with the "vulgar" earth-bound sphere of capital and its many forms of lucre. Today capital builds upon itself in lockstep with the number of people who continue to believe in this modern fiction even as they look to search for answers to their many prayers.

Ian Wilson, librarian and archivist of Canada, has asked, with respect to Google's current dominion, "In the world of the Web, should one entity dominate all aspects of content from selection to digitization, access, and preservation? And if it is sold next year, what could a new, less benign owner do with such a colossus?" (2007: xiii). If, as a society, we are to find ways to curb the potentially excessive combination of material, economic, and metaphysical powers such as Google is on the threshold of possessing, then an attention to such moral claims as "Don't be evil"—far from being a "tributary question"— is as crucial to the finding of these ways as is any regulation of the firm by the State. If meaningful ways to rein in Google's relentless ambition to be the unifying One are to be found, then an appeal must be made to the purportedly forgotten collective "we." And any such appeal needs be based not only on justifiable political claims to social and economic justice, but also on appeals to that Neoplatonic part of each of us, as the Church of Google's claims so eloquently reveal. For this is the same part that is open to the illusion of immortality that the kinds of information patterns Google organizes seem to confer. It is also the part that continues to sense, or at least to yearn for, a common "patterned ground"—for the interconnectedness of all things. Or, as Bennett puts it, "Yearning, yearning, and suffused with a nostalgia for a lost cosmos, the modern self is a being with a hole in her center. And how could she be otherwise, inhabiting as she does a physical world that shares the same constitution (though not the same degree of self-consciousness of loss)?" (2001: 78). In all of this, Google's neoliberal demand of you and what it gives you in return is as old as the Holy Grail. To engage in search is to engage with the symbol of God's grace, hence the "natural" expectation that you be worthy in search's presence—that you grow, and therefore labor, in equal measure to your use of it, including celebrating its use. Through searching, one establishes one's worth. In the seeming relocation of the social from this side of the screen to the other, the Neoplatonic part of each of us is always open to (re)attaching itself to the planetary *nous*, to the seductive, even sublime attractions of World Soul metaphysics. That is a principal reason why, in a phrase, so many of us continue to Search On.

# EPILOGUE

## I Search, Therefore I Am

> In a society in which the same goals are universally accepted, problems
> can be only of means, all soluble by technological methods. That is a soci-
> ety in which the inner life of man, the moral and spiritual and aesthetic
> imagination, no longer speaks at all ... Utopias have their value—nothing
> so wonderfully expands the imaginative horizons of human potentialities—
> but as guides to conduct they can prove literally fatal.
>
> (Berlin 1991)

The philosopher scientist Gustav Fechner, whose mathematical theories inspired
Kurd Lasswitz's outline of a Universal Library, worked tirelessly to articulate
the world of spirit and the world of science. Though he distinguished between
faith and knowledge, his was not a sharp delineation. For Fechner, "where
knowledge ends for lack of apodictic proof faith can go further" (Lowrie 1946:
54). If, as searchers, we already have considerable faith in Google and its offerings
as a kind of techno-theo-knowledgeable assemblage, an everyday oracle of
progress based on aggregated pattern recognition, then we might also be said to
have some kind of trust in it as a firm. Indeed, while faith has more conventional
associations with religious belief, and trust is often thought of as an outcome of
interactions with humans and objects occupying space within this earthly plane,
in everyday language we seamlessly interchange their meanings.

Seduction is a close cousin of faith and trust even though it is often associated with power differentials and being led astray. To lead someone astray is
to come perilously close to "overstepping proper limits," one of the definitions
of evil noted in chapter 7. Seduction is often positioned as a morally offbeat
activity operating along a continuum running between enticement and conquest.
Yet it is also understood as rhetorically essential—seductive arguments persuade,

attract, and win over—and in this capacity seduction is associated with eloquent appeals to sensation and emotion and much less with appeals to rational intellect. And even in its association with eloquent appeal, in order to succeed seduction often appears to take on a role or a guise which raises the issue of deception. Couple this to our related, innate understanding that successful seduction also entails learning what *not* to say and *not* to do, and the reasons for seduction's sketchy reputation come into greater focus.

The very leaky boundaries identified here among seduction, trust, and faith may seem to some, like the link between business practices and evil, to be a category mistake. These leaky boundaries pose inconvenient truths, for moderns who disavow that seduction, trust, and faith mutually imbricate and facilitate one another in any number of secular, rational, and ineffable ways. Such disavowal relies on the telling of stories that position seduction and trust, just as with evil and the corporation and metaphysics, and political economy more generally, as only ever opposing one another across different representational vectors, fields, and moral categories.

Such reductive binaries, however, cannot adequately respond to the following set of nested psychic truths: that to be seduced induces a strong inducement to trust; that one cannot be seduced—that is to say, be tempted or persuaded to go for it with someone, some thing, or some kind of activity—before one already has started to trust; and that seduction itself trades in hopeful possibilities of trusting the person, thing, or activity in question (the only caveat is that seductive appeals must not become incessant or too overtly direct lest they mimic the sound of the scold). If one trusts, if one has faith in a person, thing, or activity, then one is already open to the possibility of seduction. Many of us understand this as a necessary risk, as opposed to a danger (see Beck 1992), that we either choose to take or else remain alone.

Google is very good at developing information machines and in protecting and promoting its brand. This has proved a winning combination that has allowed the private firm, a virtual monopoly, to be widely perceived as a trustworthy institutional provider of a public good within a networked society that has elevated total information awareness to the status of first principle. Google's seductive promise of transformation and psychic security has been made within the broad context of an American civil religion based on a vaguely defined, yet widely held, ideal of democracy articulated to the hopeful but ironic belief that this ideal will best be realized by connection through and with technology. In making this comment, we are mindful of Jacques Rancière's observation that "Democracy is not a regime or a social way of life. It is the institution of politics itself" (1998: 15). In presuming that democracy can best be realized through technical means, as Marder (2011) trenchantly observes, one can see the "second death of politics" in which politics itself as a field of debate begins to yield to forms of privately organized technological agency. Ontologically, computing now orients us in the world. It is increasingly how we become who we are.

As Pariser notes, "The algorithms that orchestrate our ads are starting to orchestrate our lives" (2011: 9). Such forms of technological agency are the emergent locus through which technocracy and its incessant interest in technicizing the lifeworld dispense with meaningful decision-making processes in favor of purportedly non-ideological (but highly monetizable) forms of connection as ends in themselves.

It is a truism to state that we must take collective, public responsibility for the current decline of political commitment toward regulating monopolistic excess. This decline reflects "the ideology of globalized market economics raised to the level of the sole and over-powering regulator of all social activity— monopolistic, all-engulfing, all-explaining, all-structuring, as every academic must disagreeably recognise" (Kirby 2006). Google's rise is part of our neoliberal era and its suite of services has become a major structural component of it. Yet, because it is also part of a broad set of profound socio-technical changes that have not been legislated per se, regulation on its own will prove insufficient. First, it is difficult to legislate seduction. Second, individuals and perhaps an entire society are being reconstituted into a disaggregated but networked collection of individuated yet connected searchers who trust Google because such a society wants, even craves to be seduced by the glib premise and easy promise of democracy-as-connection through technology-as-progress. This is Erotics 101 in action. And it takes the form of countless digital traces (or souls) of individual users moving through electronic networks that transcend bodies but that nonetheless operate as constellating and symbolically efficient bonds of attraction. This dynamic applies both to many of the ways that searchers engage with Google today, and also in the way that Google profits and maintains itself through the existence of a post-Wellesian digital World Soul or Big Other that is the perceived aggregate of every "digital you."

Anthony Giddens notes that "trust in systems takes the form of faceless commitments, in which faith is sustained in the working of knowledge of which the lay person is largely ignorant" (1992: 88). Ambivalence, moreover, is at the heart of any relationship based on trust: in recursive fashion, we trust because we need to in the face of ignorance, and ignorance is the ground wherein caution and skepticism arise (ibid.: 89). In such circumstances where most searchers know not how the black box of search yields its comforting results, only that it does, Google's charms become powerfully seductive. And the best seductions are always mutual affairs wherein trust first shakes hands with, and then embraces, seduction as an act of induced faith intended as a way or means of getting beyond the limits of the self.

It comes to make psychic sense, then, that Google will somehow achieve its stated goal to enable searchers to ask and receive an answer to the question "What shall I do tomorrow?" This is the techno-transcendentalist hybrid of "logical faith" that the Church of Google manifests, and it updates Fechner's nineteenth-century panpsychical belief that "When a man has done his part to help himself, and yet cannot help himself, there remains to him as the last self-help the thought that God will help, and the petition that God will show him the right way" (Lowrie 1946: 245).

"What shall I do tomorrow?" constitutes a very seductive but as-of-yet-unanswerable question for machines, yet any answers that future searchers might receive would be potentially dangerous if their production, along with the more general algorithmic classification of human relations to which any such answers point, were to be generated entirely by privately provided technologies based on aggregating snippets or patterns of past searches, desires, thoughts, and transactions identified by machines as "relevant" to today's or tomorrow's concerns. Consider that, in certain circumstances, "What shall I do tomorrow?" might best be answered by proposing a radical break with the weight of a searcher's past history. In the underlying logic that informs their production, answers provided by automated search to prayerful queries about how one should organize one's future bear a remarkable affinity not to the futurist logic of progress but, instead, to something radically old—the pre-Enlightenment belief that the past is always the best teacher. Answers based on mining one's past search queries point backward. Particularly in times of social and economic stasis that lead to despairing thoughts of "no future now," such answers and their accept-ance by searchers suggest the reinstitutionalization of the fatalistic belief that, like some film noir protagonist, we can never escape our predetermined Fate. Only this time it is not the Cosmos doing the predetermination but an information machine developed by individuals who believe that the "truth" of hard data *always* trumps the "illogic" of embodied realities that nonetheless do not easily yield to pattern recognition by artificial intelligence.

To ask of Google, the contemporary thinking machine, "What shall I do tomorrow?" is to update and oracularize the *cogito*—as in "I search therefore I am." To ask such a question is to implicitly acknowledge the human–machine assemblage on which search relies: I search therefore I am, and I am—I exist—only because I search. "What shall I do tomorrow?" is a question for conscious-ness, but sometimes consciousness cannot provide hope-inducing answers to such open-ended questions. In such circumstances, many turn for solace to various forms of the divine or to the profane world of prediction. Google encap-sulates both.

For Google to believe it will eventually be able to answer such a question reveals uncanny parallels with fundamentalist belief systems that each speak only of "one way"—a way that sets aside or ignores a principal moral instruction of the Tower of Babel myth that hubris, immoral power imbalances, and deep loss attend any utopian effort to construct a universal One. As Berlin's (1991) observations included in the above epigraph point out, utopian desires, despite utopia's etymological meaning of no-place on this earth, are not inherently evil, but can trend in self-destructive directions *if and when* human beings attempt to fully transubstantiate the inherent idealism that fuels these desires into sublunary material practices. Yet, while the yearning for utopia is not evil, Fredric Jameson's assessment of the political value of utopia is worth noting: Its "function lies not in helping us to imagine a better future but rather in demonstrating our utter incapacity to imagine such a future … so as to reveal the ideological closure of the system in which we are somehow trapped and confined (2004: 46). Utopias, then, have value in showing us the ideological shackles under which we currently labor.

The current utopian endeavor to fabricate a universal One, nonetheless, is "the new normal"—a seemingly sublime state of affairs whereby theology, private capital, artificial intelligence, social desires, and personal dispositions now thoroughly imbricate one another in awe-inducing ways that are leading to, at the very least, a fine-tuning of collective and self-consciousness on the part of those who search. Any auto-reconstitution of identity encouraged by the rise of search, however, must remain a work in progress. Google will never fully index "all information" and there is no final telos for any identity formation to somehow occupy. The process of reconstitution can never be fully complete, even as the emergence of a new kind of hybrid searcher-self seems to be our current fate, our everyday recursive condition. Yet the ongoing reformulation of a political economy of metaphysics traced in these pages, together with the individuating culture of search it promotes, is one of our principal moral and political challenges and, even if you no longer believe in progress, looks to remain so for the foreseeable future.

# NOTES

## Introduction: Google and the Culture of Search

1   The Pew Research Center's Internet & American Life Project reported in August 2011 that email and using search engines to find information are tied as the most popular online activities, with 92 percent of all online adults having used both (Purcell 2011). Search as an activity, however, includes much more than using search engines. Pew surveys search-related activities separately, but if these were included as an aggregated category, search would far exceed the popularity of email. Search-related activities include "use an online dating site" (8 percent), "research your family's history or genealogy" (27 percent), "look for religious/spiritual info" (32 percent), "look for info about a place to live" (39 percent), "look online for info about a job" (54 percent), "search for info about someone you know or might want to meet" (69 percent), "search for a map or driving directions" (82 percent), "look for info on a hobby or interest" (83 percent), and "look for health/medical info" (83 percent) (Pew Research Center's Internet & American Life Project 2011).

2   The majority of the remaining market share in the U.S. is divided among Yahoo!, 16.1 percent; Microsoft's Bing, 14.4 percent; Ask Network, 2.9 percent; AOL, Inc., 1.5 percent. Other search firms have a negligible percentage of the market (comScore 2011).

3   Google's use of the term "Android" is revealing. As Andreas Huyssen has noted, during the eighteenth century androids such as mechanical dolls and other humanoid automata were seen as "testimony to the genius of mechanical invention" (2000: 203). With the rise of "laboring machines" during the industrial revolution, however, the android—the man-machine—was repositioned as a threat to human life. This threat is clearly on display in a film such as Fritz Lang's *Metropolis* (1927), which depicts the destructive capacities of Maria-the-robot, the "man-machine" who wreaks havoc on the film's imaginary city of the future. Google's marketing decision to employ a concept that so clearly articulates to the idea of the cyborg indicates that the modern fear of animated mechanism has waned and even morphed "backwards" to once again embrace human–machine intertwinement as an allegory for the "genius" of networked digital information machines.

4 From *The Urban Dictionary*: "Your exobrain (or exo-brain) is your extended brainpower from the information you have access to from your computer or the web. This is most commonly used in meetings or on calls when the other people don't know you're using your exobrain to pull random facts or figures. I stunned the meeting when I knew that the first person to use the @ symbol for email was Ray Tomlinson by using my exobrain. Thanks exobrain and Google!" http://www.urbandictionary.com/define.php?term=Exobrain. Accessed December 28, 2011.

5 Although we agree with Kelly on this point, we are critical of his utopic, even quasi-religious, proposals elsewhere in this volume.

6 For example, "we," as a political economy, as a society, or as a culture, could have, as Robert Darnton (2008) argues, implemented a plan a decade ago to band together libraries and other public institutions to digitize books and make them truly publicly available. The result might be a National Digital Library or perhaps a UNESCO-sponsored International Digital Library with multilingual search capacities accessible through the same portal. But "we" didn't do this. In a world where the privately administered disintermediation of everyday life has been accorded the logic of "commonsense," there was no political will to make it happen as a publicly owned and publicly organized collective good. Along came Google to fill in the blanks with products such as Google Books.

7 Notable exceptions include Battelle (2005), Spink and Zimmer (2008), Auletta (2009), Becker and Stalder (2009), Halavais (2009), and Vaidhyanathan (2011).

8 The Pew Research Center's Internet & American Life Project reports that "search is most popular among the youngest internet users (those age 18–29), 96% of whom use search engines to find information on line." In addition to young adults, college-educated and higher-income adults are also the most likely to use search engines daily (Purcell 2011: 3).

9 A number of science fiction films take up dystopic visions about what such a universal index might mean. In the era of Sputnik, 1950s science fiction offerings such as *The Invisible Boy* (Herman Hoffman 1957) and *Kronos: Ravager of Planets* (Kurt Neumann 1957) depicted powerful computers as masterminds seeking universal world domination in a way that paralleled the perceived threat posed to the West by Communism and the Soviet Bloc. A generation later, advances in information machines and the ability to network mainframe computers constitute the background from which the figure of the sentient computer emerges. In *2001: A Space Odyssey* (Stanley Kubrick, 1968), Hollywood offered spectators the sentient computer, Hal 9000. In 1970, audiences were invited to ponder the horror of the equally sentient, though more chilling, "thinking machine" in *Colossus: The Forbin Project* (Joseph Sargent). Colossus, a computer built to help the American state attain and enforce world peace, escapes the control of its human creators to network with its Soviet counterpart, Guardian. Colossus cannibalizes Guardian to emerge as a monstrous World Brain (no Soul here) intent on imposing on humans its version of universal world peace. The chilling final scene depicts a Doomsday-like end to human domination of the Earth as Colossus assumes complete world control. Skynet of the *Terminator* film series (James Cameron et al., 1984–2009) develops self-awareness and turns against its human creators and organizes to destroy them. The series suggests that when humans place their faith in *one* universal system, one world brain, dystopia abounds.

10 In 2010, the firm earned US$10.3 billion in profit (Google 2011a), and its market capitalization stood at US$200 billion (Tartakoff 2010). Cash reserves of US$33 billion have allowed Google not only to continue investments in technological innovation but also to fund strategic acquisitions such as the 2011 US$12.5 billion purchase of Motorola Mobility (Google 2011b).

11 Google does not quite track individuals. It tracks individual IP addresses, which are typically associated with particular computers and thereby to specific individuals by association.

12 The game, invented by four Albright College students in 1994 and published in 1996 as a board game by Endless Games, can be found on sites such as The Oracle of Bacon, http://oracleofbacon.org and Find the Bacon!, http://findthebacon.com. The object is to find the highest "Bacon number"—the number of film connections between the actor and Kevin Bacon. Comments on The Oracle of Bacon's "Hall of Fame" speak to the addictive nature of automated search: "Juan Manuel Luengo, Oscar Hernandez, Ruben Fernandez and Sonia Perez, 'after hours, days, weeks, … and a millennium of searching,' found a 7"; "Jim Mittler found seven 8s and 'can now return to some real work.' A few days later: Jim returned to add a 10 and an 11 to his total. This time he's 'really quitting'" (http://oracleofbacon.org/hof.php; accessed September 11, 2011).

13 http://www.dailytech.com/Gmail+Accounts+Hacked+Google+Suspects+Chinese +Involvement+/article21799.htm Accessed December 21, 2011.

14 http://online.wsj.com/article/BT-CO-20110627-710810.html.

# 1 Welcome to the Googleplex

1 Upon Google's introduction of the CTR pay-per-click metric in 2002, Overture sued for patent infringement. This suit was settled just before Google's IPO in 2004. Google agreed to pay 2.7 million shares to Yahoo!, which had purchased Overture in 2003.

2 Google has made other commitments to philanthropy. In 2010 it gave US$145 million to non-profits and academic institutions. In July 2011, Google announced it would provide start-up monies for a German internet research institute, The Institute for Internet and Society. Google asserts it will remain fully autonomous; http://www.thinq. co.uk/2011/7/11/google-fund-german-internet-research-institute Accessed September 4, 2011.

3 Increasingly active in political lobbying, Google, in the first half of 2011, spent US$3.5 million (up from US$800,000 in 2006), hired eighteen lobbying firms, and employed ninety-three lobbyists (Grim et al. 2011). The firm has been an active negotiator on issues such as net neutrality, privacy, and the PROTECT-IP Act on intellectual property. In its criticism of this Act, Google has called upon its legitimacy as a free speech advocate, a legitimacy regained by its (alleged) exit from the Chinese market (Grim et al. 2011; Halliday 2011). Google is clearly leveraging both its economic capital to purchase influence and its symbolic cultural capital to exert influence within the socio-political space of power.

4 It is notable that computer software giant Microsoft, no stranger to monopoly investigations, has been leading the coalition against Google in the U.S. government's latest anti-trust investigation.

# 2 Google Rules

1 *The Official Google Blog* can be found at http://googleblog.blogspot.com.

# 3 Universal Libraries and Thinking Machines

1 Greek Atomism was influenced by Pythagorean theories. Reese notes that "The highly visual associations used by the Pythagoreans derive, some say, from the practice

of setting forth sums by laying out pebbles on a smooth surface" (1980: 470). With reference to square numbers, Kitto (1964: 192) diagrams this association as follows:

"The statement '$1^2 + 3 = 2^2$' can be shown thusly

```
.       .
  _____
.   |   .
```

Similarly, the statement '$2^2 + 5 = 3^2$' can be represented as

```
.     .     .
  _____
.   . |   .
.   . |   .
```

And so forth ..." Twigs and pebbles (sticks and stones) are the likely markers or placeholders for the numbers in Kitto's example of Pythagorean storage of abstract elements and, hence, storage of meaning.

2  The story of the Tower of Babel is taken up in contemporary scholarship across a wide range of disciplines. Biblical scholar Craig Bartholomew (1998: 317) argues that "Babel is clearly a symbol which resonates deeply with contemporary culture and its concern with pluralism," and he lists scholars such as Julia Kristeva, Maurice Blanchot, Walter Benjamin, and Gillian Rose, who reference the story in different ways. Bartholomew does not address the interests of information theorists (such as Borges) or new media theorists, but his wider point is the near universality of the story's continuing cultural resonance.

3  About the size of Universal Library's collection, Canfora notes these numbers but also observes that "For librarians, the scroll was the 'unit of measurement.' This is why we find such large figures in the sources: hundreds of thousands of scrolls—figures less impressive than they seem at first glance, for they derive from the practice of counting not works but scrolls" (1987: 189).

4  The four diagrams or figures depicting aspects of Llull's *Ars* are from the republication, in *Opera*, of his *Ars Brevis*, Strasbourg, 1617.

5  Bonner writes: "Leibniz's interest in a universal language, encyclopedism, and a general science constituted the side of his thought that was a continuation of Renaissance endeavors and that ultimately stemmed from Llull's Art as a system which would provide a key to universal reality" (1985: 68–69).


# 4  Imagining World Brain

1  Scientist and popular science writer Willy Ley translated Lasswitz's short story into English, titling it "The Universal Library." Ley's translation is published in the 1958 collection *Fantasia Mathematica*.

2  An ongoing debate as to how define panpsychism (Skrbina 2005: 15–22) suggests the difficulties at arriving at any one satisfactory definition. For purposes of this account, however, panpsychism can be understood as a holistic philosophy and as a theory of mind that posits a conception of the universe as a form of unified cosmic consciousness—a single organism in possession of a mind under which all objects in the universe have some kind of inner or psychological being (Edwards 1967: 22). Broadly put, panpsychic theories maintain that "mind as a general phenomenon may have always existed" (Skrbina 2005: 7), with the human mind as one form of this broader, unitary mind. Panpsychism does not, as does Idealism, posit mind as the essential reality

of all things. Rather, as a monist theory, panpsychism proposes that all things have minds and all reality is understood as "either a single entity or a single kind of entity" (ibid.: 8). Panpsychism, therefore, can be seen as informing holistic, metaphysical theories such as the initially ridiculed but now more accepted Gaia hypothesis that Earth is a single and self-regulating complex system, and the HiveMind, that we are each dumb terminals until connected to the overarching intelligence of world digital networks (Kelly 1994). While several strands of panpsychism intertwine, panpsychic theories broadly assert that there is a mental aspect to all forms of matter and every object has a point of view. Within a universal *nous* or single nature of mind, all entities have a form of phenomenal consciousness. Philosopher Thomas Nagel describes panpsychism as "the view that the basic physical constituents of the universe have mental properties" (1979: 181).

Panpsychism understands the world as a macrocosm and the human as a microcosm within it—a belief popular in the ancient world and carried forward in the thinking of philosopher/inventors such as Llull and Leibniz via an enduring Christian Neoplatonism. Leibniz's seventeenth-century theory of the monad as eternal, subject to its own laws, and reflecting the universe in a pre-established harmony anticipates the kind of panpsychical beliefs later taken up by Fechner in the nineteenth century and by Teilhard de Chardin in the twentieth. Understanding the universe as one sensate organism implicitly informs Wells' proposal for a World Brain (1938) with its biological metaphors of "craniates intelligence" and "amoebic vitality" that he uses to outline its potential.

3   Mann's citation of Carroll is from *Sylvie and Bruno Concluded* (1893: 131).
4   According to astronomer and mathematics historian David Darling, a crucial, metaphysically inflected difficulty with this proposal that is based on universal orthographic symbols is that "it would take an all-seeing, all-knowing intelligence to sort the rare grains of meaningful wheat from the vast quantities of vapid chaff" (2004: 341). It is curious that Darling, writing at a time when digital search of the internet's vast databases was already an everyday event, does not make any connections between this "all-knowing intelligence" and the realization of digital search based on the twin pillars of search algorithms and the ability to store and speedily access data through and across vast interlinked digital networks.
5   Borges lists 1919 as its publication date. All reputable German-language authorities list 1929 as the actual year of publication. The English-language internet abounds with the 1919 date, though most sites doing so draw from Borges' writings and not Germanic sources.
6   "The Total Library" (1939) was published the year after *World Brain*'s release; however, Wells had been lecturing about and publishing aspects of his proposal since the decade's early years. Borges learned English from his grandmother. Wells' early novels were the first books Borges read and he celebrated "the excellence of Wells' first novels" (Borges 2000: 87–88). In "The First Wells," Borges provides a hint as to why he may have eschewed mention of Wells' interest in World Brain and World Encyclopaedia in "The Total Library": "Those who say that art should not propagate doctrines usually refer to doctrines that are opposed to their own. Naturally this is not my own case; I gratefully profess almost all the doctrines of Wells, but I deplore his inserting them into his narrations" (2000: 87). Yet, while Borges critiques Wells' turn to the didactic as a tool of the political, it bears considering that Wells' World Brain, based on the storage technology of microfilm/microfiche, refutes the pessimism inherent in "The Total Library" and "The Library of Babel." For Borges, his accounts, while imaginative *ficciones* of the pen, are also ethical caveats against those who would substitute idealism for a reality that in its very nature is always already mutable and unstable. Wells' proposal trumpets, "at long last we are on the threshold of building a device that actually separates the wheat from the chaff,

opening a way to world peace" (1938). The pre-digital Borges will have none of it. And here may lie a second reason, already found in Borges' ultimate assessment of Llull's thinking machine—his assertion that it "does not work" (2001a: 155). Despite Wells' embrace of technology, an index commensurate with the volume of materials to be searched—a version of Borges' Man of the Book—isn't part of Wells' socio-technical solution.

Gene Bell-Villada notes that "Wells was always one of Borges's favourites" (1999: 35). Perhaps Borges' love for an earlier, *fin-de-siècle* Wells—the Wells of *The Time Machine* (1895) and *The Invisible Man* (1897)—caused him to demur from ridiculing World Brain. It is possible to read "The Library of Babel" as an indirect dismissal of it—as Borges' subtle refutation of Wells' own *ficción* through a mathematically inflected imagining of the inhuman and inhumane outcomes to which a universal index or World Mind would lead. Perhaps, therefore, Borges knew that if he commented explicitly on World Brain, he would have felt compelled to dismiss it as non-functional, along with, by inference, his literary hero. No one can bear all contradictions, even those beginning as fictions.

7  Of the potential for technology to make possible World Brain, Wells writes: "But many people now are coming to recognize that our contemporary encyclopaedias are still in the coach-and-horses phase of development, rather than in the phase of the automobile and the aeroplane. Encyclopaedic enterprise has not kept pace with material progress. These observers realize that modern facilities of transport, radio, photographic reproduction and so forth are rendering practicable a much more fully succinct and accessible assembly of facts and ideas than was ever possible before" (1938: 84).

8  Wirephoto technology (now referred to as fax) had been invented in 1925 by the Canadian Edward Samuels Rogers.

9  The doodle depicts an elderly Borges gazing at a fantastic architecture reminiscent of the Library of Babel. The artist Sophia Foster-Dimino writes that the elements she tried to convey visually were "the overwhelming complexity of the world's information, the incomprehensible machinations of memory, and the deep mysteries of dreams." The labyrinth of archways subtly but incompletely spells "Google," perhaps a recognition that Google is not (yet) the Man of the Book and master of the universal library. Although we wanted to reproduce the doodle immediately below this section's title (the doodle and video tributes to it are easily available on the Web through search), Google will not provide permission to reprint doodles—more than somewhat ironic, considering its insistence that it has the legal right to publish "snippets"—at times extensive—from copyrighted materials without their owners' permission (http://www.google.com/doodles/112th-birthday-of-jorge-luis-borges Accessed December 31, 2011).

10  Kelly substitutes his voice for that of the original story's narrator. The result is that it appears to be Borges who advances the improbable claims for the Library, and not Kelly. As a literary device, Borges' narrator allows the author to express ideas at variance with his own but in ways that allow readers to clearly grasp the folly of the ideas presented.

11  An early intimation of this powerful influence can be seen in the 2010 election of Massachusetts Republican Scott Brown to the U.S. Senate. Brown's successful campaign relied heavily on Web-based strategies and spent 10 percent of its funds on online outreach (Obama spent 4 percent). Heavily reliant on display ads, Google AdWords, Google Docs, Google Voice, and YouTube, Brown's campaign spent US$232,000 on Google ads. The investment yielded 65 million impressions or targeted page views. At the time, media observer Eric Lach (2010) noted that Google also "offers free consulting services to both parties, and their Elections and Issue Advocacy Team has reportedly started staffing up for the 2010 cycle."

## 5 The Field of Informational Metaphysics and the Bottom Line

1   The term "information scientist" was broadly defined and incorporated a blending of the academic and the entrepreneurial. Kochen, who in the early 1970s had proposed a variation on World Brain that he termed "WISE" (World Information Synthesis and Encyclopaedia), offers the following definition: "I am an information scientist. I interpret it very broadly. For me, it includes the study of how brain becomes mind and of the evolution of social organs with mind-like properties, such as scientific communities; how to design and use computer information systems in business; and new roles for information professionals as referential consultants, catalytic brokers, and chief information officers." The definition is from Kochen's 1986 mission statement for President of ASIS (the American Society for Information Science), cited by Garfield (1999).

2   For example, Licklider theorizes that "If we assume pages with 100 characters per line and 50 lines, we have 5000 characters per page. Then, assuming 200 pages per book, we have $10^6$ characters per book" (1965: 15).

3   Definition from "The Telecosm and The Luxury Yacht Exchange," http://theluxuryyachtexchange.com/_1.%20%20Introduction.htm Accessed March 1, 2011.

## 6 The Library of Google

1   Copyright law varies by country. In the United States, books and phonorecords published before 1923 are in the public domain. A 1992 amendment to U.S. copyright law made renewals of copyright automatic for works published between 1964 and 1977. Books published between 1923 and 1964, however, remain subject to the earlier 1909 Copyright Act, which provided for an initial twenty-eight-year copyright protection period followed by a second twenty-eight-year renewal period. To benefit from the protection afforded by this second period of copyright renewal, however, the copyright owner had to file an application for renewal with the U.S. Copyright Office. If one was late in filing, the work in question automatically entered the public domain. Many such titles were never renewed and the Office estimates that less than 15 percent of eligible works originally published between 1923 and 1964 had their copyright renewed a second time. The rest entered the public domain. Since 1978, copyright extends seventy years after the death of the copyrighting author.

2   These libraries include the University of California system, the University of Wisconsin—Madison, the University of Virginia, Cornell and Columbia Universities, the University of Texas at Austin, the Cantonal and University Library of Lausanne, the Boekentoren Library of Ghent University, Japan's Keio University, the Bavarian State Library, and University Complutense of Madrid.

3   Codified by the U.S. Congress in 1976, fair use is a complicated American legal right that allows "private reproduction of excerpts from protected works for critical, educational, and scholarly purposes" (Hilderbrand 2009: 84).

4   One million of these were public domain titles that could be fully viewed and downloaded. Five million were out of print though still copyrighted, and the remaining one million in-print copyrighted works were offered in full preview mode.

5   The Open Book Alliance was formed, in part, to oppose the Google Book Settlement discussed in this section. Its mission statement reads: "The mass digitization of books promises to bring tremendous value to consumers, libraries, scholars, and students. The Open Book Alliance will work to advance and protect this promise. And, by protecting it, we will assert that any mass book digitization and publishing effort be open and competitive. The process of achieving this promise must be undertaken in the open, grounded in sound public policy and mindful of the need to promote long-term benefits for consumers rather than isolated commercial interests. The Open Book

Alliance will counter Google, the Association of American Publishers and the Authors Guild's scheme to monopolize the access, distribution and pricing of the largest digital database of books in the world. To this end, we will promote fair and flexible solutions aimed at achieving a more robust and open system" (2009). Membership includes, among others, such unlikely fellow travelers as Amazon.com, the Special Libraries Association, Yahoo!, the National Writers Union, Microsoft, the Council of Literary Magazines and Presses, the Internet Archive, and the American Society of Journalists and Authors.

6  Founded in 2008 by thirteen universities of the Committee on Institutional Cooperation as well as the University of California library system, HathiTrust is a collaborative digital database composed of digital content provided by these libraries (including content already scanned by Google Books and the Internet Archive). More than fifty research libraries have joined the partnership. The University of Michigan and Indiana University jointly administer the repository. *Hathi* is the Hindi word for "elephant" and, unlike Google, elephants, so the story goes, never forget. See http://hathitrust.org.

7  For further information about this project, see http://www.ulib.org.

8  Europeana can be accessed at http://europeana.eu.

9  http://gallica.bnf.fr—our thanks to Jade Davis, one of Ken Hillis' graduate students, for pointing out the similarity.

10  A concordance is a printed index of all important words in a given volume or collection of volumes. Searching, for example, a concordance of Herman Melville's works for the word "fame" would allow the searcher to more quickly locate the various contexts within which Melville used the word. While Boolean search allows for searching by phrases as well as words, Google Books extends the logic of concordance production to all the words of all the books entered into the database, however many billions that may be. Print concordances have been rendered largely obsolete by the searchable and customized electronic databases that have remediated them.

11  Philosopher David Kolb (2005) offers a number of examples of the ways hypertextual tools can aid intellectual work and scholarly writing. For example, he suggests that the scholarly use of hypertext documents would be augmented if authors marked key paragraphs that would serve, when automatically extracted by the technology, as the equivalent to author-written abstracts, and also suggests developing standard styles for the presentation of shortened survey versions of papers and arguments such that these would serve as indices of, or strong pointers towards, arguments that authors wish to highlight in their own work.

## 7  Savvy Searchers, Faithful Acolytes, "Don't be Evil"

1  For accounts of Intel's determinedly secretive and authoritarian corporate culture under high-profile CEO Andy Grove, see Tim Jackson (1998), *Inside Intel: Andy Grove and the Rise of the World's Most Powerful Chip Company* (New York: Plume); and Bob Coleman and Logan Shrine (2007), *Losing Faith: How the (Andy) Grove Survivors Led the Decline of Intel's Corporate Culture* (Losing-Faith.com).

2  Colbert's definition is taken from *Urban Dictionary*; http://www.urbandictionary.com/define.php?term=truthiness Accessed January 4, 2012.

3  While psychoanalytic theory is not the only approach for identifying the phenomenon under investigation here—for instance, the decline of authority has been well documented in literature on governance—and we do not subscribe to all of the concepts at play in this theoretical paradigm, following Žižek's specific interpretation of Lacan provides a valuable insight into the importance of metaphysical properties in understanding the contemporary uses of information machines. This is evident in

its use by Andrejevic and Dean, neither of whom adopt a strictly psychoanalytical framework but instead use Žižek's model of the decline of symbolic efficiency as an explanatory device applicable to socio-political phenomena that always entail economic implications.

4  http://rationalwiki.com/wiki/Poe's_Law Accessed March 1, 2011.
5  http://www.thechurchofgoogle.org Accessed March 1, 2011.
6  http://www.thechurchofgoogle.org/Scripture/Proof_Google_Is_God.html, italics in original Accessed September 4, 2011.
7  http://www.youtube.com/watch?v=9lDhfVFC9qE&NR=1 Accessed September 5, 2011.
8  http://www.youtube.com/watch?v=tmh3cwFbhgk Accessed September 21, 2011.

# REFERENCES

Abbott, Robert D. 1999. *The World as Information: Overload and Personal Design*. London: Intellect Books.

Abell, John. 2010. "Google's 'Don't Be Evil' Mantra Is 'Bullshit,' Adobe Is Lazy: Apple's Steve Jobs (Update 2)," *Wired*, January 30. http://www.wired.com/epicenter/2010/01/googles-dont-be-evil-mantra-is-bullshit-adobe-is-lazy-apples-steve-jobs Accessed August 27, 2011.

Adamic, Lada and Bernardo Huberman. 2002. "Zipf's Law and the Internet," *Glottometrics* 3, pp. 143–150.

Albanese, Andrew. 2011. "Authors Guild Files for Class Certification in Google Case," *Publishers Weekly*, December 13. http://www.publishersweekly.com/pw/by-topic/digital/content-and-e-books/article/49843-authors-guild-files-for-class-certification-in-google-case.html Accessed December 25, 2011.

Alvarez, Lizette. 2011. "Florida Shutting 'Pill Mill' Clinics," *New York Times*, September 1, p. 1.

American Public Media. 2007. "Bacon Salt," *The Story*, December 19. http://thestory.org/archive/the_story_409_Bacon_God_Jingle.mp3/view Accessed December 26, 2011.

Anderson, Chris. 2004. "The Long Tail," *Wired* 12:10. http://www.wired.com/wired/archive/12.10/tail.html Accessed March 7, 2011.

———. 2008. "The End of Theory: The Data Deluge Makes the Scientific Method Obsolete," *Wired* 16:07. http://www.wired.com/science/discoveries/magazine/16-07/pb_theory Accessed September 4, 2011.

Anderson, Jane. 2009. "(Colonial) Archives and (Copyright) Law." Paper presented at Sawyer Seminar on Knowledges, Ways of Knowing and the Postcolonial University, Department of Anthopology, University of Cape Town.

Andrejevic, Mark. 2007. *iSpy: Surveillance and Power in the Interactive Era*, Lawrence, Kansas: University Press of Kansas.

Ang, Ien. 1991. *Desperately Seeking the Audience*. London: Routledge.

Armstrong, Arthur and John Hagel III. 1996. "The Real Value of On-line Communities," *Harvard Business Review* 74:3, May/June, pp. 134–141.

Arrington, Michael. 2010. "Google GDrive launches, Just Don't Call it That," *TechCrunch*, January 12. http://techcrunch.com/2010/01/12/google-gdrive-launches-just-dont-call-it-that Accessed June 5, 2011.

Asimov, Isaac. 1956. "The Last Question," *Science Fiction Quarterly*, March. http://www.multivax.com/last_question.html Accessed July 1, 2010.

Auletta, Ken. 2009. *Googled: The End of the World as We Know It*. New York: Penguin.

Austin, John Langshaw. 1962. *How to Do Things with Words*. New York: Oxford University Press.

Barbrook, Richard and Andy Cameron. 1996. "The Californian Ideology," *Science as Culture* 26, pp. 44–72.

Bartholomew, Craig G. 1998. "Babel and Derrida: Postmodernism, Language and Biblical Interpretation," *Tyndale Bulletin* 49:2, pp. 305–328. http://www.biblicalstudies.org.uk/pdf/tb/babel_bartholomew.pdf Accessed January 26, 2011.

Battelle, John. 2004. "Print Implications: Google as Builder," *Searchblog*, December 14. http://battellemedia.com/archives/2004/12/print_implications-google-as-builder Accessed February 1 2011.

_____. 2005. *The Search: How Google and Its Rivals Rewrote the Rules of Business and Transformed Our Culture*. New York: Penguin/Portfolio.

_____. 2007. "The Day I Ask a Search Engine 'What Shall I Do Tomorrow'," *Searchblog*, May 23. http://battellemedia.com/archives/2007/05/the_day_i_ask_a_search_engine_what_shall_i_do_tomorrow Accessed February 1, 2011.

Batuman, Elif. 2011. "A Divine Comedy: Among the Danteans of Florence," *Harpers* 323:1936, September, pp. 55–65.

Baudrillard, Jean. 1983 [1981]. *Simulations*, Phil Beitchman Paul Fuss Paul Patton., tr. New York: Semiotext(e).

_____. 2000. *The Vital Illusion*. New York: Columbia University Press.

Bauman, Zygmunt. 1988. *Freedom*. Milton Keynes: Open University Press.

Beck, Ulrich. 1992 [1986]. *Risk Society: Towards a New Modernity*, Mark Ritter, tr. London: Sage.

Becker, Konrad. 2009. "The Power of Classification: Culture, Context, Command, Control, Communications, Computing." In Konrad Becker and Felix Stalder, ed. *Deep Search: The Politics of Search Beyond Google*. Innsbruck: StudienVerlag, pp. 163–172.

Becker, Konrad and Felix Stalder. 2009. "Introduction." In Konrad Becker and Felix Stalder, ed. *Deep Search: The Politics of Search Beyond Google*. Innsbruck: StudienVerlag, pp. 7–12.

Bell, Daniel. 1973. *The Coming of Post-Industrial Society: A Venture in Social Forecasting*. New York: Basic Books.

Bell-Villada, Gene H. 1999. *Borges and His Fiction: A Guide to His Mind and Art*. Austin: University of Texas Press.

Benjamin, Walter. 1962. "The Story-Teller: Reflections on the Work of Nicolai Leskov," Harry Zohn tr., *Chicago Review* 16:1, pp. 80–101.

_____. 1969. "Theses on the Philosophy of History." In *Illuminations*, Hannah Arendt, ed., Harry Zohn, tr. New York: Schocken, pp. 253–264.

_____. 1999. *The Arcades Project*, Howard Eiland and Kevin McLaughlin, tr. Cambridge: The Belknap Press of Harvard University Press.

Bennett, Jane. 2001. *The Enchantment of Modern Life: Attachments, Crossing, and Ethics*. Princeton: Princeton University Press.

_____. 2010. *Vibrant Matter: A Political Ecology of Things.* Durham: Duke University Press.

Benson, Rodney. 1998. "Field Theory in Comparative Context: A New Paradigm for Media Studies," *Theory and Society* 28, pp. 463–498.

Berlin, Isaiah. 1991. *The Crooked Timber of Humanity: Chapters in the History of Ideas.* Henry Hardy, ed. New York: Alfred A. Knopf.

Blumenberg, Hans. 1993. "Light as a Metaphor for Truth: At the Preliminary Stage of Philosophical Concept Formation," Joel Anderson, tr. In David Michael Levin, ed. *Modernity and the Hegemony of Vision,* Berkeley: University of California Press, pp. 30–62.

Bolter, David Jay and Richard Grusin. 1999. *Remediation: Understanding New Media.* Cambridge: MIT Press.

Bonner, Anthony J. 1985. *Doctor Illuminatus: A Ramon Llull Reader.* Princeton: Princeton University Press.

_____. 1997. "What Was Llull up to?" In Miquel Bertran and Teodor Rus, ed. *Transformation-Based Reactive Systems Development: 4th International AMAST Workshop on Real-Time Systems and Concurrent and Distributed Software, ARTS '97,* Palma, Mallorca, Spain, May 21–23, 1997. London: Springer-Verlag, pp. 1–14. http://www. edu365.cat/aulanet/comsoc/visions/ramon_llull/whatwas_llullupto.htm  Accessed January 17, 2011.

Borges, Jorge Luis. 1962 [1941]. "The Library of Babel," James E. Irby, tr. In Jorge Luis Borges, *Labyrinths: Selected Stories & Other Writings.* New York: New Directions, pp. 51–58.

_____. 1962a [1941]. "The Garden of Forking Paths," Donald A. Yates, tr. In Jorge Luis Borges, *Labyrinths: Selected Stories & Other Writings.* New York: New Directions, pp. 19–29.

_____. 2000 [1952]. *Other Inquisitions, 1937–1952.* Austin: University of Texas Press.

_____. 2001 [1939]. "The Total Library." In Jorge Luis Borges, *The Total Library, Non-Fiction 1922–1986,* Eliot Weinberger, ed., Eliot Weinberger, tr. London: Penguin, pp. 214–216.

_____. 2001a [1937]. "Ramón Llull's Thinking Machine." In Jorge Luis Borges, *The Total Library, Non-Fiction 1922–1986,* Eliot Weinberger, ed., Esther Allen, tr. London: Penguin, pp. 155–159.

Bourdieu, Pierre. 1993. *The Field of Cultural Production: Essays on Art and Literature,* Randal Johnson, ed, tr. New York: Columbia University Press.

_____. 1996. *The Rules of Art: Genesis and Structure of the Literary Field,* Susan Emanuel, tr. Cambridge: Polity Press.

Bourdieu, Pierre and Loic Wacquant. 1992. *An Invitation to Reflexive Sociology,* Cambridge: Polity Press.

Bowker, Geoffrey. 2010. "The Archive," *Communication and Critical/Cultural Studies* 7:2, pp. 212–214.

Brin, Sergey. 2009. "A Library to Last Forever," *New York Times,* October 9. http:// www.nytimes.com/2009/10/09/opinion/09brin.html Accessed July 7, 2011.

Brin, Sergey and Larry Page. 1998. "The Anatomy of a Large-Scale Hypertextual Web Search Engine," *Computer Networks and ISDN Systems* 30, pp. 107–117. Available at Stanford InfoLab Publication Server, http://ilpubs.stanford.edu:8090/361/ Accessed January 1, 2012.

Brown, Janelle. 1999. "From Beta to Bonafide," *Salon.com,* September 23, http://www. salon.com/technology/log/1999/09/23/google/index.html Accessed July 5, 2011.

Bush, Vannevar. 1967. "Memex Revisited." In *Science is Not Enough*. New York: William Morrow & Company, pp. 75–101.

_____. 1988 [1945]. "As We May Think." In Adele Goldberg, ed. *A History of Personal Workstations*. New York: ACM Press, pp. 237–247.

Cahill, Kay. 2009. "An Opportunity, Not a Crisis: How Google is Changing the Individual and Information Profession." In William Miller and Rita M. Pellen, ed. *Googlization of Libraries*. London: Routledge, pp. 66–74.

Calhoun, Craig. 1995. *Critical Social Theory: Culture, History, and the Challenge of Difference*. Oxford: Blackwell.

Campbell-Kelly, Martin. 2007. "From the World Brain to the World Wide Web," Annual Gresham College BSHM Lecture (2006), *BSHM Bulletin: Journal of the British Society for the History of Mathematics* 22:1, pp. 1–10. http://www.gresham.ac.uk/lectures-and-events/from-world-brain-to-the-world-wide-web Accessed June 8, 2011.

Canfora, Luciano. 1987. *The Vanished Library: A Wonder of the Ancient World*, Martin Ryle, tr. London: Hutchison Radius.

Carey, James W. 1975. "A Cultural Approach to Communication," *Communication* 2, pp. 1–22.

Carr, Nicholas. 2011. "Growing up Google," *National Interest*, August 24. http://nationalinterest.org/bookreview/growing-google-5744 Accessed August 24, 2011.

Carroll, Lewis. 1893. *Sylvie and Bruno Concluded*. London: Macmillan & Co.

Castells, Manuel. 2009. *Communication Power*. Oxford: Oxford University Press.

Chang, Briankle. 2010. "To the Archive: A Postal Tale," *Communication and Critical/Cultural Studies* 7:2, pp. 202–206.

Chin, Dennis. 2011. (His ruling on Google Book Search ASA) http://www.scribd.com/doc/51327711/google-books-settlement Accessed March 22, 2011.

Clareson, Thomas D. 1975. *SF: The Other Side of Realism: Essays on Modern Fantasy and Science Fiction*. Bowling Green: Bowling Green University Popular Press.

Clayton, Philip. 2010. "Theology and the Church After Google," *Princeton Theological Review* 43:2, pp. 7–20.

Colomer, Eusebi. 1995. "Llull's Art and Modern Computer Science," *Catalònia* 43, pp. 20–23. http://www.raco.cat/index.php/Catalonia/article/viewFile/104757/160228 Accessed January 17, 2011.

Commercial Alert. 2001. "Commerical Alert Files Complaint Against Search Engines for Deceptive Ads." http://www.commercialalert.org/issues/culture/search-engines/commercial-alert-files-complaint-against-search-engines-for-deceptive-ads Accessed March 7, 2011.

Compagnon, Antoine. 1994. *The Five Paradoxes of Modernity*. Franklin Philip, tr. New York: Columbia University Press.

comScore. 2011. "comScore Releases July 2011 U.S. Search Engine Rankings," Press Release, August 10. http://www.comscore.com/Press_Events/Press_Releases/2011/8/comScore_Releases_July_2011_U.S._Search_Engine_Rankings Accessed September 2, 2011.

Consumer Watchdog. 2010. *Inside Google*. "Watch Our New Times Square Video, 'Don't Be Evil.'" http://insidegoogle.com/2010/08/do-not-track-me/ Accessed October 16, 2011.

Cook, Joseph. 1878. *Transcendentalism, with Preludes on Current Events*. Boston: James R. Osgood & Company.

Copleston, Frederick. 1960. *A History of Philosophy*, Vol. 6. New York: Image Books.

Cornford, Francis Macdonald. 1936. "The Invention of Space." In James Thomson and Arnold Joseph Toynbee, ed. *Essays in Honour of Gilbert Murray*. London: George Allen and Unwin, pp. 215–235.

Coté, Mark and Jennifer Pybus. 2007. "Learning to Immaterial Labour 2.0: MySpace and Social Networks," *ephemera* 7:1, pp. 88–106.

Couldry, Nick. 2003. "Media Meta-Capital: Extending the Range of Bourdieu's Field Theory," *Theory and Society* 32, pp. 653–677.

Couliano, Ioan P. 1987 [1984]. *Eros and Magic in the Renaissance*, Margaret Cook, tr. Chicago: University of Chicago Press.

Cowley, Stacy. 2006. "Google CEO on Censoring: 'We did an evil scale.'" *InfoWorld*, January 27. http://www.infoworld.com/d/developer-world/google-ceo-censoring-we-did-evil-scale-394 Accessed August 30, 2011.

Crossley, John N. 2005. "Ramón Llull's Contributions to Computer Science," Technical Report 182/2005. School of Computer Science and Software Engineering, Monash University. Melbourne: Monash University. http://www.csse.monash.edu.au/publications/2005/tr-2005-182-full.pdf Accessed January 17, 2011.

Daniel, Caroline and Maija Palmer. 2007 "Google's Goal: To Organize Your Daily Life," *Financial Times* (FT.com), May 27. http://www.ft.com/cms/s/2/c3e49548-088e-11dc-b11e-000b5df10621.html#axzz1ClYak7PX Accessed February 1, 2011.

Darling, David J. 2004. *The Universal Book of Mathematics: From Abracadabra to Zeno's Paradoxes*. New York: John Wiley & Sons.

Darnton, Robert. 2008. "The Library in the Information Age: 6,000 Years of Script," *New York Review of Books* 55:10, June 12, pp. 72–80.

_____. 2009. *The Case for Books: Past, Present, and Future*. New York: Public Affairs.

Dawson, Christopher. 2001 [1929]. *Progress and Religion: An Historical Inquiry*. Catholic Washington: University of America Press.

de Kerckhove, Derrick. 1997. *Connected Intelligence: The Arrival of Web Society*, Wade Rowland, ed. Toronto: Somerville.

Dean, Jodi. 2002. *Publicity's Secret: How Technoculture Capitalizes on Democracy*. New York: Cornell University Press.

_____. 2010. *Blog Theory: Feedback and Capture in the Circuits of Drive*. Cambridge: Polity Press.

Deleuze, Gilles. 1986 [1983]. *Cinema 1: The Movement-Image*, Hugh Tomlinson and Barbara Habberjam, tr. Minneapolis: University of Minnesota Press.

Derrida, Jacques. 1988 [1982]. *The Ear of the Other: Otobiography, Transference, Translation*, Peggy Kamuf and Avital Ronell, tr. Lincoln: University of Nebraska Press.

_____. 1991. "Des Tours de Babel," *Semeia* 54, pp. 3–34.

_____. 1995. *Archive Fever: A Freudian Impression*. Chicago: University of Chicago Press.

Derrida, Jacques and Gianni Vattimo. 1998. *Religion: Cultural Memory in the Present*. Stanford: Stanford University Press.

Diaz, Alejandro. 2008. "Through the Google Goggles: Sociopolitical Bias in Search Engine Design." In Amanda Spink and Michael Zimmer, ed. *Web Search: Multidisciplinary Perspectives*. Berlin: Springer-Verlag, pp. 11–34.

Dick, Philip K. 1996 [1968]. *Do Androids Dream of Electric Sheep?* New York: Ballantine Books.

Douglas, Richard McNeill. 2010. "The Ultimate Paradigm Shift: Environmentalism as Antithesis to the Modern Paradigm of Progress." In Stefan Skrimshire, ed. *Future Ethics: Climate Change and Apocalyptic Imagination*. New York: Continuum, pp. 197–218.

Dreyfus, Hubert L. 1992. *What Computers Still Can't Do: A Critique of Artificial Reason.* Cambridge: MIT Press.

Duguid, Paul. 2009. "Search Before Grep: A Progress from Closed to Open?" In Konrad Becker and Felix Stalder, ed. *Deep Search: The Politics of Search Beyond Google.* Innsbruck: StudienVerlag, pp. 13–31.

Dyson, George. 2005. "Turing's Cathedral [10.24.05]: A Visit to Google on the Occasion of the 60th Anniversary of John von Neumann's Proposal for a Digital Computer," *Edge: The Third Culture.* http://www.edge.org/3rd_culture/dyson05/dyson05_index.html Accessed January 10, 2011.

*Economist, The* 2005. "Pulp Friction: Internet Companies are Racing to get Books Online, but Publishers are Understandably Wary," November 10. http://www.economist.com/node/5149499?story_id=5149499 Accessed December 19, 2011.

Edwards, Douglas. 2011. *I'm Feeling Lucky: The Confessions of Google Employee Number 59.* New York: Houghton Mifflin Harcourt.

Edwards, Paul. 1967. "Panpsychism," *Encyclopedia of Philosophy*, Vol. 6:22, pp. 22–31. Macmillan: New York.

Ellul, Jacques. 1964 [1954]. *The Technological Society,* John Wilkinson, tr. New York: Vintage.

Emerson, Ralph Waldo. 1904 [1836]. *The Works of Ralph Waldo Emerson: English Traits. Conduct of Life. Nature.* London: George Bell & Sons.

_____. 1911. *Journals of Ralph Waldo Emerson, 1820–1872,* Vol. 6. Boston and New York: Houghton Mifflin.

Evans, David S. 2008. "The Economics of the Online Advertising Industry," *Review of Network Economics* 7:3, September, pp. 359–391.

Fallows, Deborah. 2005. "Search Engine Users: Internet Searchers are Confident, Satisfied and Trusting—But they are also Unaware and Naïve," *Pew Internet & American Life Project,* http://www.pewinternet.org/Reports/2005/Search-Engine-Users.aspx Accessed June 17, 2010.

Fechner, Gustav Theodor. 1882. *On Life After Death,* Hugo Wernekke, tr. London: Gilbert and Rivington.

_____. 1904 [1836]. *The Little Book of Life After Death,* Mary C. Wadsworth, tr. Boston: Little, Brown & Company.

_____. 1988 [1860]. "Psychophysics and Mind–Body Relations." In Ludy T. Benjamin, Jr., ed. *A History of Psychology: Original Sources and Contemporary Research.* New York: McGraw-Hill, pp. 156–166.

Federal Trade Commission. 2002 "Re: Commercial Alert Complaint Requesting Investigation of Various Internet Search Engine Companies for Paid Placement and Paid Inclusion Programs." June 27. http://www.ftc.gov/os/closings/staff/commercialalertattatch.shtm Accessed March 7, 2011.

Finkelstein, Seth. 2008. "Google, Links, and Popularity Versus Authority." In Joseph Turow and Lokman Tsui, ed. *The Hyperlinked Society: Questioning Connections in the Digital Age.* Ann Arbor: University of Michigan Press, pp. 104–120.

Fischer, William B. 1984. *The Empire Strikes Out: Kurd Lasswitz, Hans Dominik, and the Development of German Science Fiction.* Bowling Green: Bowling Green University Press.

Fisher, Barbara M. 1997. *Noble Numbers, Subtle Words: The Art of Mathematics in the Science of Storytelling.* London: Associated University Presses.

Foucault, Michel. 1972 [1969]. *Archaeology of Knowledge*, London: Tavistock Publications.
_____. 1978. *The History of Sexuality*, Vol. 1, Robert Hurley, tr. New York: Pantheon Books.
_____. 1986. "Of Other Spaces," *Diacritics* 16, pp. 22–27.
_____. 2000. *The Hermeneutics of the Subject: Lectures at the Collège de France 1981–1982*, Fréderic Gros and Arnold Davidson, ed., Graham Burchell, tr. New York: Picador.
Frank, Thomas. 2001. *One Market Under God: Extreme Capitalism, Market Populism, and the End of Economic Democracy*. New York: Anchor Books.
Franz, Gerald. 2011. "The Ancient Library at Alexandria: Embracing the Excellent, Avoiding its Fate." Paper presented at Association of College & Research Libraries Annual Convention, Philadelphia, March 30. http://www.ala.org/ala/mgrps/divs/acrl/events/national/2011/papers/ancient_library.pdf Accessed May 9, 2011.
Fraser, Malcolm. 2011. "America's Self-Inflicted Decline," *Project Syndicate: A World of Ideas*, August 30. http://www.project-syndicate.org/commentary/fraser2/English Accessed September 5, 2011.
Fry, Jenny, Shefali Virkar, and Ralph Schroeder. 2008. "Search Engines and Expertise About Global Issues: Well-defined Territory or Undomesticated Wilderness?" In Michael Zimmer and Amanda Spink, ed. *Web Search: Interdisciplinary Perspectives*. Berlin: Springer-Verlag, pp. 255–276.
Fuchs, Christian. 2011. "Web 2.0, Prosumption and Surveillance," *Surveillance and Society* 8:3, pp. 288–309.
Gamow, George. 1960 [1947]. *One Two Three … Infinity*. New York: Viking.
Garfield, Eugene. 1955. "Citation Indexes for Science: A New Dimension in Documentation through Association of Ideas," *Science* 122:3159, July 15, pp. 108–111. http://scimaps.org/static/docs/Garfield1955cit.pdf Accessed September 19, 2011.
_____. 1964. "Toward the World Brain." *Current Contents* 40, October 6, pp. 3–4. http://garfield.library.upenn.edu/essays/v2p638y1974–1976.pdf Accessed June 25, 2011.
_____. 1968. "'World Brain' or 'Memex?'—Mechanical and Intellectual Requirement for Universal Bibliographic Control." In Edward B. Montgomery, ed. *The Foundations of Access to Knowledge: A Symposium*. Syracuse: Syracuse University Press, pp. 169–196.
_____. 1975. "The World Brain as Seen by an Information Entrepreneur." In Manfred Kochen, ed. *Information for Action: From Knowledge to Wisdom*. New York: Academic Press, pp. 155–160.
_____. 1977. *Essays of an Information Scientist*. Philadelphia: ISI Press.
_____. 1989. "Manfred Kochen: In Memory of an Information Scientist Pioneer qua World Brain-ist," *Current Comments* 25, June 19, pp. 166–168. http://www.garfield.library.upenn.edu/essays/v12p166y1989.pdf Accessed June 27, 2011.
_____. 1999. "From the World Brain to the Informatorium—With a Little Help from Manfred Kochen." Symposium in honor of Manfred Kochen, University of Michigan, Ann Arbor, September 21. http://www.garfield.library.upenn.edu/papers/kochen_worldbrain.html Accessed April 22, 2011.
Gerhart, Susan L. 2004. "Do Web Search Engines Suppress Controversy," *First Monday* 9:1. http://firstmonday.org/htbin/cgiwrap/bin/ojs/index.php/fm/article/view/1111/1031 Accessed July 2, 2009.
Giddens, Anthony. 1992. *The Consequences of Modernity*. Cambridge: Polity Press.
Gilder, George. 1984. *The Spirit of Enterprise*. New York: Simon & Schuster.
Gleick, James. 2011. *The Information: A History, A Theory, A Flood*. Pantheon: New York.

Godoy, Maria. 2006. "Google Records Subpoena Raises Privacy Fears," *NPR*, January 20. http://www.npr.org/templates/story/story.php?storyId=5165854 Accessed January 2, 2012.

Goldman, Eric. 2008. "Search Engine Bias and the Demise of Search Engine Utopianism." In Amanda Spink and Michael Zimmer, ed. *Web Search: Multidisciplinary Perspectives*. Berlin: Springer-Verlag, pp. 121–133.

Google. n.d. "Google Chrome and Speed." http://www.google.com/chrome/intl/en/more/speed.html Accessed October 7, 2011.

Google. 2000. "MentalPlex FAQ." http://www.google.com/mentalplex/MP_faq.html. Accessed September 1, 2011.

_____. 2004. "Founder's IPO Letter." http://investor.google.com/corporate/2004/ipo-founders-letter.html Accessed August 30, 2011.

_____. 2005. "Cerf's up at Google." http://www.google.com/press/pressrel/vintcerf.html Accessed September 20, 2011.

_____. 2006. "Our Philosophy: Ten Things We Know to Be True." September 2009. http://www.google.com/about/corporate/company/tenthings.html Accessed September 3, 2011.

_____. 2008. "Introduction to Google Search Quality," The Official Google Blog. http://googleblog.blogspot.com/2008/05/introduction-to-google-search-quality.html Accessed September 11, 2011.

_____. 2009. "Google Code of Conduct," Google Investor Relations. http://investor.google.com/corporate/code-of-conduct.html Accessed September 4, 2011.

_____. 2009a. "The Official Google Blog." http://googleblog.blogspot.com/2009/06/lets-make-web-faster.html Accessed October 16, 2011.

_____. 2010. "Annual Report 2010." Google Investor Relations. http://investor.google.com/order.html#download Accessed March 25, 2011.

_____. 2010a. "The Official Google Blog." http://googleblog.blogspot.com/ Accessed October 16, 2011.

_____. 2011. "An Explanation of Our Search Results." http://www.google.com/explanation.html Accessed September 4, 2011.

_____. 2011a. "Google Announces Fourth Quarter and Fiscal Year 2010 Results and Management Changes." http://investor.google.com/earnings/2010/Q4_google_earnings.html Accessed March 25, 2011.

_____. 2011b. "Google to Acquire Motorola Mobility." Google Investor Relations, August 15. http://investor.google.com/releases/2011/0815.html Accessed August 29, 2011.

_____. 2011c. "About Google Instant." http://www.google.com/instant Accessed September 1, 2011.

_____. 2011d. "Google Code: Let's Make the Web Faster." http://code.google.com/speed/tools.html Accessed October 7, 2011.

_____. 2011e. "Introducing Page Speed Online, with Mobile Support." March 31. http://googlewebmastercentral.blogspot.com/2011/03/introducing-page-speed-online-with.html Accessed October 7, 2011.

_____. 2011f. "Finding More High-Quality Sites in Search." February 24. http://googleblog.blogspot.com/2011/02/finding-more-high-quality-sites-in.html Accessed February 25, 2011.

_____. 2011h. "Watch Lunar Eclipse from Anywhere." http://googleblog.blogspot.com/2011/06/watch-lunar-eclipse-from-anywhere.html Accessed June 20, 2011.

Grim, Ryan, Zach Carter, and Paul Blumenthal. 2011. "Spreading Freedom: Google and the War for the Web." *Huffington Post,* September 25. http://www.huffingtonpost.com/2011/09/25/google-antitrust-microsoft-war_n_976804.html Accessed October 6, 2011.

Haakonssen, Knud. 2002. "Introduction." In Adam Smith, *The Theory of Moral Sentiments*, Knud Haakonssen, ed. Cambridge: Cambridge University Press, pp. xii–xxiv.

Hagel, John III and Arthur G. Armstrong. 1997. *Net Gain: Expanding Markets Through Virtual Communities*. Boston: Harvard Business School Press.

Haigh, Gideon. 2006. "Information Idol: How Google is Making Us Stupid," *The Monthly*, February. http://www.themonthly.com.au/how-google-making-us-stupid-infomation-idol-gideon-haigh-170 Accessed December 16, 2011.

Halavais, Alex. 2009. *Search Engine Society*. Cambridge: Polity Press.

Halliday, Josh. 2011. "Google Boss: Anti-Piracy Laws Would Be Disaster for Free Speech," *Guardian*, May 18. http://www.guardian.co.uk/technology/2011/may/18/google-eric-schmidt-piracy Accesssed October 6, 2011.

Hargittai, Eszter. 2008. "The Role of Expertise in Navigating Links of Influence." In Joseph Turow and Lokman Tsui, ed. *The Hyperlinked Society: Questioning Connections in the Digital Age*. Ann Arbor: University of Michigan Press, pp. 85–103.

Hayles, N. Katherine. 1999. *How We Became Posthuman: Virtual Bodies in Cybernetics, Literature, and Informatics*. Chicago: University of Chicago Press.

Heather, Michael and Nick Rossiter. 2005. "Logical Monism: The Global Identity of Applicable Logic." In Giandomenico Sica, ed. *Essays on the Foundations of Mathematics*, Monza: Polimetrica, pp. 39–52.

Heidegger, Martin. 1977. *The Question Concerning Technology and Other Essays*, William Lovitt, tr. New York: Harper & Row.

Heidelberger, Michael. 2004 [1993]. *Nature from Within: Gustav Theodor Fechner and His Psychophysical Worldview*, Cynthia Klohr, tr. Pittsburgh: University of Pittsburgh Press.

Helft, Miguel. 2011. "Judge Rejects Google's Deal to Digitize Books," *New York Times*, March 22. http://www.nytimes.com/2011/03/23/technology/23google.html Accessed March 23, 2011.

Herring, Mark Y. 2009. "Fool's Gold: Why the Internet is no Substitute for a Library." In William Miller and Rita M. Pellen, ed. *Googlization of Libraries*. London: Routledge, pp. 29–53.

Hesmondhalgh, David. 2006. "Bourdieu, the Media and Cultural Production," *Media, Culture and Society* 28:22, pp. 211–231.

Hess, A. 2008. "Reconsidering the Rhizome: A Textual Analysis of Web Search Engines as Gatekeepers of the Internet." In Amanda Spink and Michael Zimmer, ed. *Web Search: Multidisciplinary Perspectives*. Berlin: Springer-Verlag, pp. 35–50.

Hilderbrand, Lucas. 2009. *Inherent Vice: Bootleg Histories of Videotape and Copyright*. Durham: Duke University Press.

Hillgarth, Jocelyn Nigel. 1971. *Ramon Lull and Lullism in Fourteenth-Century France*. Oxford: Clarendon Press.

Hillis, Ken. 1999. *Digital Sensations: Space, Identity and Embodiment in Virtual Reality*. Minneapolis: University of Minnesota Press.

_____. 2009. *Online a Lot of the Time: Ritual, Fetish, Sign*. Durham: Duke University Press.

Hindman, Matthew, Kostas Tsioutsiouliklis, and Judy A. Johnson. 2003. "Googlearchy: How a Few Heavily Linked Sites Dominate Politics Online," Midwest Political

Science Association conference. http://www.matthewhindman.com/index.php/2003032812/Research/Googlearchy-How-a-Few-Heavily-Linked-Sites-Dominate-Politics-Online.html Accessed August 25, 2009.

Hoff, Todd. 2010. "Google's Colossus Makes Search Real-time by Dumping MapReduce," *High Scalability* http://highscalability.com/blog/2010/9/11/googles-colossus-makes-search-real-time-by-dumping-mapreduce.html Accessed December 23, 2011.

Holiday, Robert Cortes. 1919. *Broome Street Straws*. New York: George H. Doran.

Hoofnagle, Chris Jay. 2009. "Beyond Google and Evil: How Policy Makers, Journalists and Consumers Should Talk Differently About Google and Privacy," *First Monday* 14:4. http://firstmonday.org/htbin/cgiwrap/bin/ojs/index.php/fm/article/view/2326/2156 Accessed April 7, 2011.

Huberman, Bernardo A. 2001. *The Laws of the Web: Patterns in the Ecology of Information.* Cambridge, Massachusetts: MIT Press.

Hütter, Verena. 2010. "I Link, I Like"—Peter Kruse on Cloud Culture," Jonathan Uhlaner, tr. Goethe Institut. http://www.goethe.de/wis/med/idm/fin/en6578052.htm Accessed January 25, 2011.

Huyssen, Andreas. 2000. "The Vamp and the Machine." In Michael Minden and Holger Bachmann, ed. *Fritz Lang's Metropolis: Cinematic Visions of Technology and Fear.* Rochester: Camden House, pp. 198–215.

IAB (Interactive Advertising Bureau). 2010. "IAB Internet Advertising Revenue Report: 2010 First Half-Year Results." http://www.iab.net/insights_research/947883/adrevenuereport Accessed April 7, 2011.

Introna, Lucas and Helen Nissenbaum. 2000. "Shaping the Web: Why the Politics of Search Engines Matter," *Information Society* 16:3, pp. 169–185.

James, William. 1904. "Introduction." In Gustav Theodor Fechner, *The Little Book of Life after Death*, Mary C. Wadsworth, tr. Boston: Little, Brown, & Company, pp. 13–20.

_____. 1909. *A Pluralistic Universe*. London: Longmans, Green & Co.

Jameson, Fredric. 2004. "The Politics of Utopia," *New Left Review* 25, January–February, pp. 35–54.

Jarrett, Kylie. 2008. "Interactivity is Evil: A Critical Investigation of Web 2.0," *First Monday* 13:3, March 3. http://firstmonday.org/htbin/cgiwrap/bin/ojs/index.php/fm/article/view/2140/1947 Accessed December 14, 2011.

Jarvis, Ewen. 2008. "Beyond the Lie at the Heart of the Library: Blake and Bachelard," *In/Stead* 2. http://www.doubledialogues.com/in_stead/in_stead_iss02/std_jarvis.html Accessed February 1, 2011.

Jeanneney, Jean-Noël. 2007. *Google and the Myth of Universal Knowledge*, Theresa Lavender Fagan, tr. Chicago: University of Chicago Press.

Jenkins, Holman. 2010. "Google and the Search for the Future." *Wall Street Journal*, August 14. http://online.wsj.com/article/SB1000142405274870490110457542329409 9527212.html. Accessed January 1, 2012.

Joachims, Thorsten, Laura Granka, Bing Pan, Helene Hembrooke, and Geri Gay. 2005. "Accurately Interpreting Clickthrough Data as Implicit Feedback," *Proceedings of the 28th Annual International ACM SIGIR Conference on Research and Development in Information Retrieval,* Salvador, Brazil, pp. 154–161. http://www.cs.cornell.edu/People/tj/ Accessed August 25, 2009.

_____. 1987. *The Spiritual Logic of Ramon Llull*. Oxford: Clarendon Press.

Johnson, Bobbie. 2010. "How Google Censors its Results in China," *Guardian*, January 13. http://www.guardian.co.uk/technology/2010/jan/13/how-google-censors-china Accessed November 26, 2011.

Johnson, Mark D. 1986. "The Natural Rhetoric of Ramon Llull," *Essays in Medieval Studies* 3, pp. 174–192. http://www.illinoismedieval.org/ems/VOL3/johnston.html Accessed January 30, 2011.

Kang, Hyunjin and Matthew McAllister. 2011. "Selling You and Your Clicks: Examining the Audience Commodification of Google," *tripleC* 9:2, pp. 141–153.

Keane, Mark T., Maeve O'Brien, and Barry Smyth. 2008. "Are People Biased in Their Use of Search Engines?" *Communications of the ACM* 51:2, pp. 49–52. http://portal.acm.org/citation.cfm?id=1314224 Accessed August 25, 2009.

Keating, Craig. 2000. "The Condition of Virtuality," *H-Net Reviews*. http://www.h-net.org/reviews/showrev.php?id=4517 Accessed September 19, 2011.

Kelly, Kevin. 1994. *Out of Control: The New Biology of Machines, Social Systems, and the Economic World*. Menlo Park: Addison-Wesley.

———. 1998. *New Rules for the New Economy: 10 Radical Strategies for a Connected World*. New York: Penguin.

———. 2006. "Scan This Book." *New York Times Magazine*, May 14. http://www.nytimes.com/2006/05/14/magazine/14publishing.html?pagewanted=all Accessed January 11, 2012.

———. 2010. *What Technology Wants*. New York: Viking.

Kenney, Martin. 2003. "What Goes up Must Come down: The Political Economy of the U.S. Internet Industry." In Jens Froslev Christensen and Peter Maskell, ed. *The Industrial Dynamics of the New Digital Economy*. Cheltenham: Edward Elgar, pp. 33–55.

Kirby, Alan. 2006. "The Death of Postmodernism and Beyond," *Philosophy Now* 58. http://www.philosophynow.org/issue58/The_Death_of_Postmodernism_And_Beyond Accessed December 25, 2011.

Kitto, Humphrey Davy Findley. 1964. *The Greeks*. Harmondsworth: Penguin.

Kochen, Manfred. 1972. "WISE: A World Information Synthesis and Encyclopaedia." *Journal of Documentation* 28:4, pp. 322–343.

———. 1975. "Evolution of Brainlike Social Organs." In Manfred Kochen, ed. *Information for Action: From Knowledge to Wisdom*. New York: Academic Press, pp. 1–18.

Kolb, David. 2005. "Association and Argument: Hypertext in and around the Writing Process," *New Review of Hypermedia and Mutimedia* 11:1, pp. 7–26.

Kretzmann, Edwin M.J. 1938. "German Technological Utopias of the Pre-War Period," *Annals of Science* 3:4, pp. 417–430.

Kurtzweil, Ray. 2005. *The Singularity is Near: When Humans Transcend Biology*. New York: Viking.

Lach, Eric. 2010. "What Did Google Do for Scott Brown? A Lot," *TPM LiveWire*, February 4. http://tpmlivewire.talkingpointsmemo.com/2010/02/did-google-help-scott-brown-win-in-ma.php?ref=fpb Accessed February 5, 2010.

Laffey, Des. 2007. "Paid Search: The Innovation That Changed the Web," *Business Horizons* 50, pp. 211–218.

Langford, David. 1997. "The Net of Babel." In David Pringle, ed. *The Best of Interzone*, New York: St. Martins Press, pp. 450–452.

Lasch, Christopher. 1991. *The True and Only Heaven: Progress and Its Critics*. New York: W.W. Norton & Company.

Lash, Scott. 2002. *Critique of Information*. London: Sage.

Lasswitz, Kurd. 1958 [1901]. "The Universal Library," Willy Ley, tr. In Clifton Fadiman, ed. *Fantasia Mathematica*. New York: Simon & Schuster, pp. 237–243.

Latour, Bruno. 1993. *We Have Never Been Modern*, Catherine Porter, tr. Cambridge: Harvard University Press.

Lawler, Andrew. 2010. "Tending the Garden of Technology: An Interview with Kevin Kelly," *Orion* 29:1, January/February, p. 36.

Lazzarato, Maurizio. 1996. "Immaterial Labour," Paul Colilli and Ed Emory, tr. In Paolo Virno and Michael Hardt, ed. *Radical Thought in Italy*. Minneapolis: University of Minnesota Press, pp. 133–146.

Lee, Micky. 2011a. "Google Ads and the Blindspot Debate," *Media, Culture and Society*, 33:3, pp. 433–447.

Lee, Timothy B. 2011b. "Google Tries to Kick Authors Guild out of Court in Book Case," *Ars Technica*, December 23. http://arstechnica.com/tech-policy/news/2011/12/google-tries-to-kick-authors-guild-out-of-court-in-book-case.ars Accessed December 25, 2011.

Lessig, Lawrence. 2006. *Code Version 2.0*. New York: Basic Books.

_____. 2011. *In the Plex: How Google Thinks, Works, and Shapes Our Lives*. New York: Simon & Schuster.

Lévy, Pierre. 1998. *Becoming Virtual: Reality in the Digital Age*. Robert Bononno, tr. New York: Plenum.

Ley, Willy. 1958. "Postscript to 'The Universal Library'." In Clifton Fadiman, ed. *Fantasia Mathematica*. New York: Simon & Schuster, pp. 244–247.

Licklider, J.C.R. (Joseph Carl Robnett). 1960. "Man–Computer Symbiosis," *IRE Transactions on Human Factors in Electronics* HFE-1, pp. 4–11. http://groups.csail.mit.edu/medg/people/psz/Licklider.html Accessed September 20, 2011.

_____. 1965. *Libraries of the Future*. Cambridge: MIT Press.

Licklider, J.C.R. and Welden E. Clark. 1962. "On-line Man–Computer Communication," *Joint Computer Conference Proceedings* 21, pp. 113–128.

Lister, Martin, Jon Dovey, Seth Giddings, Iain Grant, and Kieran Kelly. 2003. *New Media: A Critical Introduction*. London: Routledge.

Livingston, Jessica. 2008. *Founders at Work: Stories of Startups' Early Days*, Berkeley: Apress.

Lohr, Steve. 2010. "Interview: Sergey Brin on Google's China Move," *New York Times*, March 22. http://bits.blogs.nytimes.com/2010/03/22/interview-sergey-brin-on-googles-china-gambit Accessed August 30, 2011.

Lopes, Paul. 2000. "Pierre Bourdieu's Fields of Cultural Production: A Case Study in Modern Jazz." In Nicholas Brown and Imre Szeman, ed. *Pierre Bourdieu: Fieldwork in Culture*. Maryland: Rowman Littlefield, pp. 165–185.

Lovink, Geert. 2003. *My First Recession: Critical Internet Culture in Transition*. Rotterdam: V_2 Publishing/NAI Publishers.

_____. 2009. "Society of the Query: The Googlization of our Lives." In Konrad Becker and Felix Stalder, ed. *Deep Search: The Politics of Search Beyond Google*. Innsbruck: StudienVerlag, pp. 45–53.

Lowrie, Walter, 1946. *Religion of a Scientist: Selections from Gustav Th. Fechner*, Walter Lowrie, ed. and tr. New York: Pantheon Books.

Mackenzie, Adrian. 2006. *Cutting Code: Software and Sociality*. New York: Peter Lang.

Mann, Susan. 1989. "The Universe and the Library: A Critique of James Boyd White as Writer and Reader," *Stanford Law Review* 41:4, April, pp. 959–1020.

Mann, Thomas. 2008. "Will Google's Keyword Searching Eliminate the Need for LC Cataloging and Classification?" *Journal of Library Metadata* 8:2, pp. 159–168.

Manovich, Lev. 2002. *The Language of New Media*. Cambridge: MIT Press.

Marder, Michael. 2011. "The Second Death of Politics," *Al Jazeera.Net*, December 23. http://www.aljazeera.com/indepth/opinion/2011/12/2011121981347391640.html Accessed December 24, 2011.

_____. 2011a. "Vegetal Anti-Metaphysics: Learning from Plants," *Continental Philosophy Review* 44, pp. 469–489.

Marshall, Marilyn E. 1988. "Biographical Genre and Biographical Archetype: Five Studies of Gustav Theodor Fechner." In Ludy T. Benjamin, Jr., ed. *A History of Psychology: Original Sources and Contemporary Research*. New York: McGraw-Hill, pp. 170–177.

Martinez, Michael. 2011. "Why You Cannot Reverse Engineer Google's Algorithm." *SEO Theory and Analysis Blog*, January 7. http://www.seo-theory.com/2011/01/07/why-you-cannot-reverse-engineer-googles-algorithm Accessed September 19, 2011.

Marx, Karl and Friedrich Engels. 2007 [1848]. *The Communist Manifesto*. Bel Aire, Minnesota: Filiquarian Publishing.

Mayer, Katja. 2009. "On the Sociometry of Search Engines: A Historical Review of Methods." In Konrad Becker and Felix Stalder, ed. *Deep Search: The Politics of Search Beyond Google*. Innsbruck: StudienVerlag, pp. 54–72.

Mayer-Schönberger, Viktor. 2009. *Delete: The Virtue of Forgetting in the Digital Age*. Princeton: Princeton University Press.

Mbembe, Achille. 2002. "The Power of the Archive and its Limits," Judith Inggs, tr. In Carolyn Hamilton, Verne Harris, Michèle Pickone, Graeme Reid, Razia Saleh, and Jane Taylor, eds. *Refiguring the Archive*. Dordrecht: Kluwer Academic Publishers, pp. 19–26.

McCarthy, Tom. 2003. *Calling All Agents: Transmission, Death, Technology*. International Necronautical Society, London: Vargas Organization.

McHugh, Josh. 2003. "Google vs. Evil," *Wired* 11:1 http://www.wired.com/wired/archive/11.01/google_pr.html Accessed September 4, 2011.

McLaughlin, Andrew. 2006. "Google in China," *The Official Google Blog*, January 27. http://googleblog.blogspot.com/2006/01/google-in-china.html Accessed April 8, 2011.

McLuhan, Marshall. 1964. *Understanding Media: The Extensions of Man*. London: Routledge.

McStay, Andrew. 2010. *Digital Advertising*. Hampshire: Palgrave Macmillan.

Meddaugh, Priscilla Marie. 2010. "Bakhtin, Colbert and the Center of Discourse: Is There no 'Truthiness' in Humor?" *Critical Studies in Mass Communication* 27:4, October, pp. 376–390.

Mehl, Dominique. 2005. "The Public on the Television Screen: Towards a Public Sphere of Exhibition," *Journal of Media Practice* 6:1, pp. 19–28.

Menocal, María Rosa. 1994. *Shards of Love: Exile and the Origins of the Lyric*. Durham: Duke University Press.

Mitias, Michael H. 1984. *Moral Foundation of the State in Hegel's Philosophy of Right: Anatomy of an Argument*. Amsterdam: Rodopi.

Moore, Charles. 1921. *Daniel H. Burnham, Architect, Planner of Cities*. Boston: Houghton Mifflin.

Myerson, George. 2001. *Heidegger, Habermas and the Mobile Phone*. Cambridge: Icon Books.

Myerson, Joel, Sandra Harbert Petrulionis, and Laura Dassow Walls, ed. 2010. "Introduction." In *The Oxford Handbook of Transcendentalism*. Oxford: Oxford University Press, pp. xxiii–xxxiii.

Nagel, Thomas. 1979. *Mortal Questions*. Cambridge: Cambridge University Press.

Nelson, Victoria. 2011. *The Secret Life of Puppets*. Cambridge: Harvard University Press.

Nietzsche, Friedrich. 1976. "Twilight of the Idols." In Walter Kaufmann, ed. *The Portable Nietzsche*. New York: Penguin Books, pp. xi–xxxix.

Nikoltchev, Susanne. 2006. "Editorial," *IRIS plus: Legal Observations of the European Audiovisual Laboratory* 2. http://www.obs.coe.int/oea_publ/iris/iris_plus/iplus2_2006.pdf.en Accessed December 19, 2011.

Noble, David F. 1999 [1997]. *The Religion of Technology: The Divinity of Man and the Spirit of Invention*. New York: Penguin.

Open Book Alliance. 2009. "Mission." http://www.openbookalliance.org/mission Accessed July 7, 2011.

Orwell, George. 1937. *The Road to Wigan Pier*. Orlando: Harcourt.

O'Sullivan, Anne. 2010. "Is Google Building a Library of Babel?" *LISNews: The Vaudeville of Social Media*. http://www.lisnews.com/google_building_library_babel Accessed January 25, 2011.

Ouellet, Maxime. 2010. "Cybernetic Capitalism and the Global Information Society: From the Global Panopticon to a 'Brand' New World." In Jacqueline Best and Matthew Paterson, ed. *Cultural Political Economy*. London: Routledge, pp. 177–196.

Page, Larry. 2011. "Larry Page is Using Google+," July 14. https://plus.google.com/106189723444098348646/posts/dRtqKJCbpZ7#106189723444098348646/posts/dRtqKJCbpZ7 Accessed November 11, 2011.

Pal, Amitabh. 2010. "Google Tarnished by Its Hypocrisy," *Toronto Star*, January 16. http://www.thestar.com/opinion/article/751448--google-tarnished-by-its-hypocrisy Accessed November 25, 2010.

Pan, Bing, Helene Hembrooke, Thorsten Joachims, Lori Lorigo, Geri Gay, and Laura Granka. 2007. "In Google We Trust: Users' Decisions on Rank, Position, and Relevance," *Journal of Computer-Mediated Communication* 12:3. http://jcmc.indiana.edu/vol12/issue3/pan.html Accessed August 25, 2009.

Papacharissi, Zizi A. 2010. *A Private Sphere: Democracy in a Digital Age*. Cambridge: Polity Press.

Pariser, Eli. 2011. *The Filter Bubble: What the Internet is Hiding from You*. New York: Penguin.

Pash, Adam. 2011. "When Google Doesn't Have the Answer, or 'Is Idol White a Scam?'" *Lifehacker*. http://lifehacker.com/5743020/when-google-doesnt-have-the-answer-or-is-idol-white-a-scam?utm_medium=referral&utm_source=pulsenews Accessed January 28, 2011.

Peers, E. Allison. 1929. *Ramon Lull: A Biography*. Toronto: Macmillan.

Pelton, Joseph N. 1989. "Telepower: The Emerging Global Brain," *Futurist* 23:5, September–October, pp. 9–14.

*Penny Cyclopaedia of the Society for the Diffusion of Useful Knowledge*. 1837, Vol. 7. London: Charles Knight & Co.

Pew Research Center's Internet & American Life Project. 2011. "Trend Data: What Internet Users Do Online." http://pewinternet.org/Static-Pages/Trend-Data/Online-Activites-Total.aspx Accessed September 1, 2011.

Phillips, Heather. 2010. "The Great *Library* of Alexandrina?" *Library Philosophy and Practice*, August. http://unllib.unl.edu/LPP/phillips.pdf Accessed April 8, 2011.

Plato. 1965 [c. 360 BCE]. *Timaeus*, H.D.P. Lee, tr. Baltimore: Penguin Books.

Plotinus. 2004. *The Six Enneads*, Stephen MacKenna and B.S. Page, tr. Whitefish, Montana: Kessinger Publishing.

Pogue, David. 2011. "A Laptop, Its Head in the Cloud," *New York Times*, June 15. http://www.nytimes.com/2011/06/16/technology/personaltech/16pogue.html?pagewanted=all Accessed August 24, 2011.

Postman, Neil. 1992. *Technopoly: The Surrender of Culture to Technology*. New York: Knopf.

Press, Larry. 1993. "Before the Altair—The History of Personal Computing," *Communications of the ACM* 36:9, September, pp. 27–33.

Price, Gary. 2011. "Official: The Google Wonder Wheel is Gone," *Searchengineland*. http://searchengineland.com/official-the-google-wonder-wheel-is-gone-84105 Accessed January 4, 2012.

*Princeton Theological Review*. 2010. "The Church After Google." Special Issue, Elizabeth Dias, ed. 43:2.

Purcell, Kristen. 2011. "Search and Email Still Top the List of Most Popular Online Activities," *Pew Research Center's Internet & American Life Project*, August 9. http://pewinternet.org/Reports/2011/Search-and-email.aspx Accessed August 30, 2011.

Quine, W.V. 1987. *Quiddities: An Intermittently Philosophical Dictionary*. Cambridge: Belknap Press.

Ramoneda, Josep. 1999. "Prologue—The Tower and the City," *Exhibition Catalog for The City of K. Franz Kafka and Prague*. Barcelona: Centre de Cultura Contemporània de Barcelona. http://www.cccb.org/rcs_gene/25-kafka-ramo-ang.pdf Accessed February 2, 2011.

Rancière, Jacques. 1998. *Disagreement*, Julie Rose, tr. Minneapolis: University of Minnesota Press.

Rayward, W. Boyd. 1999. "H.G. Wells's Idea of a World Brain: A Critical Re-Assessment," *Journal of the American Society for Information Science* 50, May 15, pp. 557–579.

———. 2008. "The March of the Modern and the Reconstitution of the World's Knowledge Apparatus: H.G. Wells, Encyclopedism and the World Brain." In W. Boyd Rayward, ed. *European Modernism and the Information Society: Informing the Present, Understanding the Past*. Aldershot: Ashgate, pp. 223–239.

Reese, William L. 1980. *Dictionary of Philosophy and Religion*. Atlantic Highlands: Humanities Press.

Reilly, Paul. 2008. "'Googling' Terrorists: Are Northern Irish Terrorists Visible on Internet Search Engines?" In Amanda Spink and Michael Zimmer, ed. *Web Search: Multidisciplinary Perspectives*. Berlin: Springer-Verlag, pp. 151–175.

Ricoeur, Paul. 2006. *On Translation*, Eileen Brennan, tr. London: Routledge.

Robertson, Adi. 2011. "Google Moves to Strike Authors Guild and Other Organizations from Books Suit," *The Verge*, December 25. http://www.theverge.com/2011/12/25/2659404/google-books-motion-strike-authors-guild-copyright-organizations-lawsuit Accessed December 25, 2011.

Rogers, Richard. 2004. *Information Politics on the Web*. Cambridge: MIT Press.

———. 2009. "The Googlization Question: Towards the Inculpable Engine?" In Konrad Becker and Felix Stalder, ed. *Deep Search: The Politics of Search Beyond Google*. Innsbruck: StudienVerlag, pp. 173–184.

Röhle, Theo. 2009. "Dissecting the Gatekeepers: Relational Perspectives on the Power of Search Engines." In Konrad Becker and Felix Stalder, ed. *Deep Search: The Politics of Search Beyond Google*. Innsbruck: StudienVerlag, pp. 117–132.

Rose, Gillian. 1993. "Architecture to Philosophy—The Post-Modern Complicity." In *Judaism and Modernity: Philosophical Essays*. Oxford: Blackwell, pp. 225–240.

Rose, Nikolas. 1999. *Powers of Freedom*. Cambridge: Cambridge University Press.

———. 2007. *The Politics of Life Itself: Biomedicine, Power, and Subjectivity in the Twenty-First Century*. Princeton: Princeton University Press.

Rosenberg, Scott. 1998. "Yes There is A Better Search Engine: While the Portal Sites Fiddle, Google Catches Fire," *Salon.com*, 21 December http://www.salon.com/21st/rose/1998/12/21straight.html Accessed July 5, 2011.

Rosnay, Joël de. 2000. *Symbiotic Man: A New Understanding of the Organization of Life and a Vision of the Future*. New York: McGraw-Hill.

Rothenberg, David. 1993. *Hand's End: Technology and the Limits of Nature*. Berkeley: University of California Press.

Rottensteiner, Franz. 2008. "A Short History of Science Fiction in German." In *The Black Mirror and Other Stories: An Anthology of Science Fiction from Germany and Austria*. Middletown: Wesleyan University Press, pp. xi–xxxix.

Russell, Bertrand. 1945. *A History of Western Philosophy*. New York: Simon Schuster.

Sales, Ton. 1997. "Llull as Computer Scientist or Why Llull Was One of Us." In Miquel Bertran and Teodor Rus, ed. *Transformation-Based Reactive Systems Development: 4th International AMAST Workshop on Real-Time Systems and Concurrent and Distributed Software, ARTS '97*, Palma, Mallorca, Spain, May 21–23, 1997. London: Springer-Verlag, pp. 15–21.

Samuelson, Pamela. 2009. "Google Books is Not a Library," *Huffington Post*, October 13. http://www.huffingtonpost.com/pamela-samuelson/google-books-is-not-a-lib_b_317518.html Accessed July 7, 2011.

Sark, Kat. 2011. "Google: Building the Digital Future," *Suites Culturelles*, May 14. http://suitesculturelles.wordpress.com/2011/05/14/google-building-the-digital-future Accessed October 16, 2011.

Scholem, Gershom. 1965. *On the Kabbalah and Its Symbolism*, Ralph Manheim, tr. New York: Schocken Books.

Sconce, Jeffrey. 2000. *Haunted Media: Electronic Presence from Telegraphy to Television*. Durham: Duke University Press.

Searle, John. 1995. *The Construction of Social Reality*. New York: Free Press.

Shapiro, Carl and Hal Varian. 1999. *Information Rules: A Strategic Guide to the Network Economy*. Boston: Harvard Business School Press.

Skrbina, David. 2005. *Panpsychism in the West*. Cambridge: MIT Press.

Sloterdijk, Peter. 1987 [1983]. *Critique of Cynical Reason,* Michael Eldred, tr. Minneapolis: University of Minnesota Press.

Smith, Adam. 2009 [1759]. *The Theory of Moral Sentiments*. New York: Penguin.

Smith, Catherine and Bianca Bosker. 2010. "Google Instant REVIEWS: Users Rate Google's New Search Tool" *Huffington Post*, September 8. http://www.huffington-post.com/2010/09/08/google-instant-reviews-us_n_709372.html#s136237 Accessed November 5, 2011.

Smith, David. 2009. "Google Plans to Make PCs History," *Observer*. January 25. http://www.guardian.co.uk/technology/2009/jan/25/google-drive-gdrive-internet/print Accessed January 25, 2009.

Smythe, Dallas W. 1981. *Dependency Road: Communication, Capitalism, Consciousness and Canada*. Norwood, New Jersey: Ablex.

Sowa, John F. 2000. *Knowledge Representation: Logical, Philosophical and Computational Foundations*. Pacific Grove: Brooks/Cole.

Spink, Amanda and Michael Zimmer, ed. 2008. *Web Search: Multidisciplinary Perspectives*. Berlin: Springer-Verlag.

Stabile, Susan J. 2008. "Google Benefits or Google's Benefit?" *Journal of Business and Technology Law* 3:1, pp. 97–107.

Staikos, Konstantinos. 2004. *The History of the Library in Western Civilization: From Minos to Cleopatra*, Timothy Cullen, tr. New Castle, Delaware: Oak Knoll Press.

Stalder, Felix and Christine Mayer. 2009. "The Second Index: Search Engines, Personalization and Surveillance," In Konrad Becker and Felix Stalder, ed. *Deep Search: The Politics of Search Beyond Google*. Innsbruck: StudienVerlag, pp. 98–115.

StatCounter. 2011. *Global Stats*. http://gs.statcounter.com/ Accessed August 28, 2011.

Sterne, Jonathan. 2003. "Bourdieu, Technique and Technology," *Cultural Studies* 17:3, pp. 367–389.

Stirling, Greg. 2011. "Google Book Search Settlement Rejected by Court," *Searchengineland*. http://searchengineland.com/google-book-search-settlement-rejected-by-court-69446 Accessed June 2, 2011.

Sullivan, Danny. 2003. "Yahoo To Buy Overture," *Search Engine Watch*, July 14. http://searchenginewatch.com/article/2067396/Yahoo-To-Buy-Overture Accessed December 28, 2011.

_____. 2011. "Google: Bing is Cheating, Copying our Search Results," *Searchengineland*. http://searchengineland.com/google-bing-is-cheating-copying-our-search-results-62914 Accessed November 1, 2011.

Swift, Mike. 2009. "Surge in Innovation Leads to Intense Search Engine Battles." *San Jose Mercury News*, October 31. http://smallbizlink.monster.com/news/articles/516-surge-in-innovation-leads-to-intense-search-engine-battles Accessed August 29, 2011.

Szeman, Imre. 2007. "'Do No Evil': Google and Evil as a Political Category," *Topia* 18, pp. 131–139.

Tapscott, Don. 1998. "Introduction." In Don Tapscott, Alex Lowy, David Ticoll, and Natalie Klym, eds, *Blueprint to the Digital Economy: Creating Wealth in the Era of e-Business*. New York: McGraw-Hill, pp. 1–16.

Tartakoff, Joseph. 2010. "Google's Schmidt on the State of the Mobile Phone: 'It's Like Magic,'" *paidContent.org*, February 16. http://paidcontent.org/article/419-googles-schmidt-the-new-rule-is-mobile-first-in-everything Accessed September 28, 2011.

Taycher, Leonid. 2010. "Books of the World, Stand up and Be Counted! All 129,884,860 of You," *Inside Google Books*, August 5. http://booksearch.blogspot.com/2010/08/books-of-world-stand-up-and-be-counted.html Accessed September 9, 2011.

Teilhard de Chardin, Pierre. 1964. *The Future of Man*, Norman Denny, tr. New York: Harper & Row.

_____. 1970 [1963]. *Activation of Energy*, René Hague, tr. London: Collins.

Thiem, Jon. 1999. "Myths of the Universal Library: From Alexandria to the Postmodern Age." In Marie Laure Ryan, ed. *Cyberspace Textuality: Computer Technology and Literary Theory*. Bloomington: Indiana University Press, pp. 256–266.

Toobin, Jeffrey. 2007. "Google's Moon Shot: The Quest for the Universal Library," *New Yorker*, February 5. http://www.newyorker.com/reporting/2007/02/05/070205fa_fact_toobin Accessed July 7, 2011.

Turing, Alan M. 1950. "Computing Machinery and Intelligence, *Mind* 59, pp. 433–460.

_____. 1969 [1948]. "Intelligent Machinery." In B. Meltzer and D. Michie, ed. *Machine Intelligence*, Vol. 5. Edinburgh: Edinburgh University Press, pp. 3–23.

Turner, Fred. 2009. "Burning Man at Google: A Cultural Infrastructure for New Media Production," *New Media and Society* 11:1–2, pp. 73–94.

Upstill, Trystan, Nick Craswell, and David Hawking. 2003. "Predicting Fame and Fortune: PageRank or Indegree?" *Proceedings of the 8th Australasian Document Computing Symposium*, Canberra, December 15, pp. 31–40. http://cs.anu.edu.au/~Trystan. Upstill/pubs/upstill_adcs03.pdf Accessed July 5, 2011.

Vaidhyanathan, Siva. 2011. *The Googlization of Everything (And Why We Should Worry)*. Berkeley: University of California Press.

Vallee, Jacques F. 1979. *Messengers of Deception*. Berkeley: Ronin Publishing.

van Couvering, Elizabeth. 2004. "New Media? The Political Economy of Internet Search Engines," paper presented at the International Association of Media and Communications Researchers Conference, Porto Alegre, Brazil, July 25–30.

_____. 2007. "Is Relevance Relevant? Market, Science and War: Discourse of Search Engine Quality," *Journal of Computer-Mediated Communication* 12:3, pp. 866–887. http://jcmc.indiana.edu/vol12/issue3/vancouvering.html. Accessed April 18, 2011.

_____. 2008. "The History of the Internet Search Engine: Navigational Media and the Traffic Commodity." In Amanda Spink and Michael Zimmer, ed. *Web Search: Multidisciplinary Perspectives*. Berlin: Springer-Verlag, pp. 177–206.

Virilio, Paul. 1997. *Open Sky*, Julie Rose tr. London: Verso.

Warde, Alan. 2004. "Practice and Field: Revisiting Bourdieusian Concepts," *Centre for Research on Innovation and Competition Discussion, Discussion Paper No. 65*. http://www.cric.ac.uk/cric/abstracts/dp65.htm Accessed April 18, 2011.

Weiner, Norbert. 1964. *God & Golem, Inc.: A Comment on Certain Points Where Cybernetics Impinges on Religion*. Cambridge: MIT Press.

Wells, H.G. (Herbert George). 1938. *World Brain*. Garden City: Doubleday, Doran & Co.

Wheeler, John Archibald. 1989. "Information, Physics, Quantum: The Search for Links." In Shirō Kobayashi, H. Ezawa, Y. Murayama, and S. Nomura, eds, *Proceedings of the 3rd International Symposium of the Foundations of Quantum Mechanics*. Tokyo: Physical Society Japan, pp. 354–368.

Whitaker, Reg. 1999. *The End of Privacy: How Total Surveillance is Becoming a Reality*. New York: New Press.

White, Lynn Townsend. 1971. *Medieval Religion and Technology: Collected Essays*. Publications of the Center for Medieval and Renaissance Studies 13. Los Angeles: University of California Press.

Williams, Raymond. 1960. *The Long Revolution*. London: Chatto & Windus.

Wilson, Ian E. 2007. "Foreword." In Jean-Noël Jeanneney, *Google and the Myth of Universal Knowledge*. Chicago: University of Chicago Press, pp. vii–xiii.

Winner, Langdon, 1995. "The Enduring Dilemmas of Autonomous Technique," *Bulletin of Science and Technology Studies* 15:2–3, pp. 66–72.

Wiseman, D.J. 1996. "Babel." In I. Howard Marshall, A.R. Millord, J.I. Packer, and D.J. Wiseman, eds, *New Bible Dictionary*, 3rd edn. Downers Grove: Inter-varsity Press, pp. 109–110.

Wolff, Theodor. 1929. *Der Wettlauf mit der Schildkröte (The Race with the Tortoise)*. Berlin: Scherl.

World Digital Library. 2011. "Mission." http://www.wdl.org/en/about/ Accessed December 3, 2011.

Wright, Quincy. 1957. "Project for a World Intelligence Center," *Conflict Resolution* 1:1, pp. 315–325.

Wright, Robert, 2010. "Building One Big Brain," *Opinionator.* July 6. https://opinionator.blogs.nytimes.com/2010/07/06/the-web-we-weave/?hp Accessed July 7, 2010.

Yap, Alexander Y. 2002. "Enabling e-Commerce Growth Through the Social Construction of a Virtual Community's Culture," *Journal of Electronic Commerce Research* 3:4, pp. 279–294.

Yates, Frances A. 1982. *Lull & Bruno: Collected Essays,* Vol. 1. London: Routledge & Kegan Paul.

YouTube. 2010. "Google Chrome Speed Tests." May 3. http://www.youtube.com/watch?v=nCgQDjiotG0 Accessed July 8, 2010.

Zimmer, Michael. 2008. "The Gaze of the Perfect Search Engine: Google as an Infrastructure of Dataveillance." In Amanda Spink and Michael Zimmer, ed. *Web Search: Multidisciplinary Perspectives*. Berlin: Springer-Verlag, pp. 77–99.

Žižek, Slavoj. 2008 [1997]. *The Plague of Fantasies*. London: Verso.

_____. 2008a [1999]. *The Ticklish Subject: The Absent Centre of Political Ontology*. London: Verso.

# INDEX

Web of Science 127
Weiner, Norbert 153
Wells, H.G. 11, 109–14, 117, 123,
    129, 135, 136, 142, 145, 155, 192;
    and biological metaphors 136; and
    influence on search 116, 120–1, 127,
    128; and Jorge Luis Borges 109, 208n6;
    and metaphysics 112, 115, 141; and
    microfilm 113, 132, 137; and science
    fiction 113; and World Brain 15, 29,
    82, 97, 105, 127
Wheeler, John Archibald 79
Wilson, Ian 198
Winner, Langdon 11, 13, 139, 144
WISE (World Information Synthesis
    and Encyclopaedia) 127, 132, 136;
    as linking device 134; as prefiguring
    Google and Wikipedia 133; as storage
    device 134
Wolff, Theodor 78, 91, 109
World Brain 10, 28, 105–6, 109, 110–11,
    112–14, 115, 152; and biological
    metaphors 112, 136; and ideology of
    efficiency 111; and lie of unity 112;
    and metaphysics and science 115; and

searchability 112–13; and sentience 114;
    as inspiration for universal library 106;
    as manifestation of Symbolic order 180;
    as precursor to World Wide Web 114;
    as publically owned 132; as substitute
    for political decisions 111; *see also*
    cloud computing; Garfield, Eugene;
    index; Lasswitz, Kurd; universal library;
    memex; Neoplatonism; Royal Library
    at Alexandria; Wells, H.G.
World Digital Library 161
World Encyclopaedia *see* World Brain
World Intelligence Center 143
World Soul 10, 28, 107, 114, 124,
    201; metaphysics of 198; see also
    metaphysics, Neoplatonism, panpsychic
    philosophy

Yahoo!: as a Web librarian 69
YouTube 43, 50, 63, 86, 168, 196

zeitgeist 16, 31, 32, 125, 129, 168, 182;
    *see also* habitus; structure of feeling
Zipf's law 65
Žižek, Slavov 179, 180, 181